Spain

modern architectures in history

This international series examines the forms and consequences of modern architecture. Modernist visions and revisions are explored in their national context against a backdrop of aesthetic currents, economic developments, political trends and social movements. Written by experts in the architectures of the respective countries, the series provides a fresh, critical reassessment of Modernism's positive and negative effects, as well as the place of architectural design in twentieth-century history and culture.

Series editor: Vivian Constantinopoulos

Already published:

Spain

modern architectures in history

David Cohn

REAKTION BOOKS

To Amelia

Published by Reaktion Books Ltd
Unit 32, Waterside
44–48 Wharf Road
London N1 7UX, UK

www.reaktionbooks.co.uk

First published 2024
Copyright © David Cohn 2024

Printed and bound in Great Britain by Bell & Bain, Glasgow

A catalogue record for this book is available from the British Library

ISBN 978 1 78914 581 6

Contents

Note on Translations

Whenever possible, the accepted local versions of place names and personal names are used, in Spanish, Catalan and other regional languages: Catalunya instead of Catalonia; Sevilla instead of Seville; Felipe II instead of Philip II; Josep Lluís Sert instead of José Luis Sert. In the case of Basque place names, I use their Spanish alternatives for the sake of clarity (few will recognize Donastia as San Sebastián, for example). Unless noted, all original texts in Spanish are translated by me and edited for succinctness.

Glossary of basic place-marking terms

SPANISH	CATALAN	ENGLISH
Avenida	Avinguda	Avenue
Calle	Carrer	Street
Casa	Casa	House / Apartment Building
Ciudad	Ciutat	City
Edificio	Edifici	Building
Ensanche	Eixample	Urban Extension
Palacio	Palau	Palace
Plaza	Plaça	Plaza
Plaza Mayor	Plaça Major	Main Square
Torre	Torre	Tower

chapter one

A Short History, 1750–1925

It is the fashion to walk every evening until dark in the Prado – a long, broad space with six rows of trees each side enclosing a walk – the middle space is for carriages and has some handsome fountains at certain distances which supply water for the trees, and it is conducted to their roots every morning and evening by channels cut and kept in order for the purpose. This space on one side is supplied with a great number of cane chairs where any person may sit down when tired. Lord Wellington regularly attends the Prado and it is very flattering to see the attention with which he is treated.

John Aitchison, 1812[1]

General histories of the Modern Movement trace its origins to the eighteenth-century Enlightenment, and follow its early development through the emergence of industrialized European states and the critical social and cultural movements that arose in response to problems created by rapid industrialization and urbanization in the nineteenth century.[2] The spirit of Reason, which animated Neoclassical architecture and early projects of urban reform during the Enlightenment, coincided with the appearance of the new liberal bourgeois class, as seen in projects such as the terraces of John Nash in England (Regent Street, London, 1817–19) or Charles Percier and Pierre-François-Léonard Fontaine's rue de Rivoli in Paris (1805). Later in the nineteenth century, Romanticism and other intellectual movements joined in a broad critique of the Enlightenment and the limits of its practical and technical accomplishments, focusing instead on the subjective dimensions of human experience and sentiment. At the same time, the social problems created by industrialization motivated reform movements in which architecture and urbanism played important roles. These different critical strands were brought together in architecture by the neo-Gothic movement and its derivatives and descendants, as advocated by Eugène-Emmanuel Viollet-le-Duc, John Ruskin and others, and arguments for a non-alienating, organic, functional and honest use of materials, crafts and styles. The new bourgeoisie also produced a broader historic eclecticism in architecture, in a restless search for appropriate national and contemporary styles, incorporating new materials and methods, new building typologies and

Juan de Villanueva, Prado Museum, 1785–1808. Lithograph by Léon August Asselineau, 1833, after original painting by Fernando Brambilla.

needs, and a new scale of construction. By the beginning of the twentieth century, the social and structural conflicts that culminated in the First World War and the Russian Revolution combined to create a climate of crisis for the bourgeois order, a situation that gave early modern architecture its social and moral agenda.

Spain began as an important participant in this history, but the work of Enlightenment reformers in the eighteenth century was cut short, and the country's political instability, poverty and isolation prevented its full participation in the construction of the European bourgeois state until late in the nineteenth century. Spain's architecture reflects this situation: the early, interrupted promise of Neoclassical reforms, the dependence on foreign models, especially from the French Academy, and a late flourishing of invention at the end of the nineteenth century and first decades of the twentieth, mainly in Barcelona. The Modern Movement arrived in Spain only in the mid-1920s in a subdued form, and it was not until the brief, idealistic and conflictive period of the Second Republic (1931–6), with the work of Josep Lluís Sert and GATEPAC in Barcelona, that the Modern Movement took on something of the urgency and excitement it had acquired in Weimar Germany or in the early years of the Soviet Union.

The Spanish Enlightenment

The seeds of the Enlightenment were brought to Spain by the Bourbon dynasty, established by Louis XIV's grandson, the Duke of Anjou, who took over the Spanish throne as Felipe V in 1701. The Bourbons promoted the French model of a centralized state. They cut back the power of the Church and ancient regional rights and instituted political, social, economic and cultural reforms that favoured the modernization of the country and the emergence of a bourgeois entrepreneurial class. But the Bourbon kings and the *afrancesados* (enlightened Francophiles) of their court were not strong enough to overcome the conservative forces of the country or reverse its centuries-long decline. Their project of reform was met with resistance from not only the religious and regional interests they fought, but the popular classes. The period of reform came to an end following the disastrous reign of Carlos IV (1788–1808), with the invasion of Napoleon and the War of Independence (1808–14), followed by the reactionary monarchy of Fernando VII (1814–33), who abolished many intellectual freedoms in his efforts to prevent a French-style revolution. His reign set the tone for conservative resistance to reform throughout the nineteenth century.

The Bourbons brought contemporary French and Italian architectural fashions to Spain, breaking with the cultural isolation of the country and its local, late Baroque styles. With the establishment of Madrid's San

Fernando Royal Academy of Fine Arts in 1744, architectural training was removed from its traditional craft and guild base in the royal workshops, and systematized in theoretical rather than practical terms, following French models, under the direction of the architectural theorist Diego de Villanueva. In the mid-eighteenth century, military engineers, many born or trained outside Spain, brought a severe Neoclassicism to military buildings, ports and fortifications, and to royal industrial initiatives such as Catalunya's tobacco factory. They also introduced early rational city plans related to naval constructions in El Ferrol, Barcelona's Barceloneta and elsewhere.

The reign of Carlos III (1759–88) marked the culmination of the Bourbon modernizations. He came to the throne after ruling the Spanish territories of the kingdoms of Naples and Sicily, where he presided over the excavations of Herculaneum and Pompeii and the construction of the Royal Palace of Caserta, designed by Luigi Vanvitelli in a restrained late Baroque style. He embellished Madrid with many works by Vanvitelli's son-in-law, Francisco Sabatini, who also completed the new Royal Palace that Felipe V had begun on the western edge of the city. Carlos instituted programmes of paving and lighting streets, building sewers, creating new plazas and *paseos* (tree-lined avenues) and relocating cemeteries outside the city, as well as other measures designed to improve hygiene and comfort. One of his most interesting projects is the Salón del Prado (1767–82), designed by José de Hermosilla with sculptural fountains by Ventura Rodríguez, an outdoor evening salon for the upper classes situated near the royal palace of El Buen Retiro. The salon, which partially survives today as the Paseo del Prado boulevard, was a model for parks and *paseos* in other cities sponsored by new liberal 'Economic Societies of Friends of the Country', such as the Paseo de Floridablanca in Valladolid, or the reform of Barcelona's Ramblas (1775). At a national level, Carlos built the road network that remained the backbone of Spanish highways well into the twentieth century.

Carlos was also the chief patron of Juan de Villanueva, Diego's brother and Spain's most significant Neoclassical architect. Villanueva was pensioned in Rome from 1759 to 1764, then the centre of the Neoclassical movement. He is best known for the scientific campus he built for the king around the Salón del Prado: the Royal Observatory (1790–1808) in the Buen Retiro Park, the Royal Botanical Garden (1785–9) and the Cabinet of Natural History (1785–1808), which became the Prado Museum in 1819. With its elegantly modelled central and end pavilions connected by long galleries, the Prado exemplifies Villanueva's rational compositions of linearly assembled elements. Its unusual brick massing, a material that Villanueva adapted from the nearby royal palace and whose use dates to Spain's Islamic period, set an influential precedent for later Madrid architecture.

Students and members of the academy produced a large collection of visionary projects in emulation of their French colleagues. These drawings, and works such as Sabatini's vast, incomplete San Carlos Hospital in Madrid (1769–88, today the Reina Sofía Museum of Contemporary Art), initiated the transformation of the architectural profession from its origins in royal patronage and religious work into a civic service. Unchecked by material limits, these projects maintained and even enlarged the monumental conceptions of court practice, setting a precedent for an endogamic, academic grandiosity that echoed through the nineteenth century and beyond.

Basque communities were the most receptive to Neoclassical reforms, many of which were sponsored by the liberal Royal Basque Society of

Plan of Madrid, 1848, detail showing the Salón del Prado, Prado Museum and Royal Botanical Garden.

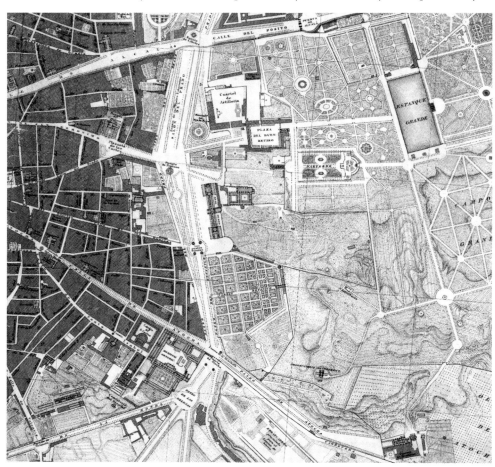

Pedro Manuel de Ugartemendía, Plaza de la Constitución, 1815, San Sebastián, with the former city hall by Silvestre Pérez and Ugartemendía, constructed 1819–32.

Friends of the Country established in 1763. Influential urban projects include the Plazas Nuevas (New Plazas) of Vitoria and Bilbao, the first designed by Justo Antonio de Olaguíbel (1781–1829) and the second by Silvestre Pérez and Antonio de Echevarría (begun in 1781). These were Neoclassical versions of Spain's traditional *plazas mayores* (main squares), enclosed on four sides by uniform facades, with regular balcony windows and ground-floor galleries. Basque architects also proposed two innovative, though unrealized, rational city plans: Pérez's project for the Port of Peace in Bilbao (1801–7) and Pedro Manuel de Ugartemendía's plan for rebuilding San Sebastián following its destruction by British 'liberators' under Wellington in 1813. Though the rebuilt city followed existing street lines, it incorporated Ugartemendía's ordinances for regularizing new building, as seen in his own Plaza de la Constitución.

Economic Growth and Liberal Reform

Spain's history following the war against Napoleon is marked by instability, with dramatic alternations between liberal and conservative rule, set against a background of conflict, underdevelopment and isolation. The country went through at least three periods of civil war in the nineteenth century, the 'Carlist Wars', launched by rural traditionalists of the Basque Country, Navarra and Catalunya. There were six successful military coups, seven constitutions, two abdications, the short-lived First Republic (1873–4) and a subsequent Bourbon restoration. Economic recovery did not begin until the reign of Isabel II (1833–68), and sustained economic growth was not achieved until the relative stability of the Restoration, under the reigns of

Alfonso XII and Alfonso XIII (1874–85; 1886–1931). But Spain's industrial development and economy lagged far behind its northern European neighbours.

During this period, British capital and technology created Bilbao's iron industry; British and French firms built Spain's railways; and French investors expanded Catalan industry from its eighteenth-century base in textiles into machinery and other goods. This moderate economic success reached a high point during the First World War, when Spain's neutrality fuelled business. Nevertheless, as the historian Raymond Carr points out, in 1930, half of the nation's income was still derived from its backwards agricultural system: more than half the population was rural, and hunger was widespread among landless agricultural labourers, small landowners and impoverished urban classes, as it had been throughout the nineteenth century.[3]

These conditions created fertile ground for popular unrest. In the early twentieth century, the anarchist movement spread rapidly in both the countryside of Andalucía and the factories of Barcelona. Founded in 1910, the anarchist trade union CNT (Confederación Nacional del Trabajo, or National Confederation of Labour) had over 700,000 members by 1919, and crippled Barcelona in a series of general strikes between 1916 and 1923.[4] The growing confrontation between the forces of revolutionary change and repression set the stage for the Civil War (1936–9).

Moments of progress and reform usually coincided with periods of liberal rule, widely spaced in time and generally short in duration. There were five such progressive intervals in the nineteenth century, led first by the emerging bourgeois class and later, once this class had consolidated its position, by a new group of petty-bourgeois revolutionaries and reformers. The liberals launched the most daring projects of modernization, such as Ildefons Cerdà's mid-century plan for the expansion of Barcelona or the educational and housing programmes of the 1910s, while the traditional elites and new industrialists patronized the grandiloquent decorative styles of the Restoration, including the singular movement in Barcelona known as Modernisme.

The effects of Spain's gradual economic and political recovery after 1833 are first evident in urban planning initiatives within city cores. The 'disentailment', a sweeping public seizure and auction of Church properties carried out under the brief, radically liberal government of Juan Álvarez Mendizábal in 1836–7, delivered the land needed for urban growth into the hands of the bourgeoisie, although at a high cost to the nation's historic patrimony. The measure increased the schism between liberals and Catholic conservatives and fed a conservative fervour for church building in succeeding decades, as seen in the career of Antoni Gaudí, for example.

The sites of religious buildings were used for municipal markets, barracks, hospitals, plazas and other public facilities. In Madrid, slightly more than half of the city's 64 monasteries and convents were sold, demolished or turned over to new uses.

In Barcelona, the disentailment was preceded by the anti-clerical riots of 1835 in which many convents and monasteries were burned. All told, 80 per cent of the Church's properties in the city were seized. Notable urban projects resulting from the measure include the Boqueria market and the Plaça Reial, both near the Ramblas. The Boqueria's 1860 glass-and-iron structure occupies an incomplete market plaza with an Ionic portico, built by the city government from 1836 to 1840. The Plaça Reial (1848–64) was designed by Francesc Daniel Molina i Casamajó. As with other works of the period, these urban projects show the persistence of Neoclassicism into the nineteenth century.

Alignment plans were another tool of urban growth and reform, in which principal streets were widened and regularized in the interests of circulation, hygiene and development. An early example, begun by a short-lived liberal government in Barcelona in 1823, is the Vía Transversal, which cuts east–west across the Gothic Quarter (Carrers Ferran and Jaime I). Quite narrow by later standards, it opened access to the Plaça Sant Jaume, site of the city hall and Generalitat, or regional government. In Madrid, the central plaza of the Puerta del Sol took on its present semi-circular form in a project of 1857–62.

From Cerdà's Eixample to Soria's Linear City

While Spanish cities generally did not follow the contemporary example of Georges-Eugène Haussmann's Paris in cutting wide new boulevards through existing urban fabrics, they undertook urban planning projects of a similarly transformative scale in the latter half of the century, in the form of large *ensanches* (planned extensions) following the demolition of their walls. Spain's municipalities lacked the economic and legal means to operate freely in consolidated urban fabrics, as the two major street-cutting projects undertaken at the end of the century demonstrate: Madrid's Gran Vía and Barcelona's Via Laietana took decades to plan and legislate and further decades to build, extending well into the twentieth century.

The liberal epoch's most important contribution to urban design was Ildefons Cerdà's plan for Barcelona's Eixample (extension), approved in 1860, which would become a model for the rest of Spain. The initiative for the plan arose during the Progressive Biennial of 1854–6; it reflected both the pressures of growth and the reawakening of Catalan nationalism among the city's leaders as they gained economic power and political voice following the Bourbon repressions of the eighteenth century. Barcelona had joined in a military alliance with the Austrian Habsburgs against the Bourbon dynasty in the War of Succession (1702–14). After conquering the city, Felipe v made it a heavily fortified *plaza fuerte* (stronghold). He demolished the neighbourhood of La Ribera to build the Ciutadella fort and built massive zig-zagging defensive walls and earthworks around the city's perimeter. Construction was prohibited in a radius of 2 kilometres (1¼ mi.) outside the walls to maintain an open field of fire, effectively restricting growth to the dense and insalubrious medieval core. Felipe's repression of the city's rebellious spirit also included the abolition of historic Catalan rights and political institutions, the prohibition of the Catalan language and the closing of the University of Barcelona. Today, these measures remain a historic reference point for the revindication of the region's rights and culture.

The move to demolish the Bourbon walls and enlarge the city, first proposed in 1841, was promoted as a step forward in these revindications. It brought together ideas of progress, hygiene and social improvement – the city was plagued by outbreaks of cholera, strikes and popular uprisings – with the Catalan nationalist spirit first openly evoked by Buenaventura Carles Aribau's wistful romantic ode 'La Patria' (The Fatherland, 1833).

The city organized a competition for the new plan in 1859, which was won by the municipal architect Antoni Rovira i Trias. But Madrid's Ministry of Development, still under the influence of liberal engineers, commissioned Cerdà to design a separate plan and imposed it on the city over its bitter opposition, in another affront to its pride and autonomy. Cerdà was a progressive pro-Catalan engineer who had been commissioned by Madrid to make a topographic survey of the plain around the city in 1855, in preparation for the Eixample. He had carried out a pioneering study of the living conditions of Barcelona's working classes, *A Statistical Monograph on the Working Class of Barcelona in 1856*, a contemporary of Friedrich Engels's *The Condition of the Working Class in England* of 1845.

Rovira's and Cerdà's proposals juxtaposed architectural and engineering approaches to the city, as well as conservative and progressive visions. The former, with its hierarchy of plazas and avenues radiating from the existing city, was monumental, articulated and contextual, the latter was regular, egalitarian and functional, as well as 'monotonous', according to later detractors. It emphasized the importance of circulation over representation in public spaces and treated the city as a non-hierarchical territory, with hypothetically equal conditions of access and land value.

Cerdà proposed a uniform grid like those of Spain's planned colonial cities in the Americas, much larger in extension than Rovira's plan and essentially bypassing the existing city, which was to be incorporated via a

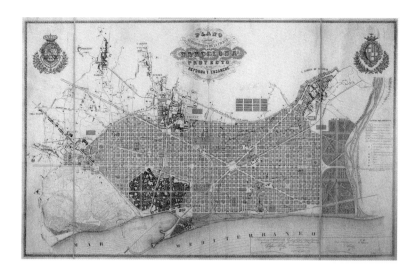

Ildefons Cerdà, plan for the expansion of Barcelona, 1859.

series of circulation axes cut through its fabric (including the future Via Laietana, the only one to be fully realized). Filling the plain between the hill of Montjuïc on the southwest and the Besòs river to the northeast, the new city was crossed by two diagonal thoroughfares and a transversal avenue serving the principal points of entry. The large blocks – 113 square metres (1,216 sq. ft) with celebrated chamfered corners and large interior gardens – were intended to be open to the streets on at least two sides, with a low density of construction. They were developed, however, as fully enclosed units, and only a handful of interior gardens were realized.

Cerdà accompanied his proposal with one of the first general treatises on urban planning, the *General Theory of Urbanization, and the Application of Its Principles and Doctrines to the Reform and Expansion of Barcelona* (1867). Many of its concepts were incorporated into the national legislation that governed the ensanches of Spanish cities after 1864. These measures included pragmatic systems for financing urbanizations and redistributing parcels among landowners, which the urbanist Fernando de Terán considers an advance over the more authoritarian methods used by Haussmann in his urban reform of Paris, and a forerunner of such practices today.[5]

Parallel to Barcelona's Eixample, in 1860 Madrid implemented a similar plan by the engineer Carlos María de Castro, although it incorporated zoning for the different classes, industry and agriculture. The ensanche became an instrument for urban growth in virtually all of Spain's major cities into the 1930s, and it set the precedent for the notable degree of municipal control over urban planning in Spain today, contributing to the highly defined urban mass and boundaries of Spanish cities. Other important ensanches in the nineteenth century are those for San Sebastián, Vitoria, Bilbao and Santander, and in the twentieth century, the plans for Valencia, Pamplona, A Coruña, Tarragona and Alicante, among others.

But the ensanches grew slowly, and actually diverted growth elsewhere. By 1890, only some sixty blocks around the Passeig de Gràcia in Barcelona had been developed, and Madrid's was only half filled by 1900, with many streets yet to be laid out. In the same period, uncontrolled industrial building and working-class slums grew up on the outer edges of the ensanches and within the far-flung northeastern sector of Cerdà's plan in Poblenou, escaping the higher land prices and restrictive building ordinances of parcels in the ensanches and forgoing essential infrastructures such as water, sewers, paving and lighting. In Barcelona, these slums were the centre of revolutionary workers' movements at the turn of the century. The ensanches thus proved to be a formula valid only for creating the bourgeois city, while the problems of hygiene, health and deprivation of the old city were recreated in the new slums, demonstrating the failure of the liberal system to effectively address the basic inequalities that produced these contrasts. At the same time, the relation of the ensanche to older fortified city cores, especially in smaller provincial capitals of the interior, offered a physical portrait of the division between progressives and conservatives, as the Spanish writer Pío Baroja pointed out in a 1918 article on Cuenca: 'on the heights, the aristocracy, the clergy, the representatives of the militias and the state; below, democracy, commerce, industry'.[6]

The progressive impulse also gave rise to Spain's most original contribution to urban planning, Arturo Soria's Ciudad Lineal (Linear City), which was built in a modest form on the eastern outskirts of Madrid at the turn of the century. Soria had participated in the national government produced by the Revolution of 1868, and he founded one of Madrid's first streetcar lines during the short-lived First Republic in 1873. In 1882, he published his concept for the Ciudad Lineal in the Madrid newpaper *El Progreso*. Soria proposed to decentralize settlement along a multi-level spine of local and express railway and streetcar lines between existing cities. A single row of large blocks on each side of the rail lines would accommodate individual houses set in gardens for all the different classes. After winning the concession for a circumferential suburban tram line in 1894, he organized the Madrid Metropolitan Urbanization Company and began to sell lots for a linear city 48 kilometres (30 mi.) long. Typical house plans were designed by Mariano Belmás Estrada, a veteran of other experimental housing ventures. By 1911, a first phase of 3.2 kilometres (2 mi.) was complete, and its outlines, together with some of the original houses, can still be seen today. Soria's ideas anticipated both the Constructivist linear cities

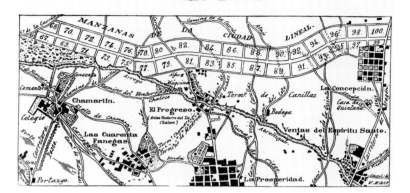

PLANO GENERAL DE LA PRIMERA BARRIADA DE LA 'CIUDAD LINEAL,, Y SUS INMEDIACIONES

Arturo Soria, Linear
City plan, 1894.

of the Soviet Union and Ebenezer Howard's Garden City, proposed in 1898 and first built at Letchworth, England, in 1903.

The Engineers

Together with the ensanches, the railway was the other great engineering work that restructured Spain during the latter half of the nineteenth century. Early railway lines, including stations and bridges, were largely financed, designed and fabricated by English firms, beginning with the first, which connected Barcelona to Mataró in 1848. After the 1868 Revolution, French and Belgian firms replaced the British. Madrid's Delicias station of 1879, for example, was designed by the engineer Émile Cachelièvre and introduced the de Dion truss, the most advanced of its time, which was assembled from elements fabricated in Belgium.

A dependence on foreign technology extended to other engineering projects. Sevilla's Triana Bridge, the first permanent crossing of the Guadalquivir river since Roman times, was modelled on Antoine-Rémy Polonceau's 1834 Pont du Carrousel in Paris. Opened in 1852, it is the only surviving example of the system of cast iron arches Polonceau introduced in that work. When Madrid's revolutionary government of 1869 built the first covered markets of Cebada, Mostenses and Olavide (all since demolished), they were modelled on the markets of Paris and built with cast-iron elements imported from France.

Several works involving the Spanish engineer Alberto de Palacio form an interesting footnote to this reliance on foreign know-how. With the French engineer Ferdinand Joseph Arnodin, he built the remarkable Puente Transbordador (Transporter Bridge) in Portugalete near Bilbao (1887–93).

Gustavo Steinacher and Ferdinand Bennetot (engineers), Triana Bridge with Polonceau trusses, Sevilla, 1852.

12 MADRID.—Estación del Mediodía.

Alberto de Palacio and Henry Saint James (engineers), Atocha train station (formerly known as Mediodía), Madrid, 1888–92.

Still in operation, the structure consists of a floating platform guided across the river by cables hung from a truss suspended 45 metres (148 ft) above the water. With its slender steel towers, 57 metres (187 ft) high, it was the forerunner to Arnodin's 1905 *pont transbordeur* in Marseille, whose daring use of naked steel trusses made a profound impression on Sigfried Giedion in the 1920s.[7] With a British engineer, Henry Saint James, De Palacio designed the Atocha train station in Madrid, whose shed was the largest ever spanned by de Dion trusses, thanks to the introduction of laminated steel (1888–92). And in collaboration with the Spanish architect Ricardo Velázquez Bosco, he was the engineer for the iron and glass Palacio de Cristal in El Retiro Park, built for the Philippine Exposition of 1887. The capstone of this intense decade of work is an unrealized monument to Christopher Columbus of 1892 for El Retiro, a globe 300 metres (984 ft) high – matching the Eiffel Tower – and occupied by museums, a zoo and botanical garden, libraries, observatories, a theatre, a hotel, restaurants and a church, and crowned by a full-scale replica of the Santa María.[8]

Madrid Eclecticism

The growth of the ensanches in the latter half of the nineteenth century was accompanied by some of the new architectural styles and tendencies flourishing elsewhere in Europe. The most coherent and original developments took place in Barcelona, where a robust economy and high cultural aspirations contributed to the emergence of Modernisme, as we shall see below. Madrid's architecture of the period, by contrast, was characterized by a repertoire of academic historicist styles derived almost entirely from French models.

Antonio Celles, first director of Barcelona's Lonja School of Architecture (opened in 1817), introduced the classical rationalism of Jean-Nicolas Louis Durand to Spain. Led by Antonio Zabaleta and Aníbal Álvarez, the group of 'young Romantics' who gave the first impetus to the Madrid School of Architecture, which succeeded the Royal Academy of San Fernando in 1844, followed the evolution of the French Academy towards what the historian Julio Arrechea terms a 'Romantic historical' perspective, awakened by Victor Hugo's *Notre-Dame de Paris* (1832).[9] In this evolution, the academy's traditional focus on classical models opened towards a broader historical perspective that laid the foundations for Eclecticism.

Elsewhere in Europe, Hugo's work helped to spark a broader rejection of Neoclassicism in favour of the Gothic and other medieval styles, by thinkers such as Eugène Viollet-le-Duc in France or Augustus Pugin and Ruskin in England. This movement idealized the medieval period as a model for spiritual and social renewal, as well as for an architecture based on natural, rational principles of construction, as Viollet-le-Duc argued. Significantly, however, this path was not followed in Madrid. The argument that medieval styles were native to northern Europe, and thus more genuinely 'national' in character than classicism, had less meaning to architects in central Spain, where the Gothic was one imported style among many. Madrid architects, again following the example of the French Academy, therefore remained loyal to an essentially Neoclassical outlook.

In this academic Eclecticism, different styles were applied according to building programme and type: Gothic for important religious works; variations on Neoclassical and French Renaissance models for state buildings; and Mudéjar, the style created by Islamic craftsmen under Catholic rule, for the simple ornamental brickwork of factories, schools and other religious works, as well as occasional excursions into more exotic Islamic styles for private mansions and places of entertainment. Following the compositional rationalism taught in France by Durand, these decorative programmes were applied over the same symmetrical layouts, with grand entry porticos, central patios, corner pavilions and other predictable elements of distribution, with an occasional timid nod to picturesque massing in private houses. Madrid architects were pluri-stylists, an attitude that persisted in various guises throughout the twentieth century. Francisco de Cubas, creator of the first Gothic design for Madrid's long-incomplete cathedral (1883), built neo-Renaissance mansions in the 1860s, the mansard-roofed, Neoclassical Museum of Anthropology in 1873 and a series of convents, churches and church orphanages in budget brickwork, with styles ranging from Mudéjar, Gothic and Renaissance to a severe proto-functionalism.

The few notable buildings of nineteenth-century Madrid reflect this background. Belatedly modelled on the ideal museum of Durand's 1802 treatise, *Précis of the Lectures on Architecture*, Francisco Jareño's sober, grandly scaled National Library and Museums (1865–92) is the great public work of the Isabelline era, cited also for its early use of cast iron in the bookstacks (demolished) and light courts, and for its brick fabric, inspired by both Spanish precedents and contemporary German building.

Ricardo Velázquez Bosco, Ministry of Development (today Ministry of Agriculture), Madrid, 1893–7.

Later public works of the Restoration emulated the sumptuous Beaux-Arts spirit of Charles Garnier's Paris Opera, including the Bank of Spain (Eduardo de Adaro and Severiano Sainz de la Lastra, 1884–91); the Palacio de la Bolsa, or Stock Exchange (Enrique María Repullés, 1884–93); and several buildings by Ricardo Velázquez Bosco, such as today's Ministry of Agriculture, originally built for the powerful Ministry of Development (1893–7), with a central portico crowned by a trio of oversized winged allegorical figures.

Barcelona Modernisme

While rejected in Madrid, the more radical strains of nineteenth-century architectural thinking, medievalist and anti-classical, found a receptive audience in Barcelona, where architects sought to give expression to the city's growing Catalan nationalism. Unlike central Spain, local examples of Romanesque and Gothic architecture offered a plausible basis for a native style. The movement that culminated in Modernisme began as a medieval revival, led by the architects Elíes Rogent and Joan Martorell in the 1870s and '80s. It reached its peak from 1890 to 1910 in the work of Lluís Domènech i Montaner, Antoni Gaudí, Josep Puig i Cadafalch, Gaudí's disciple Josep María Jujol and others. Caught up in the period's romantic idealization of medieval society and religious faith, the Modernistes sought to create a contemporary, native style, using the materials and crafts of the industrial age according to the principles of organic, 'rational' construction that Viollet-le-Duc had found in medieval architecture.

Several of these architects became principal leaders in Catalunya's regionalist politics. Their patrons belonged to Barcelona's deeply conservative and pious ruling elite, figures such as the slave trader and shipping magnate Antonio López (slavery was not abolished in Spanish Cuba until 1886), for whom Martorell, Domènech and Gaudí built an important complex of buildings in his native Comillas, in Cantabria. Eusebi Güell, Gaudí's chief patron, was son of Joan Güell, founder of Barcelona's machine industry, and became López's son-in-law.

Though these early regionalists sought greater Catalan autonomy and an independent cultural identity, they were also among the strongest backers of the Bourbon Restoration in 1874, with its promise of political and economic stability. Later in the century, and especially following Spain's defeat by the United States in the war of 1898, the Catalan movement became a political force with Enric Prat de la Riba's Lliga Regionalista (Regionalist League), which portrayed a modern, vital Catalunya taking the lead over a corrupt and decadent Castilla, and proposed the renewal of the Spanish monarchy as a decentralized federation of regions.

Modernisme was intimately implicated in the projects of social, religious and cultural self-justification of this ruling class, and in the general project to forge a Catalan national identity. These programmes included archaeological research and restoration of the region's neglected medieval monuments, carried out by successive generations of architects from Rogent to Domènech and Puig. Wagnerian mythologies of national origin make up the decorative programmes of many Moderniste works. Mythic elements from the epic poem *L'Atlàntida*, written in 1877 by López's in-house poet and priest, Jacinct Verdaguer, a key figure in the revival of the Catalan language, turn up frequently in Gaudí's projects for Güell, for example.[10] In urban terms, with its decorative richness, Modernisme was in striking contrast to the sobriety of the Cerdà plan, endowing the Eixample with the kind of hierarchical, symbolic configurations that the city's leaders had originally sought in Rovira's rejected plan. And of course, the programmes of Moderniste buildings – ranging from sumptuous palaces and new Catalan cultural institutions to religious works, charities and paternalistic experiments in social reform, offered in the face of growing workers' unrest – reflected upper-class preoccupations.

A case in point is the workers' colony that Eusebi Güell built in Santa Coloma de Cervelló early in the twentieth century, for which Gaudí designed the unfinished church. Güell was inspired by Prat de la Riba's *The Law of Industry* (1893), in which he proposed such colonies as a return to a medieval, feudal and paternalistic relation between industrialists and workers, a conservative utopianism that had its sources in the revindications of ancient rights and practices of the Carlists.[11] With its schools, church and community services, together with workers' residences and factories, the Colònia Güell anticipated the socialistic programmes of the Falangists in the 1930s, also heirs of the Carlists, and the new towns of the 1950s designed by José Luis Fernández del Amo for the National Institute of Colonization under Franco.

The first architect to break with Neoclassicism was Elíes Rogent, in his design for the re-founded University of Barcelona (1860–71), the first public building in the Eixample. Though modelled on Friedrich von Gärtner's Romanesque university buildings in Munich and arranged in a conventional symmetrical plan, it shows the influence of Viollet-le-Duc's structural rationalism in its use of modern materials such as exposed iron. The colourful decoration of the main lecture hall, with freely interpreted mixtures of medieval and Islamic motifs, is considered a harbinger of Modernisme. Rogent went on to restore the Romanesque Monastery of Santa María de Ripoll in the Pyrenees following Viollet-le-Duc's methods, and its inauguration in 1881 was an occasion for major celebration of Catalan identity. As the first director of the Barcelona School of Architecture, founded in

1871, and director of commissioning works for the Universal Exposition of 1888, Rogent was an influential link between leading architects and the city, setting a precedent for later power brokers such as Domènech, Puig, Sert and Oriol Bohigas.

The transition from Rogent's more archaeological use of past styles to designs based on a freer range of sources, and the incorporation of modern crafts and materials, was begun by the neo-Gothic architect Joan Martorell, in works such as the Salesas Church in Barcelona (1882–5), with his use of polychrome colouring and decorative patterns. His extravagant projects for Antonio López in Comillas comprise the Sobrellano Palace, the Seminary for the Poor and the Pantheon (1881–9). Martorell was a mentor to both Lluís Domènech i Montaner and Antoni Gaudí, both of whom succeeded him at Comillas. Domènech finished the Seminary and Gaudí built the Capricho (1883–5), a palace for the López family, two works that show their development towards greater formal and decorative inventiveness. These experiments continued in the most singular work of the 1888 Exposition, Domènech's brick mock-fortress of the Café Restaurant in the Ciutadella Park.

Modernisme came into its own at the turn of the century as an inventive new style in Domènech's mature, richly ornamented work. Within it, all of the formal and ornamental elements of design were integrated in a fluid, organic whole, in the manner of Wagner's *Gesamtkunstwerk* or 'total work of art'. A prime domestic example is the Casa Lleó Morera (1903–5, on the Passeig de Gracia beside buildings by Puig and Gaudí), which incorporates facade sculptures by Eusebi Arnau, interior furnishings by Gaspar Homar

Lluís Domènech i Montaner, Santa Creu i Sant Pau Hospital, Barcelona, 1901–12.

Lluís Domènech i
Montaner, Palau de
la Música, Barcelona,
1905–8.

and elaborate carpentry, glasswork and other decoration. In Domènech's
public buildings, he added modern functional innovations to ambitious
decorative programmes. His new general hospital for Barcelona, Santa
Creu i Sant Pau (1901–12), adapts the English garden city as a model for a
curative and hygienic environment, separating wards into 48 pavilions distributed in a park-like setting, all oriented to the south and connected by
underground passages for medical personnel. Underneath the Wagnerian
riot of all-over decorated surfaces and mythic references in the Palau de
la Música (1905–8, built for the Orféo Catalan chorus) is a steel-frame
structure with proto-curtain walls of stained glass.

Gaudí's sources of inspiration often approach the extremes of clichéd
exoticism seen in the Lunar Parks and Coney Islands of the day, but he
develops these themes not through the visual mimicry of historic models
but rather through a process of creative invention guided by an organic
unity between structure, material, ornament and form, derived from
Viollet-le-Duc's call for an architecture true to constructive logic.

He was a genuine structural innovator. In his designs, forms follow the
natural lines of their loads, as in the angled pergola-retaining walls of the

Parc Güell (1900–1914), the vaults of the crypt in the unfinished Colònia Güell Church (1908–15) and the Sagrada Família (1883–1926, unfinished at his death), where he was able to eliminate the need for flying buttresses. Similarly, in other works he used catenary arches, which minimized the horizontal structural forces present in Gothic pointed arches, improving on their structural performance. He experimented with hyperbolic paraboloids, which he derived from traditional thin ceramic Catalan vaults, as in the bridges of the Parc Güell and the atrium of Colònia Güell Church. As with Domènech's Palau de la Música, the Casa Milà on the Passeig de Gràcia (1905–10) is a steel-frame building, in this case with an irregular grid of displaced columns and a heavy stone curtain wall.

Domènech and Gaudí were involved in the Catalan nationalist movement in markedly different ways. Domènech was president of the Unió Catalanista (Catalanist Union Party) in 1892, and he presided over the drafting of a proposed Catalan constitution, the Bases of Manresa, one of the founding documents of Catalan nationalism. A decade later, the Bases formed the political platform of Prat de la Riba's Lliga Regionalista, which Domènech represented as a delegate in the Madrid parliament from 1901 to 1904. Among his other public activities, he taught at the Barcelona School of Architecture and was its director in 1900 and from 1905 to 1919.

As with Jacinct Verdaguer, Gaudí was a person of modest provincial origins, and like Verdaguer he took up the militant conservative religious faith

Antoni Gaudí, Parc Güell, Barcelona, 1900–1914. Early 20th-century postcard.

94 BARCELONA. — Parque Güell. — Vista general. LL.

Josep Puig i Cadafalch, Palau Nacional, Montjuïc, Barcelona, 1929. View of evening light show at the International Exposition. The fair was originally planned to celebrate the electrification of Barcelona.

of Barcelona's ruling class, a position that has recently made him a candidate for sainthood. The incomplete Sagrada Família was one of several overly ambitious church projects launched by wealthy conservatives of the era, including De Cubas's unfinished project for the Madrid cathedral. As we have mentioned, Gaudí also embraced the hermetic, mythic identity fantasies of his patrons in projects such as the Parc Güell, intended by Güell as a luxury garden suburb, modelled on those he had seen in England, where elevated roads, sunken pergolas and a covered Greek market hall invoke telluric native spirits.

A generation younger than Domènech, Josep Puig i Cadafalch followed him into the leading public roles of society architect, politician, teacher and scholar. The mansions and apartment buildings he designed in the Eixample, with their elaborate, finely chiselled yet conventional ornament, were derived from the Catalan Gothic (Quadras Palace, 1899–1906) and elements from northern Europe, such as the Flemish stepped gable of the Casa Amatller on the Passeig de Gràcia (1898–1900), or the conical-roofed towers and grouped English gables of the Casa Terrades (1903–5).

Puig was the architect of the Casa Martí (1895–6) in the Gothic Quarter, where the Quatres Gats café was opened in 1897 by Barcelona's leading artists of the time, Santiago Rusiñol and Ramón Casas. This was one of the few points of contact between Moderniste architecture and the artistic movement that gave it its name. The term first appears in the Fetes Modernistes that the two artists organized in the nearby fishing village of Sitges in 1892.

Puig's political career with the Lliga Regionalista brought him to the Barcelona County Council in 1901, where he headed the Department of Public Works and directed the founding of new Catalan cultural institutions. Prat de la Riba won a measure of autonomy for Catalunya in the form of the Mancomunitat (Commonwealth) in 1914, and Puig was its second president from 1917 until 1923, when General Miguel Primo de Rivera seized national power and abolished it. Until then, Puig was also chief architect of a new International Exposition, for which planning began in 1907, though it was not held until 1929, following several postponements and Madrid's purging of its pro-Catalan programming. Despite these changes, the fairgrounds' monumental axial ascent of Montjuïc remains true to Puig's extravagant vision of towers, domes and colonnades.

Noucentisme and the New Century

By this period of his career, Puig himself had abandoned Modernisme for the discrete, modernized Mediterranean classicism of Noucentisme. The Viennese Secession, founded in 1897, had a major impact on this movement, together with German Neoclassicism, French Art Deco and the American Beaux-Arts. Named for the new century, invoking a new collective spirit of renovation in the arts and literature, Noucentisme was taken up as the unofficial cultural movement of the Lliga. It was championed by the art critic Eugeni d'Ors in the pages of the party newspaper *La veu de Catalunya* as early as 1906. D'Ors promoted Noucentisme as a direct repudiation of Modernisme and its perceived excesses, in an attack that was, ironically, the first to identify Modernisme as a coherent style.

Given Modernisme's popularity today, it may be hard to understand the revulsion it provoked in the decades that followed its prime. Its fate is similar to that of Art Nouveau, whose rapid eclipse has been ascribed to both the pressures of technological change and the trauma and social conflicts of the First World War, which jolted the conservative bourgeoisie out of its reveries. Writing on the European movement as a whole in 1935, Walter Benjamin dissected the 'phantasmagoria' of the bourgeois interior, where 'the private individual, who in the office has to deal with reality, needs the domestic interior to sustain him in his illusions.'[12] In the case of Barcelona, which experienced violent political conflict in those years, Noucentisme recast these illusions in a more modest and collective form. In technological terms, like Art Deco and the other simplified academic classicisms of the period, it offered a temporary resolution to the tensions of what Benjamin calls 'an art besieged in its ivory tower by technology',[13] substituting the craft-oriented organicism of Modernisme with a clear separation between the straight lines of the structural frame and the more organic and decorative forms of artistic expression applied over it. Emerging elsewhere in Europe at roughly the same time, early manifestations of the Modern Movement were a more radically purgative response to these tensions. These two divergent paths gave rise to the cultural abysm that, during the 1929 Exposition, separated Mies van der Rohe's German Pavilion and the fair pavilions by Puig that form its immediate backdrop.

Noucentisme emerged following the 1901 election victory of the Lliga, which initiated a period of political turmoil that did not end until Primo de Rivera's 1923 military coup. The Lliga's rise coincided with the growing violence protagonized by popular anarchist and republican movements, and countered by the repressive measures of the Madrid-controlled local police and army, both of which, the historian Gerald Brenan observes, may have secretly abetted this violence as part of an underhanded strategy to defeat the Lliga's ambitions for greater Catalan autonomy.[14] Outstanding among the events that shook Barcelona in this period was the 'Tragic Week' of July 1909: five days of uncontrolled rioting in which 56 churches and convents were burned and more than 125 people killed. The period saw more than 2,000 bombings of Catalan factories and other Lliga interests, initiated with the 1893 anarchist bombing of a performance at the Liceu opera house; a series of crippling general strikes by the anarchist unions; and the deaths of hundreds of people in episodes of street warfare and assassination carried out by uncontrolled unionists and mercenary gangs.

Despite this climate, the leaders of the Lliga forged ahead in the consolidation of Catalan national identity through the promotion of primary education, the establishment of new cultural institutions and a united aesthetic vision under the banner of d'Ors's Noucentisme. They also pushed for the technological modernization of the Mancomunitat. The 1929 Exposition combined both ambitions in its exhibitions and was originally conceived to celebrate the electrification of Barcelona, which was showcased in its fountains of colour and light.

The Lliga thus laid the foundations for the official promotion of Catalan culture and modernization, which was resumed during the Second Republic and taken up again after the death of Franco. The exhortations

of d'Ors, under the pseudonym Xènius, in the pages of *La veu* in 1907 still echo in the fervour of cultural institution-building of pre-Olympic Barcelona in the 1980s:

> We Catalans, having been left behind on the shore, will we renounce with cowardly resignation our share of Humanism's booty? No! Quick, Quick! Bring on the Museums, bring on the Academies, bring on the Expositions. Let there be Education, let there be Urbanity, let there be Frivolity, let there be Galleries of Comely Catalanas, let there be the desire of all and the efforts of all, because today we, all saintly ambitious Catalans, propose to reach, on the way towards Humanism, the ships of Pantagruel, son of Gargantúa![15]

Many Barcelona buildings of the early twentieth century are loosely termed Noucentiste but more accurately reflect the influence of contemporary Viennese, French and American models of commercial buildings, rather than the more earthly, feminine Mediterranean spirit that d'Ors embodied in the protagonist of his allegorical novel *La ben plantada* (1912), also invoked in the stocky nudes of the Noucentiste artist Aristide Maillol. Public projects stand out amid the few clear examples of Noucentisme in architecture. Their detailing tends to be more delicately ornamental than classically sturdy, however, as in the Barcelona schools for the Mancomunitat designed by Josep Goday and others (1917–32), with *sgraffiti* ornamental stuccowork of cherubs and floral motifs over stolid, functional academic designs. Also worth mentioning are the Romantic gardens and the Greek amphitheatre created on Montjuïc for the 1929 Exposition by the French architect J.C.N. Forestier and the local landscape architect Nicolau M. Rubió i Tudurí (1914–29); and Rubió's later garden work, such as the Brunelleschian monastery he designed with Raimon Duran i Reynals for the Benedictines of La Verge de Montserrat (1922–40).

Oriol Bohigas's childhood memories of the traces of Noucentisme in a progressive Montessori school during the Republic are evocative of d'Ors's more rustic, Virgilian ethos: 'In the Montserrat Institute we began to appreciate the virtues, at once popular and aristocratic, of pergolas and arbours, of potted geraniums, of cypresses and hydrangeas.'[16] A similar aesthetic permeated the modern architecture of Madrid from the 1910s through the 1930s, especially among the architects associated with the Institución Libre de Enseñanza (Free Institution of Teaching, or ILE), as we shall see in the next chapter.

Though d'Ors's cultural activism had much in common with his progressive contemporaries of the ILE, with whom he was in contact, he went on to become a leading aesthetic ideologue of Francoism after the Civil War. With its rooted traditionalism and nationalist rhetoric, d'Ors movement can be seen as foreshadowing some of the aesthetic trends of fascism. Such a relation was more clearly established in the Italian Novecento, exemplified by the work of the architect Giovanni Muzio in Milan, which was inspired by the 'metaphysical' Mediterranean classicism of Giorgio de Chirico's paintings, and which later developed into the stark classicism of Mussolini's official architecture.

Other Nationalisms, Other Modernisms

The project to define an intrinsically Spanish style of architecture did not become a serious issue of debate outside Catalunya until Spain's humiliating defeat in the 1898 Spanish–American War, which produced a movement among the conservative architects of Madrid and elsewhere to revindicate national identity and pride. Their effort was launched in opposition to the use of French and other imported styles that had set the standard for advanced architecture at the beginning of the century, as seen in some of Madrid's most visible commissions. The first headquarters of La Unión y el Fénix at the head of the Gran Vía, by the French architects Jules and Raymond Février (1906–10; today the Edificio Metrópolis), and the Hotel Palace, one of Madrid's first grand hotels, built by Belgian promoters and engineers (1910–12), were sophisticated examples of the French empire style that featured pioneering structures of reinforced concrete and other technical advances.

The challenge after 1898 was to come up with a national style that would favourably position Spain among modern empire-building nations, at least to local eyes, in the contemporary global context of jingoistic posturing and military and economic competition. One side of this debate was taken up by the traditionalists, who sought to promote various historic regional styles, an approach that had its greatest success in upper-class domestic architecture. Civic architecture, on the other hand, was dominated by different versions of a modernized academic practice under the influence of broader international trends, but with reference to historic Spanish sources. The rivalry between the proponents of these approaches was celebrated in highly publicized competitions, which encouraged the kind of academic grandstanding revived by Velázquez Bosco in the nineteenth century and later carried to new heights in the early Franco era.

The traditionalists sought to base a national style on ideas of inherent 'racial' character and reference to more 'heroic' imperial times. But given Spain's cultural diversity, no single historic style could be considered definitive. The traditionalists' efforts, as championed by Vicente Lampérez, author of the monumental *History of Spanish Christian Architecture* (1908–9), and his disciples Leonardo Rucabado of Cantabria and Aníbal González of Sevilla, came to focus on the scholarly minutiae of historic details, classified in regional terms and superficially applied over contemporary building typologies.

Lampérez was behind the 1911 competition of ideas organized by the Society of Friends of Art for various projects 'to be realized in one of the traditional Spanish styles'.[17] Rucabado's winning entry for a 'Palace for a Noble in the Mountains' was the result of his research into the seventeenth- and eighteenth-century architecture of Cantabria and the Basque Country. The design is an amalgam of quotes that struck even Lampérez as an 'excess of archeology', including 'the shield of arms of Rubalcaba, the gateway of Puente Arce, the *solanas* [sun galleries] of Santillana, the tower of Elsedo, the cross of Pámanes, the porticos of Toranzo and the chapel of Gajano'.[18]

Rucabado studied architecture in Barcelona in the 1890s under Domènech and Puig, and his work brought their richness of detail to the north, in contrast to the austerity of his original regional models, as some critics have pointed out. His mansions in Santander and Bilbao are characterized by the deep eaves, towers, *solanas* and porticos he found in the region, which he adapted to the conventions of the upper-class English suburb and its houses that had become popular in Spain. Examples include the Casa Tomás Allende in the development of Las Arenas in Bilbao (1911), his own house, La Casuca, in Santander (1915) and a commercial building for Tomás Allende in Madrid's Plaza de Canalejas (1916–20), which used historic motifs from central Spain.

Aníbal González applied a similar enthusiasm to the creation of an Andalucian style for private houses and Sevilla's Ibero-American Exposition of 1929. He began designing the fairgrounds as its chief architect in 1911, but, as in Barcelona, the event was repeatedly postponed due to workers' strikes, political manoeuvring and the First World War. In the Exposition's monumental Plaza de España (1914–28) and three buildings of the Plaza de América (1912–22), González drew from local Islamic, Mudéjar, Plateresque (Spain's primitive Renaissance style) and Baroque models to adorn a standard Beaux-Arts repertoire of colonnades, towers and monumental axes, vividly finished in brick and brightly coloured glazed tile, as in the designs of his Madrid master, Velázquez Bosco.

The traditionalists' position was challenged by the Galician-born architect Antonio Palacios, another pupil of Velázquez Bosco, whose verbose formal brilliance dominated Madrid's architecture during the first decades of the century. Following cues from Germany and Vienna, Palacios based his proposal for a monumental national style on a florid Beaux-Arts base, which he personalized with idiosyncratic elements, an unorthodox, eclectic classical grammar and references to historic Spanish styles. His career was launched by the 1904 competition for the Palacio de Comunicaciones, or central post office, in Madrid's Plaza de Cibeles (designed with Joaquín Otamendi, 1904–18). In the academic composition he abstracted and combined Spanish Gothic and Plateresque elements in an arcing fan of towers, pavilions and wings. Inside, the multi-storey glass-roofed operations nave is interwoven with a matrix of modern technical services. The building became Madrid's City Hall in 2011.

Antonio Palacios with Joaquín Otamendi, Palacio de Comunicaciones (central post office), Madrid, 1904–18.

This superposition of compositional and functional elements was raised to a new level in his competition-winning design for the nearby Círculo de Bellas Artes (Circle of Fine Arts) on Calle de Alcalá (1919–26). Palacios superimposed the different programme elements vertically – a theatre and gymnasium, exhibition salons, a ballroom, dining and gaming rooms, artists' studios and so on – and expressed them volumetrically on the exterior in an asymmetrical, Beaux-Arts compositional wedding cake that approaches the simplicity of Art Deco in its upper reaches. These two buildings, among Madrid's most representative monuments, were joined on Alcalá by a number of competition-winning bank and commercial buildings, designed by Palacios and others with similar ostentation.

Palacios's projects eclipsed the new buildings of the nearby Gran Vía, cut from Alcalá to the Plaza de España from 1910 to 1954 (after a period of planning dating back to 1866). Behind the exuberant prow of La Unión y el Fénix, its first blocks are an unremarkable mix of eclectic Spanish and French styles typical of the era. As with Barcelona's Via Laietana, it acquired a more monumental and cosmopolitan scale along the blocks built in the 1920s, with buildings designed by Palacios's pupils and rivals, many of whom were beginning to experiment elsewhere with more modern designs, as shall be seen later. Examples include Teodoro de Anasagasti's Madrid-Paris Department Stores (1920–24; enlarged 1933–5), Secundino Zuazo's Palacio de la Música cinema (1924–8) and Pedro Muguruza's Palacio de la Prensa, or Press Building (1924–8), with its mixed-use programme incorporating offices, apartments and a large cinema, whose main feature is a brick tower designed around a single soaring arch.

However, the project that attracted the most attention on the Gran Vía, the 90-metre-tall (295 ft) Edificio Telefónica (1925–9), was largely designed in the United States. The publicly held Spanish telephone company was organized under contract with International Telephone & Telegraph. Their New York architects, Weeks & Day, directed the project for its new headquarters following American standards, working with a young in-house architect, Ignacio de Cárdenas. The result is a small New York sky-scraper, typical of the 1920s, combining regular fenestration and setbacks with Cárdenas's smattering of Spanish Baroque details. As with the Hotel Palace a decade earlier, its modern mechanical services, steel structure and flexible office layouts – all designed in New York – made Spain's technical and economic backwardness painfully evident. Writing about the Spanish construction industry during these years, the young architect Luis Lacasa noted that elevators and boilers were imported from Germany and Switzerland, specialized pavements and metalwork were American, metal windows were English and even cork, a Spanish resource, was manufactured into linoleum and insulation by foreign firms. 'Only bricks, cement and

Antonio Palacios,
Círculo de Bellas Artes
(Circle of Fine Arts),
Madrid, 1919–26.

36

Ignacio de Cárdenas. Arquitecto.

some metal products are left for national production,' he lamented.[19] Seen against this economic and technical inferiority, the heroic posturing of Spain's leading architects struck a younger generation as excessive, and by the mid-1920s a sizeable group was ready to adapt the Modern Movement's purgative cure.

Weeks & Day (New York)
with Ignacio de Cárdenas,
Edificio Telefónica,
Madrid, 1925–9.
Contemporary postcard
rendering.

chapter two

The First Modernists, 1910–25

At mid-afternoon on the banks of Lake Ch'ing Tsao, on a terrace overhung by the blossoming branch of a cherry tree, the two friends talk and read to one another. These are the happy days of the Ch'ing Dynasty. The youngest recites the fragment of a poem:

'I want to see the table clean, crisp, the crystal must gleam. On the tablecloth I place a clutch of roses and wild herbs.'

'Admirable!' exclaims his friend. 'No one better than AZORÍN to express the refinement of China'.

Jorge Guillén, 1951[1]

The works that constitute what contemporaries and historians call the 'modern' or 'rational' architecture of the 1920s and '30s in Spain are the product of two different impulses, the first local in origin and the second responding directly to international modernism.[2] The first emerged from the same critical intellectual movement of 'Regeneration' that produced the writers of the Generation of '98 and the Silver Age in Spanish literature (1898–1936), the progressive political thinkers and leaders of the Second Republic and Spain's first important scientists. Its origins can be traced to architects associated with Madrid's Institución Libre de Enseñanza (ILE) in the 1910s, including Antonio Flórez, Leopoldo Torres Balbás and Teodoro de Anasagasti. Adapting ideas taken by the ILE from progressive currents of European thought – and English and German education reformers in particular – these men quietly introduced concepts of functional design and non-academic thinking to architectural practice and education. They also reformulated the contemporary debate over a national architectural style, which they integrated into the broader question of the regeneration and modernization of Spain in response to the 'crisis of 1898' provoked by Spain's humiliating defeat in the Spanish–American War.

Although this Madrid-based modernism was similar in its origins to the Noucentiste movement in Barcelona, and was influenced by the same international trends, its younger practitioners were more radical in their rejection of ornament and overt historic or stylistic references. This group included Carlos Arniches, Martín Domínguez, Rafael Bergamín and

Children in the patio of the Cervantes School in Madrid, designed by Antonio Flórez (1913–16), built following the school reform principles of the Free Institution of Teaching.

others, who came to be known as the Generation of 1925, in emulation of the so-called Generation of 1927 in Spanish poetry led by Federico García Lorca. These architects diluted the compositional habits of their academic training with rational design methods and an interest in popular architecture to create a conservative modernism that featured simple, volumetric masonry forms. The overall trajectory and outlook of the movement in the 1910s and '20s can thus be compared in range to that of older pioneers of modern architecture, such as Peter Behrens and Otto Wagner, and near contemporaries, such as Robert Mallet-Stevens and Ernst May.

Spain's reception of the more radical proposals of international modernism was filtered through this outlook. The ideas and works of modernism were introduced by young architects in the 1920s such as Fernando García Mercadal, who travelled widely in Europe from 1920 to 1927, establishing contacts with leading figures and publishing their work in the pages of the magazine *Arquitectura*, and Josep Lluís Sert, who worked in Le Corbusier's Paris office in 1929.

The combination of a local impulse towards a forceful simplicity of forms and the often poorly understood lessons taken from bolder European experiments resulted in what to many has seemed to be a rather tepid contribution from Spain to the Modern Movement in these years.[3] In Spain's defence, however, some have argued that its modernism, appearing late in Europe and interrupted by the outbreak of the Civil War, did not have time to fully develop.[4] Writing from a Catalan perspective, Oriol Bohigas maintains that the only bona fide Spanish modern architecture is that which was produced by the members of GATEPAC (Group of Spanish Architects and Technicians for the Progress of Contemporary Architecture), specifically Sert and his group in Barcelona and José Manuel Aizpurúa in San Sebastián, since they were integrated in the official European movement of the Congrès Internationaux d'Architecture Moderne (International Congresses for Modern Architecture, or CIAM), and correctly understood and applied its radical formal and social programmes.[5] Others argue that the basic ingredients of Spanish modernism, with its debt to popular architecture and local climate and tradition, constitute a Mediterranean alternative to the 'machine aesthetic' of northern Europe – an argument that Sert also proposed in his time.[6] Of course, as in the Modern Movement as a whole, this first Spanish modernism was by no means uniform in character; its practitioners ranged from original innovators such as the engineer Eduardo Torroja, a pioneer in thin-shell concrete vaults and cantilevers, to an abundant and varied commercial modernism, led by figures such as Luis Gutiérrez Soto, which was practised in a spirit of fashionable Eclecticism, at times rivalling the best commercial work of Weimar Germany in its formal exuberance.

The Origins of Madrid's Local Modernism

The ILE anticipated and exemplified the reform spirit of the Generation of '98. It was founded in Madrid in 1876 by Francisco Giner de los Ríos and other professors who had been expelled from Madrid's Universidad Central for their liberal convictions, following the failure of the Revolution of 1868 and its ensuing First Republic. Known as Krausians for their allegiance to the ideas of the obscure German philosopher Karl Christian Friedrich Krause – a choice indicative of the intellectual isolation of Spain at mid-century – they used his idealist, humanist philosophical system as an ethical guide and model for the rational reform of society. According to Raymond Carr, the project of the ILE was 'the most serious and consistent attempt to create the intellectual preconditions of a liberal democracy' in Spain. Given the Revolution's failure to transform Spain from above, the ILE's founders determined that a more profound reform based on modern methods of education was the necessary first step.[7]

At the time, Spain's illiteracy rate was 70 per cent.[8] With a financially weak state, primary and secondary education was limited and largely in the hands of the Church, which firmly resisted new ideas. The founders of the ILE began by offering private, non-sectarian primary and secondary education for Spain's literate classes, an elitist approach intended to sow the seeds for wider reforms in the future. Its teaching system replaced the dogmatic instruction of Church schooling and Spanish universities, based on copying and memorization, with intuitive methods that relied on the innate intelligence and curiosity of pupils and that respected their individual liberty of conscience, in the tradition of Rousseau. The ILE sought to address the complete formation of the child in its psychological, ethical and intellectual dimensions.

The loosely formed group of intellectuals who made up the Generation of '98 found a rallying point in the national crisis of identity provoked by the Spanish–American War. One of its leaders was the social historian Joaquín Costa, a founder of the ILE and a driving force behind the Regenerationist movement, who called for drastic 'iron surgery' of an implicitly dictatorial nature on the ills of the existing social and political order. Other members included the writers Miguel de Unamuno, Pío Baroja and Azorín, the playwright Ramón del Valle-Inclán, known for his portrayals of the *esperpéntico* (grotesque) in Spanish society, and the younger philosopher José Ortega y Gasset. Carr describes their writings as 'the protest of a literary minority against the conformism, emptiness, rhetoric, and ignorance of the existing educational and literary establishment, which, in its turn, reflected the "organized corruption" of the structure created by the Restoration statesmen'.[9] But such criticism was matched by vehement opposition from the right, the conservative heirs of Carlism and other militant defenders of the Church, who saw the post-republican Restoration, with its gentlemen's agreement of alternating conservative and liberal rule, as a betrayal of Catholic Spain. The Church, simultaneously under attack from revolutionary workers' movements and traumatized by church burnings, murders and other violence, mobilized its upper-class base in a crusade of evangelizing and political campaigning. After 1900, writes Carr, 'The old language of a battle to the end reappeared on both sides.'[10]

In reaction to the deceptions of the 1868 Revolution and the high-pitched political confrontations of the time, Giner de los Ríos and his colleagues avoided direct political and religious debate; instead, they cultivated a civilized atmosphere of good manners and respect for others, and an ethical code of behaviour, developed from their Krausist principles, that had an implicit aesthetic dimension. In an article that appeared in *Arquitectura* in 1918, Azorín praised the ILE's promotion of 'good taste, order and simplicity' in all spheres: 'The influence of this Institute has been translated into a thousand diverse and gratifying manifestations. Simple manners, sober speech, truthfulness, sincerity, the well-ordered house, silence – that "marvelous silence" Cervantes spoke of – the simple, clean suit, the elegantly printed book.'[11] This mild moral asceticism also imbues the architecture promoted by the ILE.

The Schools of Antonio Flórez, 1910–15

Following the turn of the century, under the sponsorship of liberal governments, members of the ILE had a direct role in shaping national education policy, which resulted in building programmes in which ILE principles had their first impact on architecture. In 1907, following one of Giner's proposals, the Ministry of Public Education and Fine Arts founded the Junta for Advanced Studies and Scientific Research (Junta para Ampliación de Estudios e Investigaciones Científicas, or JAE), whose campus on the 'Hill of the Poplars' in the northern suburbs of Madrid grew to include the Residencia de Estudiantes (Students' Residence), the state high school known as the Instituto-Escuela and other institutions that adopted ILE teaching principles. In 1910, the ministry built two model schools in Madrid using ILE ideas, and in 1920 it launched a nationwide school-building programme.

Antonio Flórez, himself a pupil of the ILE, was the architect in charge of these programmes and dedicated his career to school-building. A classmate of Antonio Palacios (Madrid, class of 1904[12]) and winner of the Rome Prize, which included several years of residency there and European

Antonio Flórez, Menéndez y Pelayo School, Madrid, 1922–8.

travel, he won a competition on his return in 1910 for a Froebel school in Pontevedra (not built), based on the nursery teaching system of the German educator Friedrich Froebel, the inventor of the Froebel blocks that Frank Lloyd Wright used as a child, and a basic reference for the ILE. This competition brought him to the attention of Manuel B. Cossío, Giner's main disciple and a key consultant on the experimental school programme of 1910. Working with Cossío, Flórez designed two model schools, the Cervantes and the Principe de Asturias (1913–16), for poor Madrid neighbourhoods.

In his pioneering history of the period, the architect Bernardo Giner de los Ríos, a nephew of the ILE founder who worked under Flórez in later years, described these schools as precursors to functionalism: 'an architecture conceived and realized in a scientific manner'.[13] Following English and French models, banks of classrooms were oriented towards indirect northern light, breaking the otherwise symmetrical composition of the building, with wide south-facing circulation galleries, modern sanitary facilities and ample playgrounds. The galleries were designed to accommodate special activities and serve as play areas on rainy days. As in his later schools and at the Residencia de Estudiantes, Flórez used inexpensive, rough local brick with simple rectangular openings (incorporating iron lintels for the large spans of classroom glazing) and minimal regionalist details – deep eaves, hipped tile roofs, a few simple decorative string courses of brick and the occasional Mudéjar-style stair tower or upper gallery of round-arched windows. The aesthetic impact of the building thus relied on the quality of its construction and its massing and proportions, rather than on an ornamental system.

Florez's proto-functionalism was the result of applying ILE educational ideas to the problem of the school building, as sketched in the writings of Francisco Giner and Cossío. In 1882, Giner recommended that school buildings should avoid 'unnecessary expense' and 'superfluous adornment'. He called for ample playgrounds and 'hygienic' desks for correct posture, arranged in a circle around the teacher rather than in rows.[14] In 1911, Cossío wrote: 'the schoolhouse should display the greatest simplicity, and everything in it should be subservient to its hygienic and pedagogic conditions.'[15] Cossío was also a pioneering professor of art history – he established El Greco's modern standing as a major artist – and the schools he built with Flórez were more than functional exercises, if one takes into account the didactic benefits of their aesthetic qualities. Bernardo Giner credits both men with seeking to make their schools 'an element of inspiration for the teacher, an aesthetic reference in the teacher's lessons to students, and, indirectly, to encourage the love of the child for the school'.[16] In 1920, Flórez was named director of the newly formed State Technical Office for School

Construction, a conduit for building funds and technical assistance to municipalities, which were ultimately responsible for local public schools. Working with Bernardo Giner, Torres Balbás and others, Flórez designed prototypes that accounted for regional climates, materials and styles throughout Spain. General Miguel Primo de Rivera accelerated financing for the programme after taking power in 1923, and it was further expanded during the Second Republic. Giner notes that in his area of project supervision in Alicante, 101 out of 111 municipalities built schools during the 1920s.[17] While the overall quality of these buildings was distinguished, the best documented and most influential were the six school groups Flórez built in Madrid, particularly the Menéndez y Pelayo School (1922–8), where he introduced a steel-frame structure to allow floor-to-ceiling north-facing walls of glass in the multi-storey classroom block.

The Residencia de Estudiantes

A division of the Junta for Advanced Studies and Scientific Research, the Residencia de Estudiantes (founded in 1910) was modelled on English colleges. It was intended to house students and young professors coming to Madrid from the provinces, as an improvement on unsupervised boarding house accommodation. It was established to encourage contact and exchanges with other European universities, and sponsored grants, language studies and the like, an idea promoted by Giner to help overcome Spain's intellectual isolation. Under the direction of Alberto Jiménez Fraud, a teacher formed in the ILE and Cossío's son-in-law, the Residencia offered a community for learning based on ILE ideas. Complementing the offerings of Madrid's university schools, it held classes and provided a library, laboratories and other facilities, and organized cultural and athletic programmes, excursions and informal *tertulias* (discussions) designed to foment multidisciplinary intellectual exchange. The campus was an important part of the concept, with its natural setting and ample athletic grounds. The parallel Residencia de Señoritas was established with the same aims in 1915, on a separate site of existing buildings in northern Madrid. The Junta as a whole was directed by the neurologist Santiago Ramón y Cajal, winner of the 1906 Nobel Prize in Physiology or Medicine.

The Residencia was a leading centre of Madrid intellectual life and the flagship of the ILE's ideals. Its most famous student residents were Federico García Lorca, Luis Buñuel and Salvador Dalí, who met and became friends there in the late 1910s, and the scientist Severo Ochoa, another Nobel winner (in 1959), who studied there under the physiologist and future Republican leader Juan Negrín in the 1920s. Other occasional residents included Unamuno, the poets Rafael Alberti, Juan Ramón Jiménez (Nobel Prize in

Antonio Flórez,
'El Transatlántico',
Residencia de
Estudiantes, campus of
the Junta for Advanced
Studies, Madrid,
1913–15.

Literature, 1956) and José Moreno Villa, a poet and artist and director of *Arquitectura* from 1926 to 1930. The cultural events and tertulias of the Residencia attracted leading intellectuals and cultural figures of the period, including Ortega y Gasset, Valle-Inclán, Eugeni d'Ors and Manuel de Falla. Foreign lecturers and guests during the 1920s and '30s included Albert Einstein, Marie Curie, Henri Bergson, John Maynard Keynes, H. G. Wells, Filippo Marinetti, Paul Valéry, Paul Éluard, Louis Aragon, Max Jacob, Alexander Calder and the composers Maurice Ravel, Darius Milhaud, Francis Poulenc and Igor Stravinsky.[18] Flórez built two parallel dormitory buildings for the Residencia (1913–15) and a laboratory-residence, baptized by students as El Transatlántico for its flat central roof and open circulation galleries – taken from the *corrala*, Madrid's humble vernacular housing type – that featured 'our drying clothes flapping in the wind like the crew mounted on a ship's rigging', as Moreno Villa recalled.[19] As in Flórez's schools, the dormitories were oriented to the north along single-loaded galleries, with simple exteriors of rough brick, wood carpentry and tile roofs. In the court between the dormitories, Juan Ramón Jiménez laid out a garden of oleander and boxwood modelled on the austere Friars' Garden at the Monastery of the Escorial north of Madrid.

The ILE's moderate asceticism is evident in many of the comments of residents of and visitors to Flórez's buildings. Rafael Alberti described his room, with its 'bright, unadorned' whitewashed walls and sturdy functional furniture, as 'almost a cell, suspended between oleanders and embraced by climbing ivy'.[20] Of its exteriors, Moreno Villa praised Flórez's

Antonio Flórez, Twin Pavilions, Residencia de Estudiantes, campus of the Junta for Advanced Studies, Madrid, 1913–15.

use of unadorned brick, 'the poor material of our handsome Mudéjar monuments'.[21] Bernardo Giner quotes Alberto Jiménez Fraud's appreciation for 'the purity of the architectonic lines, the proportion of the massing, the colour of the high-fired brick, which, burned by the sun, acquired a handsome toasted colour, and the austere decoration, an achievement of sobriety and good taste.' Giner also cites Walter Gropius's praise for the buildings as an example of 'the functional' in his 1930 lecture there, 'adding that in architecture the function of colour is essential, and is only offered by noble materials such as stone and brick'.[22]

Flórez's references to the Mudéjar, the modest product of a mix of cultures rather than a potential standard of patriotic national Catholic identity, were in harmony with the progressive ideals of the ILE. But like Noucentisme, this essentially regionalist approach offered refuge in a traditional image of Spain that was distant from the proletarian strife of Barcelona, Sevilla and other cities. It reflects, like the project of the ILE as a whole, the outlook of a liberal class that was ill-prepared for what Ortega y Gasset in his 1930 book *The Revolt of the Masses* would later describe as the 'new mass man' emerging with industrialization and the appearance of large-scale political movements, and who would become one of the chief subjects of modern architecture in northern Europe and Italy after the First World War.

Torres Balbás: From Regionalism to Modernity

Flórez's utilitarian regionalism forms part of the complex response by the architects associated with the ILE to the debate over a national style. This response set the stage for the development of a particularly Spanish approach to early modernism. Leopoldo Torres Balbás presented the theoretical arguments for this response in the first issues of *Arquitectura*, which he edited from its founding in 1918 until 1926. Published by the Central Society of Architects, the main professional organization in central Spain at the time, *Arquitectura*'s editorial board was dominated by men close to the ILE, including Balbás, Moreno Villa and Teodoro de Anasagasti. Balbás (class of 1916) was a student of Cossío and Manuel Gómez Moreno, the archaeologist and director of the Junta's Centre for Historic Studies. He became professor of art history at the Madrid School of Architecture in 1931 and was the conservator of the Alhambra in Granada from 1923 to 1936. He is credited with modernizing Spain's restoration policies, replacing the interpretive method of Viollet-le-Duc with scientific principles of conservation that respected the complexities of archaeological data, and in which restorations were clearly distinguished from original artefacts.

As with the Rucabado–Palacios debate over a plausible 'national' style, Balbás's theoretical reflections grew out of a preoccupation with the renewal of Spanish identity and vitality in the modern era following the crisis of 1898. However, he took a radically different approach from both, rejecting what he decried as the traditionalists' 'pastiche' of historic details. In his article 'Mientras labran los sillares' (As They Work the Stone), he called for a deeper study of the 'essential' character and nature of Spain's 'anonymous, popular' architecture, and an openness to new ideas from abroad, which, as he pointed out, characterized the best of Spain's historic architecture:

> We propose a healthy *Casticismo* [roughly translated, 'authentic traditionalism'], open to all influences, that studies the architecture of our country, exploring its cities, towns and countryside, analysing, measuring and sketching old buildings. And not only the most monumental and elaborate, but also, and perhaps preferentially, the more modest, in which we might best perceive the constructive spirit of our race, in order to assimilate not the external forms that vary most in architecture such as the decorations and mouldings, but rather the proportions, the relation of masses and volumes, the distribution of the decoration, etc., that is to say, its essence.[23]

This call for inspiration in popular architecture would have many echoes in the development of Spanish modernism. It echoed in turn the Regenerationists' interest in popular life and culture, which sprang from their underlying belief that the country's future depended on improving the lives of its popular classes. This interest ranged from the sociological and statistical studies of Joaquín Costa to the poetry of Antonio Machado and Lorca, who combined avant-garde techniques with popular ballad and song forms, or the music of Manuel de Falla and the travel writings of Baroja, Azorín and others, who set out to explore the landscapes, cultures and peoples of Spain as if discovering an unknown country. This interest peaked during the Second Republic with programmes that brought culture to the countryside, such as La Barraca, Lorca's travelling theatre group, or Cossío's state-sponsored Pedagogic Missions that brought books, film, music, theatre and a travelling art museum to poor rural villages. In the Madrid School of Architecture, Balbás, Flórez and Anasagasti emulated the excursions of ILE schools, taking their students on trips to study historic and popular art and architecture all over Spain (though their calls for a general reform of architectural education following ILE ideas, including Anasagasti's 1923 book *The Teaching of Architecture: Modern Culture, Artistic Technique*, had little effect outside their classes).

Balbás's article is most directly indebted to Unamuno's famous 1895 essay 'En torno al Casticismo' (On Casticismo) and his call to discover 'the

Federico García Lorca (front row, second from left) and other members of La Barraca, his travelling theatre troupe, 1933.

landscape, the personages and the life of our people', a process Unamuno also linked to an opening up to the rest of Europe: 'The future of Spanish society is waiting within our historic society, in its intra-history, in its unknown people, and it will not re-emerge with force until it is awakened by the winds of a European horizon.'[24] On the other hand, as Unamuno and Balbás both made clear, Spain's renewal also depended on an end to its intellectual isolation, a basic ILE goal taken up in the foreign study programmes of the Junta for Advanced Studies and the Residencia de Estudiantes. As Ortega y Gasset famously phrased it in 1909, 'if Spain is the problem, then Europe is the solution,' with 'Europe' signifying above all modern scientific and professional training.[25]

Balbás was an acute observer of international developments and clearly saw the signs of crisis that were mobilizing the pioneers of the Modern Movement in northern Europe after the First World War, and the new directions a movement for architecture renewal should take. In a 1919 essay, 'The New Forms of Architecture', he anticipated many of the arguments of Le Corbusier's *Vers une architecture* (Towards an Architecture) of 1923, proclaiming the 'beginning of a new era' based on the 'dynamic' forms of the machine.[26] Curiously, however, he was later put off by the blunt, graphic argument of Le Corbusier's book and was the first of many Spaniards to dismiss him, in his words, as a 'journalist and charlatan', though conceding the book's polemical value.[27]

'The New Forms of Architecture' was a landmark in the introduction of modernism to Spain. Like Le Corbusier, Balbás denounced the 'decadence' of architecture as it was then practised, and saw its future in the 'beautiful forms' of 'great transatlantic ships, of gracious and energetic curves, imposing battleships, gigantic locomotives that seem to glide through the countryside, aeroplanes that imitate, like almost all the others, the forms of nature, together with metal viaducts and bridges, modern train stations, and the enormous factories built during the war'. He concluded, 'the works of this modern architecture offer the same constructive logic, the same reasoning in their forms, as the best Greek temple and the purest Gothic cathedral. And like them they are collective works whose authors remain in anonymity'.[28] Yet he dismissed the efforts of an unnamed group of architects in Germany and Austria, presumably related to the Deutscher Werkbund, whose 'search for a Modern style in which anything is allowed for the sake of originality' must 'confound the worthy bourgeoisie of Darmstadt, Munich or Weimar'. Balbás thus looked forward to the coming of a new architecture, but he was unprepared to recognize its first stirrings.

A Nascent Modernism, 1915–29

In the work of Anasagasti, Gustavo Fernández Balbuena and others in the 1910s and '20s, Torres Balbás's still vague call for renewal was translated into different combinations of a simplified regionalism, with increasingly 'modern' ideas and forms incorporated through the architects' exposure to successive developments in northern European architecture via trips and foreign magazines. This exposure ranged from the Secessionists to the work of Auguste Perret (Rue Franklin Apartments, Paris, 1903), Hendrik Berlage (Amsterdam Stock Exchange, 1897–1903) and Peter Behrens and the Deutscher Werkbund (Werkbund Exhibition, Cologne, 1914). It may also have extended to Adolf Loos (Steiner House, Vienna, 1910) and Charles Rennie Mackintosh (Glasgow Art School, 1896–1909).[29]

This first approach to a Spanish modernism was not without its formal uncertainties, as can be seen in the work of Anasagasti (class of 1906), with its often eclectic mix of regional references and modern ideas. During his travels as a winner of the Rome Prize in the early 1910s, Anasagasti immersed himself in Viennese and German architecture and brought back not only the moody monumental Romanticism of his early funerary projects but a lively interest in the possibilities of reinforced concrete and practical, functional thinking. His best work combines a simplified monumentality with a regional flavour, as in the Granada villa for the artist José María Rodríguez-Acosta with its austere, expressive massing of whitewashed towers on the terraced slopes of the Alhambra (1914–28, in collaboration with the artist and others). His Teatro Villamarta (1926) in the Andalusian city of Jerez de la Frontera is a whitewashed volume framed by a pair of tall abstract spires – slender, lightened versions of the paired towers of his early memorial projects – which anticipate later fusions of popular and modern forms in the 1950s.

Anasagasti became a specialist in cinema design, introducing one of the first large-span, exposed reinforced concrete structures for the Teatro Monumental in Madrid (1922–3). In the Teatro Pavón (1924–5), he made a pioneering foray into some of the leitmotifs of Spanish modernism – the corner window, the cantilevered bay and shading plane – together with abstractly patterned wall planes and an angled clock tower raised on legs, where an apparently Constructivist impulse was restrained by his academic training.

In Anasagasti's writings, his influence on his students as a champion of change can be seen. Already in 1914 he described simplicity as 'the most important condition of beauty' in architecture and looked forward to the promise of concrete and other new materials, and the coming of 'the ideal house of the twentieth century, the product of science', in which 'air and light exercise their beneficial influence'.[30] He quickly grasped the formal consequences of the new functional requirements of the movie theatre and exploited their shock value, writing in 1919: 'The cinema is a camera obscura where images are projected, and as such its exterior needs very few openings. Will the lack of openings harden its face? And what does this matter to us if that is the reality, which we must serve without prejudice?'[31] At the same time, he maintained his interest in popular architecture,

Teodoro de Anasagasti, Carmen Rodríguez-Acosta, Granada, 1914–28. View from the garden.

Teodoro de Anasagasti,
Teatro Pavón, Madrid,
1924–5.

which was the subject of his entry address to the Royal Academy of Fine
Arts in 1929.

The diverse ingredients of early Spanish modernism were synthesized
by Gustavo Fernández Balbuena (class of 1913) in a large apartment building (1925–7) for the Marqués de Amurrio in Madrid's Ensanche, with its
white stucco upper volumes, unadorned openings and mix of imported
and Spanish details, from vertical bands of Chicago bay windows to a rustic
base of exposed brick arches. A series of private houses he built near the
Residencia de Estudiantes before his premature death in 1931 show a more
uncertain development from restrained regionalism into an ambiguous

Gustavo Fernández Balbuena, apartments for the Marqués de Amurrio, Madrid, 1925–7.

terrain of asymmetrical brick massing and broad stone panels with a vaguely Art Deco flavour. He devoted most of his career to forming a modern urban planning department for the city of Madrid. His sense for urban street space, tectonic construction and classical rhythm, as displayed in the brick arcade of the Amurrio apartments, was taken up by his contemporary Secundino Zuazo in two of the most important works of the 1930s, the Casa de las Flores housing block and the New Ministries building, both directly related to the competition for the extension of Madrid prepared by Balbuena in 1929, as we shall discuss in the next chapter.

There were isolated modernizing initiatives outside Madrid in these years. In Gorliz, near Bilbao, Mario Camiña built an early work in reinforced concrete, the Children's Sanatorium of 1910–14, using the unadorned classicism of Perret, a project Sigfried Giedion praised in *Cahiers d'art* in 1931.[32] In Valencia, Demetrio Ribes followed a similar course in his use of reinforced concrete for the 1918 E. Ferrer department store. His most important building, Valencia Train Station (1906–17), was influenced by the decorative modern classicism of Vienna, though it is misleadingly termed Moderniste.

Secundino Zuazo (class of 1912) was the most influential figure of this generation. He was a pupil of Antonio Palacios and struggled in his early career between the formal rigour of his historicist training and the unexplored territory of modern materials and forms. Not connected with the ILE, he lacked Anasagasti's and Balbuena's interest in popular architecture, which served them as a mediator between modern ideas and their academic training. And Zuazo did not come into fruitful contact with European architecture until a 1925 visit to the Netherlands. Of his experience working under Palacios he commented, 'I began to make great use of the eraser. Palacios overworked his pencil, and my erasing perturbed him.'[33] But for his first important work, the Palacio de la Música on the Gran Vía (1924–8),

Secundino Zuazo, rendering of the Palacio de la Música cinema, Madrid, 1924–8.

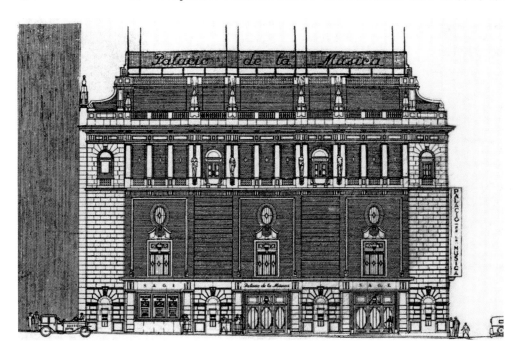

he confessed that he backed away from this purgative simplicity, fearing the loss of a specifically Spanish identity:

> My first sketches tended towards an eminently modern work. But thinking about its development and execution, in the difficulties of building the idea, and moreover, when I realized that I was moved by a tendency that was neither born nor felt in my country, I judged this path to be false. I didn't want to repeat the case of the Perrets, who had built that admirable example of modern architecture in Paris, the Théâtre Champs-Elysées, but full of German influences. In that moment, France, always in the vanguard of the nineteenth century, lost its hegemony.[34]

Like Flórez, Zuazo found a way out of this dilemma and towards what he termed 'architectonic truth' by basing his use of historic styles on the tectonic syntax of the materials and their construction, rather than a more superficial assembly of historic quotes. This can be seen in the woven brick and stone elements in the Palacio de la Música, or in his competition project for the Círculo de Bellas Artes (1919). Although related to Viollet-le-Duc's structural rationalism, this approach was arrived at by Zuazo through his direct study of Juan Herrera's sixteenth-century monastery El Escorial and the work of Juan de Villanueva, which also taught him aspects of organization and urban planning that would prove essential to his larger projects of the 1930s.

Zuazo discovered the means to refine and simplify this approach during his visit to the Netherlands, where he saw projects by Hendrik Berlage – a true disciple of Viollet-le-Duc – the School of Amsterdam and Willem Dudok. He was most impressed by Dudok's recently completed schools and bathhouse in Hilversum, which conservatively combined Neoplastic abstraction and the constructive honesty of Berlage's brickwork, creating austere cubic compositions without forgoing classical weight and dignity. On his return, in a series of private commissions in Madrid such as the house and studio for the sculptor Sebastián Miranda (1928), Zuazo brought his architecture close to the synthesis of Balbuena, with rustic brick bases supporting flat-roofed cubic blocks finished in unadorned stucco, in which the slightly asymmetrical massing was often based on the deformation of a Palladian plan.

Nevertheless, Zuazo was not willing to apply the informal simplicity of these domestic designs to public buildings. This resistance drew him into an isolated attempt to create a modern civic architecture mixing classical and Neoplastic formal concepts in his 1927 Bilbao Post Office. Here he treated the facades as autonomous brick screens that extend slightly beyond the mass of the building on the chamfered corners and around the recessed central entry. They also terminate below the roof to reveal a stucco-finished attic storey behind them. The deep eaves create a hovering horizontal plane over these panels so that the entire ensemble begins to suggest a composition of floating planes, while maintaining a traditional masonry weight and academic distribution as well as the Baroque detail of a monumental entry portal. The design seems pregnant with the revolutionary potential of modern abstraction, although still contained within an academic frame, a situation similar to that found in Frank Lloyd Wright's early Winslow House (Illinois, 1893) and Otto Wagner's Austrian Postal Savings Bank (Vienna, 1906), which appears to be a direct model for the project.

As teachers and mentors, Torres Balbás, Anasagasti and Zuazo were decisive in forming the outlook of the Generation of 1925, the name given

Secundino Zuazo, Post Office, Bilbao, 1927.

Fernando García Mercadal, 'Shacks in Valencia', from *The Popular House in Spain* (Madrid, 1930).

by historian Carlos Flores to the group of Madrid architects graduating in the years after the First World War and considered Spain's first modernists.[35] This generation embraced the ILE's calls to explore the Spanish interior at first hand, and to establish regular contacts abroad. Fernando García Mercadal (class of 1921), for example, a star pupil of Anasagasti, travelled widely through Spain as a student. His sketches of popular architecture were exhibited in the 1922 National Exhibition of Fine Arts, and he wrote a book on the subject in 1930, *La casa popular en España* (The Popular House in Spain). As a winner of the Rome Prize, he spent six-month periods studying and working in Rome, Vienna, Berlin and Paris, establishing contacts with the emerging European avant-garde.

Similarly, Mercadal's classmate Luis Lacasa recalled of his student years, 'my orientation oscillated between a Neoclassicism based on the brick and stone of nineteenth-century Madrid, and "popular" art.'[36] After graduating, he spent three months at the Bauhaus in Weimar, worked for two years in Dresden's Municipal Office of Architecture under Heinrich Tessenow and studied French, English and German urbanism and architecture.

Zuazo's impact was largely through his studio, where Mercadal, Carlos Arniches, Martín Domínguez and Manuel Sánchez Arcas worked at different times. Here the influence between the two generations was mutual, with the younger men both encouraging Zuazo's opening towards modernism in the late 1920s and '30s and absorbing his tectonic approach.

chapter three

The Generation of 1925 in Madrid, 1925–36

In June 1933, La Argentinita and her Company of Spanish Dancers produced [Manuel de] Falla's *El amor brujo*. The work opened in Cádiz, in homage to the composer and with the presence of García Lorca. Days later, the opening in Madrid was another rousing success. The press talked of Falla as La Argentinita's great new discovery, and the resurrection of authentic gypsy dancing by the three grandmothers who accompanied her. Adolfo Salazar wrote in *El Sol*: 'It must be said at once that the most essential of the Spanish character, that of the thickest fibre, the bitterest roots, the coarsest and hardest, was seen yesterday in the dances organized by La Argentinita.'

Pedro Vaquerio, 1990[1]

The emergence of the Generation of 1925 took place against a background of economic prosperity and tense stability under the relatively mild dictatorship of General Miguel Primo de Rivera (1923–30) and through the early years of the tumultuous Second Republic (1931–6). With the complicity of King Alfonso XIII, who remained on the throne, the dictator put an end to the political turmoil of the 1910s, together with all normal political activity, taking on the role of the 'iron surgeon' called for by anti-parliamentarian Regenerationists on the right. The dictatorship fuelled economic growth with major public works including expanded school-building programmes, projects of electrification and irrigation and the building of dams, railways and a highway system, as well as state-subsidized housing and the construction of a new university campus in Madrid – all programmes that gave young architects important opportunities. The dictatorship also oversaw the formation of a territorial network of Colleges of Architects: guild-like professional associations that continue to supervise architectural planning and construction today.

Though some of Primo de Rivera's policies had parallels with those of Mussolini, who took power in Italy in 1922, many of his measures enacted unrealized proposals developed in the preceding, but ineffective, parliamentary period. His vertical trade unions, which integrated owners and workers, a staple of other fascist regimes, were modelled on the Catholic trade unions of the 1910s, and his expansion of social security and retirement

Le Corbusier and Fernando García Mercadal in El Escorial, May 1928.

benefits built on the programmes of the National Institute of Prevention, founded in 1908. Spanish fascist movements inspired by Mussolini and Hitler – such as the Falange Española, founded in 1933 by Primo de Rivera's son José Antonio – did not appear until the heavily polarized atmosphere of the Republic, when political debate on the Spanish left was similarly invaded by the influence of international Communism.

After the fall of the dictatorship and the king's exile, a coalition of Socialists and Republicans – radical heirs of the Regenerationists and the Revolution of 1868 – wrote a new constitution and formed the first Republican government with Manuel Azaña as its president (1931–3). Under the banner of 'human socialism' they passed reforms including basic labour laws (the eight-hour work day, minimum wage), social provisions such as the right to vote for women, an attempt at rural land redistribution, the establishment of an autonomous government in Catalunya and, most controversially, the separation of Church and state, with measures ranging from an effort to close Church schools and the expulsion of the Jesuits to the legalization of divorce.

Despite the economic constraints of the world depression, Azaña's government worked at a frantic pace to accelerate and expand the infrastructural programmes initiated during the dictatorship. School building was its greatest priority. Bernardo Giner de los Ríos oversaw the construction or adaption of some two hundred schools in Madrid alone, and 23,000 were planned for the country as a whole.[2] Projects for hospitals, markets and other public services were undertaken at a local level, and the planned extension of Madrid proposed during the dictatorship was pushed forward with strong state backing. The introduction of holidays and shorter working hours led to new concepts of mass recreation, which in turn led to such developments as the artificial 'Madrid Beach', built along the Manzanares river by the architect Manuel Muñoz Monasterio (1932–5, altered), or the unrealized public plans to create seaside holiday resorts for the masses in Barcelona and Alicante.[3] This initial impulse was cut short by the right-wing government of Alejandro Lerroux that succeeded Azaña in 1933. The electoral victory of the Popular Front, a coalition of Republicans, Socialists and Communists, in February 1936 set the stage for the military coup in July that precipitated the Civil War (1936–9).

Primo de Rivera's dictatorship coincided with a flourishing cultural life in Madrid that continued through the Second Republic, as seen in literary magazines such as Ernesto Giménez Caballero's *La Gaceta Literaria* and Ortega y Gasset's *Revista de Occidente*, the cultural programmes of the Ateneo (although initially closed by the dictator) and the Residencia and a busy publishing industry. Political debate flourished, especially after 1930, when intellectuals took sides both for and against the Republic. The most lasting literary work of the period was produced by the young poets of the Generation of 1927, led by Lorca, Alberti, Luis Cernuda and the future Nobel laureate Vicente Aleixandre.

This cultural excitement, together with the airs of efficient modernization projected by the dictatorship, encouraged the country's reception of the new architectural ideas appearing elsewhere in Europe. The first important point of reference for these ideas was the 1925 Exposition Internationale des Arts Décoratifs in Paris, visited by many architects and amply reported on in the pages of *Arquitectura*, where the early examples of Art Deco stood out in visitors' chronicles over the pavilions of Le Corbusier or Konstantin Melnikov.[4] After 1923, *Arquitectura* opened its pages to reports on new European architecture, mainly from young architects who had travelled abroad and joined its editorial board in 1926, including Rafael Bergamín, Luis Blanco-Soler, Luis Lacasa and Manuel Sánchez Arcas. This coverage included a 1924 piece on Erich Mendelsohn by Blanco-Soler, who spent two years working in the Netherlands and Germany. Lacasa wrote an article on Bruno Taut in 1926. There were pages on Dutch architecture by Theo van Doesburg in 1927 and 1928, and a series of ten reports on the German scene by the German correspondent and Bauhaus graduate Paul Linder. García Mercadal sent dispatches from Munich, Berlin, Vienna, Paris, the Netherlands and Italy throughout the decade. Among them were articles on Le Corbusier (featured in Ortega y Gasset's newspaper, *El Sol*, in 1925), André Lurçat, Hans Poelzig, the Fiat Factory in Turin and the Weissenhof housing settlement at the 1927 Werkbund exhibition in Stuttgart.[5]

After 1927, contact with European modernism was more direct; this was due in large part to Mercadal's efforts, especially the series of lectures by leading European modernists that he organized for the Residencia de Estudiantes. Le Corbusier's two lectures in 1928 caused a sensation and marked a decisive moment of encounter with the Modern Movement. They were followed over the next two years by the visits of Van Doesburg, Gropius and Mendelsohn. This coverage, together with trips abroad and access to foreign books and magazines, gave the architects of the Generation of 1925 a thorough exposure to the evolving Modern Movement in Europe, although their understanding of and receptivity to its precepts varied.

By the late 1920s, the idea of a new architecture had become a subject of popular debate in the general media and in literary circles, where it was associated with emblems of modernity such as the skyscraper, the transatlantic liner and the 'American bar'.[6] One of the high points of this public interest was the April 1928 issue of *La Gaceta Literaria*, which was dedicated entirely to modern architecture, under the direction of Mercadal. In addition to Mercadal's survey questionnaire on modernism, sent to his Madrid colleagues and several literary figures, the issue included works and texts by Le Corbusier, Mies, Gropius, Taut and others. The generally cool response of the invited participants was reflected in Ortega y Gasset's introduction, where he associated the new architecture with 'the triumph of the average man [in whom,] one knows not how, a fine sensibility has suddenly awakened for pure form and pure colour, as well as life in the open air'.[7]

The University City

The modernizing spirit of the dictatorship gave rise to a number of exceptional opportunities for young architects to explore new ideas. One of the first, although rather tentative in formal results, was the construction of a new Ciudad Universitaria or University City in Madrid, which was announced by royal decree in 1927. The vast endeavour moved the existing university from the centre of the city to a 320-hectare (790 ac) estate on its northwestern edge, on the slopes above the Manzanares river. The project's goals of dignifying higher education, creating a controlled natural setting for student life and providing advanced modern facilities, especially for the sciences and medical education, can all be traced to the model of the Residencia de Estudiantes.

The project's junta of directors appointed Modesto López Otero (Madrid, class of 1910[8]), then head of the School of Architecture, as the chief architect. He put together a group of promising recent graduates to design buildings, including Manuel Sánchez Arcas, Agustín Aguirre and

Agustín Aguirre, Faculty of Philosophy and Letters, University City, Madrid, 1931–3; rebuilt 1941–2 (rear facade).

Manuel Sánchez Arcas and Eduardo Torroja (engineer), San Carlos Clinical Hospital, Madrid, 1928–36; rebuilt and completed 1941–6.

Miguel de los Santos (all class of 1920), Luis Lacasa (1921) and the structural engineer Eduardo Torroja (1923), who was responsible for structural calculations and site work. López Otero called for designs of 'a great simplicity and extreme sobriety, with nothing superfluous'.[9] The group took an extended trip to the United States in 1928 to study the technical characteristics of new campus buildings there, and most had already travelled and worked in Europe. Construction had barely begun when the Republic was declared in 1931. The new government accelerated work while eliminating various elements, including López Otero's monumental *paraninfo*, or central lecture hall. The campus was the principal battlefront during the siege of Madrid throughout the Civil War and had to be completely rebuilt afterwards, although it was reconstructed following the original designs, under López Otero's direction.

The general layout of the complex is unremarkable, comprising López Otero's conventional park-like master plan, and buildings of red brick embracing a mild, stripped-down classicism. Among the projects with notably modern tendencies are Sánchez Arcas's San Carlos Clinical Hospital and Aguirre's Faculty of Philosophy and Letters. The hospital, still unfinished in 1936 (it was completed by others between 1941–6), combined the technical focus of American facility planning with skilfully composed brick volumes that show the architect's familiarity with contemporary Dutch and German housing. Its disciplined severity is relieved by the jaunty asymmetrical corner balconies of the projecting ward wings and the circular operating theatres, with 20-metre (65 ft) roof spans designed by Torroja. Aguirre's building, the first to be completed in 1933, featured such American innovations as air conditioning and a modular 'unit system' for the interior distribution and furnishings. The simplicity of the exteriors, with windows grouped in horizontal bands, is comparable to Guiseppe Capponi's School of Botany at the University of Rome (1931–5). Its modernity shocked the conservative governing Junta, López recalled later, with the result that Neoclassical elements were added to other projects, such as the stocky monumental entry colonnade of Miguel de los Santos's sprawling Medical School (1928–35).[10]

Student housing was modelled on the Residencia de Estudiantes, including Lacasa's handsome, unassuming Residencia (1932–5) and Bergamín and Blanco-Soler's Fundación del Amo, with custom furnishings such as tubular steel auditorium seating fabricated by Thonet (1928–9, destroyed in the Civil War). Also worth noting is the frank, industrial rationalism of Sánchez Arcas and Torroja's Thermal Power Plant (1932–5). Torroja's site work included the graceful concrete arch of the Viaducto del Aire, built without balustrades for the streetcar line to the campus, and the 'Viaduct of the 15 Arches' (both with López Otero and Aguirre, 1929–33), the latter comprising a long row of high, unadorned round arches, like a Roman aqueduct. This variation on the brick arcade of Balbuena's Amurrio apartments, present also in the treatment of the ground floor openings of the Fundación del Amo, became a leitmotif of Madrid architecture in these years.

Lacasa, Sánchez Arcas and the American Standard

The trip to the United States by the architects of University City offered a counter-model of technical modernization to the formal revolution of the European avant-garde, helping to reinforce the resistance of some early Madrid modernists to the most radical European proposals. This defensive attitude is seen in Luis Lacasa's writings on American and European architecture in 1928. In one of the first uses of the term, he took European 'Rationalists' to task for hiding formal aims in their methods, and praised American works in contrast, 'in which the detail – Classical or Romantic – loses importance beside their perfect Rationalism'. He accused Le Corbusier, who had just given his lectures in Madrid, of 'adorning his technical poems with scientific images that are images only', and mocked 'his lyric of technique, his triumphant "discovery" of the "standard"' when American industry already has voluminous catalogues of 'standardized' products. Beneath this disdain lay Lacasa's discomfort in the face of a radical break with tradition. Citing the 1925 Paris Exposition and the work of Henri Sauvage, Victor Bourgeois and Robert Mallet-Stevens, he wrote in another article that 'the preoccupations of a "Modern Architecture", lamentably separated from any traditional idea, though perhaps sincerely thought, are very difficult to feel.'[11]

For Manuel Sánchez Arcas, who was working with Lacasa at this time on the hospital of Toledo (1926–31), the alternative suggested by American architecture was to take the call for the use of rational principles at its word: 'There are works of architecture that don't develop any aesthetic formula *a priori*. Their aim is simply to "give form to new programmes", creating a new aesthetic on a base more solid than that of Oud, Poelzig, Le Corbusier, Taut, Dudok, Frank, Hoffmann or Mies van der Rohe.'[12]

Lacasa and Sánchez Arcas put this 'American' approach to the test in their competition-winning design for the Rockefeller Foundation's Institute of Physics and Chemistry on the campus of the Junta for Advanced Studies (1927–30). The two concentrated on the technical requirements of the laboratories and designed the exterior as a simple expression of the modular plan, as can be seen with particular force on the rear elevation, its rough brick evocative of Flórez's Residencia buildings. On the main facade, they added the aesthetic accessory of an American Colonial entry portico, awkwardly interpreted, in honour of the building's donor – 'a concession I think of little importance', Lacasa wrote, 'though I confess, unnecessary'.[13]

Luis Lacasa and Manuel Sánchez Arcas, Institute of Physics and Chemistry, Rockefeller Foundation, campus of the Junta for Advanced Studies, Madrid, 1927–30.

The Styleless Architecture of Rafael Bergamín

In his works of these years, Rafael Bergamín (class of 1918) explored the idea of a more thoroughly 'styleless' architecture derived from a European perspective, but again distanced from the most radical experiments in abstract composition and anchored instead in the tectonic qualities of traditional masonry construction. In a 1924 article in *Arquitectura*, he wryly counterposed the expectations of his academic education to the simple line drawings of Robert Mallet-Stevens and the functional principles of Le Corbusier's 'machine for living', advocating 'NOT making architecture' an architecture free of such presumed 'articles of prime necessity' as 'jambs, columns and capitals'.[14] A 1925 trip to the Netherlands encouraged him to experiment with exposed brick massing and flat roof terraces for the Casa del Marqués de Villora (1927–8, altered), which is radically unadorned when compared to the contemporary mansions of Gustavo F. Balbuena nearby. Bergamín made note of the project's advanced technical features, such as standardized steel windows from Germany, cork insulation and centralized hot water and heating, and the solar orientation and functional distribution of the rooms. He wrote of the design, 'its only aim is to afford the inhabitants a maximum "comfort" at a minimum cost, procuring to comply exactly with the programme of necessities imposed by the owner.'[15]

Bergamín took these principles a step further in two *colonias* (colonies, or garden suburb developments), situated just north of the Residencia de Estudiantes, beyond the limits of Madrid's Ensanche: the Parque-Residencia (with his frequent partner Blanco-Soler and others, 1931–3) and El Viso (1933–6). In these blocks of single and attached houses with small gardens, Bergamín and Blanco-Soler abandoned exposed brick for stucco, which was closer to the abstract planes of European rationalism, as were details such as the ship-rail balustrades of the first development and the rounded bays, strip windows and thin projecting shading canopies of the second, although the massing remained masonry and volumetric in character. The architects explored the standardization and simplification of many elements, but the results struck even Bergamín as 'a little dry', as he noted in 1967, an effect he sought 'to mitigate by painting the facades in different colours'.[16]

During the short interim before the Civil War, the two colonies were home to an intellectual and cultural elite that included Ortega y Gasset, the artist Ángel Ferrant, Eduardo Torroja and the architects Luis Feduchi and García Mercadal, as well as Bergamín and Blanco-Soler. Bergamín was active in Madrid's cultural life, frequenting the writer Ramón Gómez de la Serna's literary *tertulia* at the Café Pombo, for example, while his brother José was a noted poet, writer and literary editor. Together with a handful

Rafael Bergamín and
Luis Felipe Vivanco,
Colony El Viso, Madrid,
1933–6.

of other projects, the two colonies have thus become a symbol of Madrid's
cultural life during the Republic.

The colonies were built under state-subsidized housing programmes
initiated with the 1911 Law of Cheap Housing. They were financed by the
home buyers and the National Institute of Prevention with state-backed
low-interest loans. This legislation was intended to promote low-cost workers' housing, but its subsidies were mainly used by builders to finance more
profitable developments for middle-class professionals. Similar colonies
of the 1920s, mainly in Madrid, Bilbao and Santander, mixed regional and
English styles in modest garden-suburb-type developments. The National
Institute of Prevention and its affiliated savings banks also financed a few
notable apartment blocks that introduced modern concepts of 'hygiene'
and functional planning, including Zuazo's Casa de las Flores in Madrid,
discussed below.

Arniches, Domínguez and Popular Architecture

The joint studio of Carlos Arniches and Martín Domínguez (both class of
1922) explored a third route towards modernism, finding in popular architecture a model for an elegant and understated functionalism, an option

Carlos Arniches and
Martín Domínguez,
Albergue de Carretera
(small roadside hotel),
Manzanares, 1928–31.

close to the tradition of Flórez and the ILE, with which both were associated. Domínguez had lived at the Residencia as a student, and both worked
in the office of Zuazo after graduating (Arniches was the son of the popular
playwright of the same name, and his sister married José Bergamín). The
essence of their approach is captured in Domínguez's recollections of Le
Corbusier's 1928 visit to Madrid and his identification with Spain's popular
architecture:

> He spoke to us with great surprise of having found that
> much of what he considered his personal contribution to
> the contemporary architectural lexicon – plain, Purist forms,
> the new-born whiteness of whitewashed walls, openings which
> puncture them with eloquent decision – he had seen from the
> moving train as it raced towards Madrid, in town after town
> along the trajectory.[17]

This is the formula that Arniches and Domínguez used in their winning
competition project of 1928 for the prototype *albergue* (small roadside
hotel) commissioned by the National Board of Tourism: neat, whitewashed volumes, low hip roofs without eaves, the dynamic modern
projections of a dining wing with a rounded end and outdoor pergola
on one side, and a porte cochère at the entry, a thin triangular concrete
plane that rises slightly in its long span as if shrugging off its weight. For
the interiors, the architects reinterpreted traditional furnishings with a

stylish modern simplicity. The first albergue was built in the rural town of Manzanares (1928–31), followed by ten others begun during the Republic. Equipped with a gas pump and lodging for chauffeurs, the albergues were introduced by the dictatorship as part of its system of national *paradors*, or state-owned luxury hotels, installed in historic monuments, and its highway modernization programme.

Arniches and Domínguez translated the albergues' combination of simple massing and bold modern elements to the brick of Flórez's Residencia in several additions to the campus of the Junta for Advanced Studies initiated by the Republican government. For the model high school of the Instituto-Escuela (School Institute; 1931–3, altered), they raised the classroom blocks on round concrete pilotis over covered outdoor areas, and enclosed them in a grid of oversized glazed openings, 5 metres (16 ft) wide, creating a striking contemporary silhouette on the Hill of the Poplars (1934–41). The classrooms were equipped with the architects' custom-designed tubular steel furniture. Working with Eduardo Torroja on the Instituto's linear nursery-school block (1933–5), they introduced a row of long, hovering concrete planes with rounded ends that are daringly cantilevered from a central wall to shade the classrooms' outdoor play areas.

An auditorium and library for the Residencia de Estudiantes (1932–3) was organized around a garden cloister with a central fountain and galleries of unadorned brick arches, superficially related to the De Chirico-inspired work of fascist Italy but evoking architectural tradition at a more

Carlos Arniches and Martín Domínguez, High School Pavilion, Instituto-Escuela (today Ramiro de Maeztu Institute), campus of the Junta for Advanced Studies, Madrid, 1931–3.

Instituto-Escuela
High School, covered
recreation patio,
Madrid, 1931–3.

human scale. The auditorium was rebuilt as a church after the Civil War, but the cloister survives, and it is tempting to imagine audiences lingering here after screening an early René Clair film, brought from Paris by Luis Buñuel, a concert by Igor Stravinsky, or La Argentinita's production of Manuel de Falla's *El amor brujo*.[18]

While Domínguez spent a year in Hollywood designing film sets, Arniches built a small dormitory for the Residencia de Señoritas (1932–3), which was more unabashedly rationalist in its use of smooth stucco walls, continuous horizontal openings and cantilevered balconies, while remaining masterfully unassuming and disciplined in its form. The contrast between this fashionable rationalism and the rough stucco of the albergues or the brick arches of the Residencia's cloister reveal an architecture shaped as much by context, character and propriety as by functional orthodoxy. In this sense, the work of Arniches and Domínguez still subtly echoes the mindset of liberal Eclecticism.

The Exceptional Structures of Eduardo Torroja

Arniches and Domínguez opened their work further to the radical structural experiments of Eduardo Torroja in their 1934 competition-winning design for the Zarzuela Hippodrome outside Madrid. Torroja's innovations in thin-shell concrete during the Republican years claim their place beside the pioneering work of Eugène Freyssinet, Robert Maillart and Pier Luigi Nervi. The Hippodrome design is dominated by his wing-like cantilevered shading vaults over the grandstands, which span nearly 14 metres (45 ft) and taper to a thickness of only 5 centimetres (2 in.). The vaults are composed of hyperboloids, surfaces that curve in two directions, and are counterbalanced by an ingenious system that involves suspending the roof vault of the betting hall, situated below the grandstands, from tension bars tied to the rear flanges of the vaults. Unfinished at the outbreak of the war, the structure withstood heavy artillery bombardment during the Battle of Madrid. The vaults were punctured by 26 shells, but Torroja was able to repair them by introducing stiffeners to areas that were sagging or cracking.[19]

Alongside Secundino Zuazo, Torroja built the Frontón Recoletos in Madrid, a sports hall for the Basque game of Jai Lau; it opened a few months before the war but collapsed after heavy aerial bombing.[20] The popularizing details of Zuazo's facades did little to disguise the radical, eccentric roof

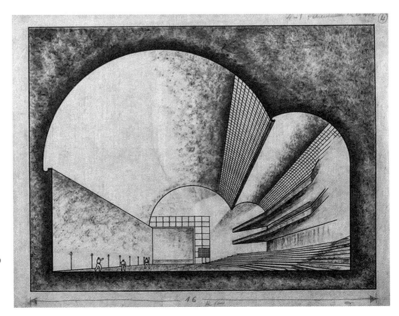

Secundino Zuazo (architect) and Eduardo Torroja (engineer), Frontón Recoletos (Jai Lau court), Madrid, 1936, demolished.

Carlos Arniches and Martín Domínguez (architects), and Eduardo Torroja (engineer), Zarzuela Hippodrome, Madrid, 1934–5.

Cross section of the Zarzuela Hippodrome grandstand by Eduardo Torroja showing canopy cantilever counterbalanced by tension rods on the opposite side.

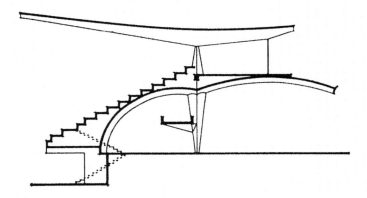

structure, which was composed of two parallel thin-shell barrel vaults, incomplete in section and of different radii, with the higher vault over the playing court and the lower over the spectators. The two vaults met asymmetrically at a smooth angle, without a mediating beam, and spanned an area of 55 by 32.5 metres (180 by 106 ft). Grandstands and intermediate floors were suspended from the lower vault on tension rods, while a large section of each vault was perforated by a skylight composed of a grille of prefabricated concrete triangles infilled with glass.

The sources for Torroja's innovations were varied. His father was a noted mathematician specializing in the geometry of curved surfaces, and his principal teacher, José Eugenio Ribera (1864–1936), was a pioneer in reinforced concrete. Torroja developed his thin-shell vaults from techniques introduced in the 1920s by the German engineers Franz Dischinger and Ulrich Finsterwalder, although their work lacks the light, graceful elegance of Torroja's designs, as seen in their barrel-vaulted Market Hall in Frankfurt (the architect was Martin Elsaesser, 1927–8).[21] Torroja's vaults are also related to the artisan tradition of Spanish masonry, as seen in the thin, brick parabolic stair vaults of Barcelona's Gothic palaces and the shallow brick vaults of vernacular floor construction. These craft techniques also inspired Gaudí and the Gustavino brothers, the Valencian masons who brought their patented system of tile vaulting to New York at the beginning of the twentieth century. Torroja's designs were thus not completely out of step with the outlines of a Spanish approach to modernism through popular architecture.

The Fabric of the Modern City: Commercial and Public Work

Modernism had its greatest success in Madrid and other cities in the architecture of entertainment and recreation, both popular and exclusive, and particularly in new typologies that ranged from the movie theatre to the petrol station. In these venues, Art Deco, the stylized Expressionism of Erich Mendelsohn's contemporary commercial architecture and Le Corbusier's more literal nautical references all provided inspiration.

The master of this commercial modernism was Luis Gutiérrez Soto (class of 1923), who became a convert to the new architecture after trips to Germany, Austria, London and Paris, where he was particularly impressed by the 1925 Exposition Internationale and buildings by Le Corbusier and Mallet-Stevens.[22] For the Cine Europa (1928) and Cine Barceló (1930), he introduced a Deco-type stylized modernism that utilized rounded corners, smooth planes of stucco and thin projecting soffits in a sophisticated counterpoint of horizontal and vertical elements that brought traditional Eclectic composition up to date.

Luis Gutíerrez Soto,
Cine Barceló, Madrid,
1930.

Luis Gutíerrez Soto,
La Isla Swimming
Pool, Madrid, 1932,
demolished.

Luis Gutíerrez Soto,
Casablanca Tea and
Dancing Salon, Madrid,
1933, demolished.

For his nightclubs and bars, Gutiérrez Soto employed black-and-white finishes inspired by contemporary Hollywood film sets, with chrome trim, large areas of glass and prominent signage in stylized modern lettering, as can still be seen in the Bar Chicote on the Gran Vía (1932), one of Hemingway's hangouts during the Civil War. The Casablanca Tea and Dancing Salon (1933), frequented by Lorca and his friends,[23] featured a glass vitrine filled with exotic birds and monkeys, a glass roof with retractable sunshades and a tall neon palm tree at the entrance. Gutiérrez Soto used imported tubular furniture manufactured by Thonet for many of these clubs, and his own designs for Chicote, made by the Madrid firm Rolaco.[24]

Outside urban confines, Gutiérrez Soto's designs stretched out with low wings, expansive terraces and unbroken strip windows, anchored by a

rounded central volume. His approach was nautical for La Isla Swimming Pool (1932, demolished), and more aerodynamic for his competition-winning design for Barajas Airport (1929–32, demolished). La Isla was another of the Republic's pioneering projects in mass recreation. It occupied a small island in Madrid's Manzanares river and was outfitted by Gutiérrez Soto like an elegant barge, with curving white lines and a super-structure trimmed with life preservers and pendants.

Casto Fernández-Shaw (class of 1919) explored a more Expressionist and Eclectic vein of commercial design. For the Porto Pi petrol station (1927, demolished; rebuilt in 1996), he declared, with the enthusiasm of an Italian Futurist: 'The superposition of planes of the canopy recalls the wings of a biplane. The tower recalls the ventilation tubes of boats, the mechanisms that administer gasoline, petrol, oils, water, pressurized air and the fire extinguishers decorate the facility. The automobiles, the loudspeakers, the lights will give it life.'[25]

His designs alternated between conventional work for private commissions, based on his academic training under López Otero and in the office of Antonio Palacios, and experiments in Structural Expressionism when the occasion arose. The first category includes the Edificio Coliseum on Madrid's Gran Vía (1931–3, with Pedro Muguruza), which was a study in miniature of the American skyscraper. The second is exemplified by the Salto del Jándula hydroelectric dam in the province of Jaén (1925–33, with engineer Carlos Mendoza), in which he explored 'hydrodynamic' forms in the undulating stone berms that enclose the turbines. His entry for the 1927 Columbus lighthouse competition in Santo Domingo, a hyperbolic cone 180 metres (590 ft) high, accessed by spiralling ramps and rotating on its vertical axis, anticipated the beefy metallic curves of mid-century American industrial design. Finally, his wartime exile in London, he imagined futuristic shell-like cities armoured against bombardment.

The most impressive landmark of modern architecture built during the Republic is the sixteen-storey Edificio Capitol (1931–3), the rounded prow of which still presides over the Gran Vía, with its continuous ribbon windows and limestone soffits, intended from the beginning as a support for large-scale illuminated advertising. The building was the work of two young architects, Luis Feduchi and Vicente Eced (both class of 1927), who adapted the language of Mendelsohn's commercial Expressionism to win the competition for the project in 1929. It was celebrated as Madrid's first modern skyscraper, marking 'the definitive entry of Madrid into the modern world', the literary historian José Carlos Mainer notes.[26] The developer Enrique Carrión spared no expense, from the Vierendeel trusses spanning 31 metres (101 ft) that support the upper floors of offices and apartments over the 1,360-seat cinema to the advanced mechanical systems, including

Luis Feduchi and Vicente Eced, Edificio Capitol, Madrid, 1931–3.

full air conditioning, which required an independent electrical substation and consumed 20 per cent of the budget. The architects travelled to France and Germany to study new cinemas, particularly Mendelsohn's Universum in Berlin (1926–8), and came back with innovations such as fireproof fabrics and a sequence of lighting in the theatre, based on optical studies, that faded from white to yellow, green, blue, violet and finally to black. Feduchi was already a specialist in interior design, and he custom designed all the furnishings and furniture. Made by Rolaco, these were inspired in the tubular metal designs of Breuer and Mies, which by this time were readily available in Madrid.[27]

These exuberant commercial projects were accompanied by more modest works of 'rational' or 'modern' architecture in residential design, in which architects abandoned ornamental programmes in favour of regular openings, planar facades and simple compositional gestures such as curving corners. Such projects had a substantial impact on the urban fabric of many neighbourhoods as Madrid's Ensanche, still one-third empty in 1930 according to one estimate, slowly filled.[28] One example was Bergamín and Blanco-Soler's Hotel Gaylord's in the exclusive residential neighbourhood of the Calle de Alfonso XII (1931, demolished), which was taken over as the Soviet Union's headquarters during the Civil War, as depicted in Hemingway's *For Whom the Bell Tolls* (1940). Gutiérrez Soto was already a prolific residential designer in the 1930s. His many projects culminated with a building on the Calle de Almagro (1935–41) that anticipated the wide balcony terraces of his post-war production. Public projects contributed to the city's modern aspect, especially the increasingly Rational school designs of Giner and the markets of the municipal architect Francisco Ferrero (class of 1916), including the neighbourhood market of Olavide with its roof of hovering concrete rings (1931–4, demolished) and the functionalist brick and concrete structures of his wholesale markets for fruit (1926–35) and fish (1931).

Zuazo: The Architecture of the State

Despite the achievements of the Generation of 1925, the figure best placed to address the challenges of the period, in terms of renovating architecture to meet urgent new social demands, turned out to be Secundino Zuazo. In his interrelated roles as author of a new housing prototype in the Casa de las Flores (House of Flowers, 1930–32), urban planner of the expansion of Madrid (1930–34) and architect of the most ambitious public building of the Republic, the Nuevos Ministerios (New Ministries, 1932–6; completed by others 1940–42), Zuazo decisively influenced Madrid's urbanism and architecture both during the Republic and in the years following the war.

These three projects form different pieces of a single problem: that of how to give adequate form to the unprecedented scale of urban growth marshalled by state intervention, whether in the fields of housing, urban planning or expanding government institutions. Through them, Zuazo systematically confronted, for the first time in Spain, the full dimensions of the social problems being addressed by the Modern Movement elsewhere in Europe. At the same time, the contradictions of Zuazo's position in relation to both modernism and the academic tradition present an extreme example of the ambivalence inherent in the Generation of 1925's outlook, a response very different from that which occurred in Barcelona in the same period.

Zuazo had specialized in city planning since 1920, when he attended a world congress of the National Housing and Town Planning Council in London, and he designed unsuccessful projects to expand Bilbao and Sevilla in the early 1920s. His visit in 1926 to the socialist housing projects of Amsterdam South, planned by Hendrik Berlage and featuring the Expressionist works of the Wendingen Group, impressed him with the interrelation between housing types and urban form, a relation that became integral to his work.

Occupying a full block of the Ensanche not far from the new university, the 288-unit Casa de las Flores gave Zuazo the opportunity to adapt modern European housing standards regarding natural light, ventilation and functional layout to produce one of the first examples of rational collective housing in Spain. For its massing, he returned to Cerdà's original proposals for developing Barcelona's Eixample, with two linear north–south volumes arranged around a central garden. Despite the project's high density, all apartments are cross-ventilated, with main living areas overlooking the street and central garden and secondary spaces facing interior patios. In formal terms, Zuazo adapted the discipline of German public housing, the monumentality of the Viennese superblocks and the modelled brickwork of the Dutch Expressionists to Madrid's popular housing tradition. He gave character to the simple brick massing with ground-floor arcades of Dutch-inspired decorative brickwork and striking corner terraces, whose railings are lined with holders for the potted geraniums that inspired the project's popular name. Openings maintain the vertical proportions of traditional Madrid window balconies. Shelled during the war, the damaged building was famously invoked by Pablo Neruda, who lived there as Chilean Consul during the Republic, in his wartime poem 'España en el corazón' (Spain in the Heart, 1937).

In the competition for the expansion of Madrid, Zuazo again brought contemporary European ideas to bear on local urban problems. He was following the lead of Gustavo F. Balbuena and his municipal planning staff, who had assiduously prepared the competition with an international symposium and technical studies that incorporated regional planning, zoning and other concepts of the period. Through the recommendation of Mercadal, Zuazo accepted the invitation of the Berlin urban planner Hermann Jansen to work together on the competition. Jansen was the author of the 1910 plan for Greater Berlin and had just won the competition to lay out the new Turkish capital of Ankara in 1928.[29] The chief features of their proposal were the definitive structuring of the city's growth along the axis of the Paseo de la Castellana (the northern continuation of Carlos III's Salón del Prado, converted into a boulevard in the nineteenth century), as called for in the municipal technical studies, and the creation of a ring of satellite communities around the city, separated by a green belt and connected by railway lines. This regional growth plan built on Jansen's work in Berlin and other German cities, as well as reinforcing the initiative of Arturo Soria's Linear City.

For the Castellana, the two proposed a monumental axis lined with housing and structured around representative buildings. The new centrality of this artery was reinforced by a railway tunnel under the boulevard linking northern and southern lines to the rest of Spain, with several stations along its route – an innovative solution, in urban terms, to the long-standing problem of Madrid's terminal stations. The plan's most radical element was the proposal to organize new housing in strict linear blocks facing north and south, both on the Castellana and in other areas. They presented the

Secundino Zuazo, Casa de las Flores (House of Flowers), Madrid, 1930–32.

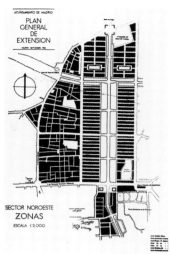

Secundino Zuazo and Hermann Jansen, perspective rendering, extension of the Paseo de la Castellana.

Secundino Zuazo and Hermann Jansen, plan for the expansion of Madrid, 1929. Detail of the extension of the Paseo de la Castellana.

buildings complete with rational plan types and elevations for different classes of occupants, carrying the ideas of the Casa de las Flores a step closer to the more radical proposals of European modernism.

The Zuazo–Jansen plan was recognized by the jury as the best of the twelve submissions, although none met the city's overdemanding competition bases. The last Madrid mayor under Primo de Rivera's dictatorship enlisted Zuazo in his unsuccessful efforts to put a limited plan for the Castellana into effect. Finally, in 1931, Zuazo was commissioned by the Republic's Minister of Public Works, the socialist Indalecio Prieto, to head work on the railway tunnel, the avenue itself and the New Ministries complex beside it, which Prieto pushed forward in large part as an emergency employment measure. These projects established the Castellana as the axis of future growth in Madrid. The more far-reaching regional implications of the Zuazo–Jansen proposal were taken up in the post-war planning for the capital directed by Pedro Bidagor, who worked in Zuazo's studio in these years. Through Jansen's collaborators and students, the plan also influenced German urban planning in the Nazi era.[30]

The New Ministries brought together four of the government's ten ministries in a single complex, headed by the Ministry of Governance, creating a representative centre for the Republic equivalent to the role of the Royal Palace as the symbolic seat of the monarchy (President Azaña was meanwhile incongruously installed in the palace). In the absence of any programme, Zuazo used the project to anchor and shape the urbanization of the Castellana and gave free rein to the rhetorical monumentalism of his academic training, although with a rigour and restraint inspired by Juan de Herrera's El Escorial rather than by his master, Antonio Palacios. Thus, while the Casa de las Flores can be seen as an update of the vernacular-accented functionalism of Antonio Flórez, presented by Zuazo as a Spanish response to European modernism, the New Ministries complex offered a Spanish version of the simplified, inflated, academic state architecture built in the capitals of other countries during the 1930s, from Washington, DC, and Moscow to Berlin and Rome.

The Castellana site, roughly four blocks long, lay in a valley beside Bergamín and Blanco-Soler's Parque Residencia, then in construction, an example of the contradictions marking Madrid's urban growth. It was occupied by the Royal Hippodrome, which was demolished for the project and replaced by Arniches and Domínguez's new racetrack. Zuazo set the long continuous wall of the buildings a full block back from the Castellana to create a large Plaza del pueblo (of the People), which he separated from the street and its traffic with a monumental one-storey arcade. This space was a condensed version of the open areas he and Jansen had proposed along the Castellana axis. He developed its design from studies of the Lonja facing the Escorial, as well as other Spanish and Italian plazas. As he wrote in his unpublished papers, 'Only architecture, bare earth and stone

Secundino Zuazo,
New Ministries arcade,
Madrid, 1932–42.

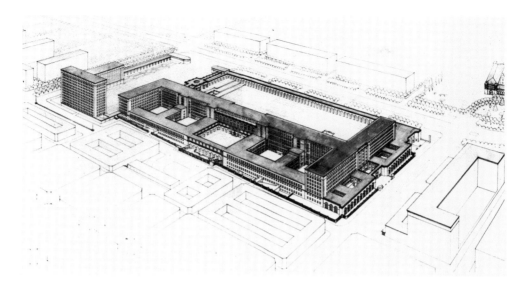

New Ministries, perspective drawing.

pavements, without gardens, without trees. Plazas without any traffic, peaceful for the citizen, reserved only for the most important events.'[31]

While Zuazo focused his attention on a 'Court of Honour' and other ceremonial details, the overall axial focus of the project was diluted by its size and linear distribution, as well as by the rationalism of its modular plan and the regular steel skeleton under its granite walls. Zuazo's volumetric layout in an elongated 'T' is asymmetrical, assuming something of the more fluid, dynamic massing he was experimenting with in his contemporary proposals for urban reforms in central Madrid. Bidagor credited the simplified detailing of the arcade along the Castellana to Arniches and Domínguez, who also worked with Torroja on the large, barrel-vaulted railway station underneath.[32] With its endless line of arches cut out from the flat plane of the granite, proportioned like those of a Plaza Mayor but coursing in isolation through the cityscape, the arcade is the most De Chiricoesque of the galleries built in Madrid in the 1930s. Zuazo intended the overall restraint of the New Ministries' design to foment a sense of 'tranquillity' and 'repose';[33] however, its superblock scale and the numbing rhythm of its countless windows (including the small attic windows of the prison cells over the General Directorate of Security, though it was never used as such) can also be interpreted, from the misleading distance of the present, as an image of apparently limitless state power that seems closer to the spirit of Franco's regime than to that of the Republic. Following the Civil War, the representation of the state in architecture could no longer be treated as so innocent a problem.

chapter four

The Provinces and Barcelona: Stylists versus Revolutionaries, 1929–39

A climate of violence that fascinated me, launched me into streets feverish with students and barricades, confronting the horses of the Civil Guards and the bullets of their Mausers. Amid those days of battle, Luis Buñuel arrived from Paris like a comet, his head shaved, his face even stronger. He had come to show his first film [*Un chien andalou*], made in collaboration with Salvador Dalí. It was one of those unforgettable sessions of the Cine Club. The film impressed and disturbed many, and all were shaken by that image of the moon cut in two by a cloud, immediately followed by that other, terrible image of the eye cut by a shaving razor. When the public asked Buñuel for a few words of explanation, he straightened up in his box seat for a moment and said something like this: 'It only has to do with a desperate, a passionate call to crime.'

Rafael Alberti, 1975[1]

Outside Madrid, modern styles rapidly became fashionable throughout Spain, especially for commercial and residential architecture. A number of architects who had graduated in the late 1910s and early 1920s, and who had begun their careers in regional or academic styles, began to experiment with modern designs in the 1930s, if not before, although many continued to mix these efforts with more conventional work as circumstances demanded. This tendency was cut short by the Civil War, however, and among those who were not forced into exile by the conflict, virtually all returned to more conventional academic styles in the 1940s in the face of Francoist purges in the profession, as we shall see in Chapter Five.

A few slightly younger architects who finished their studies in the late 1920s discovered the work of Le Corbusier and other leaders of the Modern Movement while still students, at a more formative and impressionable age, and went on to promote a more orthodox modernism inspired directly by the modernist vanguard in the rest of Europe. The main protagonists of this international approach were the most active members of the Group of Spanish Architects and Technicians for the Progress of Contemporary Architecture (GATEPAC), founded in 1930, including José Manuel Aizpurúa

Josep Renau, 'Todos en pie de guerra' (Everyone Get Ready for War), 1937. Renau was Spain's director of fine arts in the Ministry of Culture during the Civil War.

and Joaquín Labayen in San Sebastián, and the group in Barcelona led by Josep Lluís Sert and Josep Torres Clavé. These architects attended the congresses and debates of CIAM (Congrès International d'Architecture Moderne) and integrated their work in CIAM's agenda of state-sponsored social and urban reform. They promoted their activities through an ambitious publication, *AC: documentos de actividad contemporánea* (1931–7), with a modern layout and militant rhetoric modelled on contemporary Dutch and German magazines, which assured the group a lasting impact both within Spain and abroad.

Modernism in the Provinces

Fernando García Mercadal was a key player in the founding of GATEPAC and, as we have seen, one of the most important links between Spanish and European architecture in the 1920s. Nevertheless, his career offers an example of the difficulties that would-be modernists faced in conservative provincial capitals. Following his return to Madrid from his European travels in 1927, he plunged into activities promoting the new architecture. He joined the board of *Arquitectura* and organized the lecture series of the Residencia de Estudiantes. He represented Spain (with the young Bilbao architect Luis Vallejo) at the founding meeting of CIAM at the castle of La Sarraz, near Lausanne, in 1928, where he was entrusted with establishing the Spanish group of affiliates that became the GATEPAC group, and he attended subsequent congresses in Frankfurt and Brussels in 1929 and 1930, respectively, with Aizpurúa, Sert and others. For the Frankfurt congress, focused on social housing under the banner of the *Existenzminimum* (minimal dwelling), he organized a Spanish competition on the theme and presented the winning designs, by Vallejo and Juan de Madariaga, at the meeting. But his unrealized modern projects of the mid-1920s, such as the 1924 imaginary exercise, 'House by the Sea', lacked the sophistication of similar works by his Madrid contemporaries, instead remaining closer to an austere Art Deco with superficially modern details.

These formal limitations may have contributed to the cold reception of his first built project, the Rincón de Goya (Goya's Corner), a small park pavilion dedicated to Francisco de Goya in his native Zaragoza (1927). His intention, he recalled, was to create 'a different kind of monument, without rhetoric', but 'naturally, it caused only scandal.' A local paper found it 'simple, monotonous and crushingly heavy, a construction that says nothing to the heart or the understanding'.[2] Irate local citizens covered its walls with insults, and the city virtually abandoned it. By 1932, Mercadal was no longer active in GATEPAC, retreating to a secure position as Madrid's Chief Architect for Urbanism, Parks and Gardens (1932–40). 'After the Rincón

Fernando García Mercadal, Rincón de Goya (Goya's Corner), Zaragoza, 1927.

Regino and José Borobio, Hydrographic Confederation of the Ebro, Zaragoza, 1936–46.

de Goya,' he remembered in 1967, 'the dilemma became, either GATEPAC or work.'[3]

Only a few years later, this hostile provincial climate had softened, at least for some. In Mercadal's Zaragoza, Regino Borobio (Madrid, class of 1919) and his younger brother José (class of 1931) built several works close to the 'styleless' simplicity of Madrid, most notably the headquarters building for the Hydrographic Confederation of the Ebro, won in a competition

Regino and José Borobio, Casa Hernández Luna, Zaragoza, 1932.

Enrique Viedma, Finca Roja (Red Estate), Valencia, 1929–33.

Víctor Eusa, San Miguel Seminary, Pamplona, 1931–6.

organized by Indalecio Prieto's Ministry of Public Works (1933; built 1936–46). Regino's 1929 pavilion for the Hydrographic Confederation at the Barcelona International Exposition was one of the few clearly modern works there, and the brothers' 1932 Casa Hernández Luna approaches the compositional sophistication of its Corbusian and Miesian models.

As in Madrid, a discrete, functional rationalism appeared in a number of provincial apartment buildings. A few, such as the Borobios's 1931 Casa Calvo in Zaragoza, were surprisingly abstract in their use of continuous strip windows and balconies. Others exploited the compositional opportunities of corner sites, as in the smooth, rounded Mendelsohnian prow of the Adriática in Alicante (1935–6) by Miguel López González, or the staggered, blocky massing of the Edificio de La Equitativa by Manuel Ignacio Galíndez in Bilbao (1934). Subsidized housing on the scale of Zuazo's Casa de las Flores included Enrique Viedma's so-called Finca Roja, or Red Estate in Valencia (1929–33), financed, like Zuazo's project, by the National Institute of Prevention, which mixed an outdated Barcelona Modernisme with details from Dutch Expressionism and Vienna's socialist housing.

Emiliano Amann,
Solocoeche public
housing, Bilbao, 1932–3.
Render of competition-
winning design.

PRIMER PREMIO.   Arq., *Sr. Amann.*

Some of the most flamboyant examples of Art Deco expressionism
were designed by Víctor Eusa (Madrid, class of 1920) for various religious
institutions in the conservative northern city of Pamplona. For the San
Miguel Seminary (1931–6), he embellished the main facade with a backlit
cross several storeys high, with flattened mouldings rippling around it – a
feature he added during construction in response to growing attacks on
the Church.[4]

In Bilbao, a few public works were built during the Republic following
more sober functional principles, continuing the progressive civic spirit
reflected in the large number of garden city workers' housing cooperatives
built there in the 1920s under subsidized housing legislation, all in regional
styles and several by the local architect Tomás Bilbao (Madrid, class of
1918). Examples of the civic modernism of the 1930s include Pedro Ispizua's
Ribera Municipal Market (1930) and his Luis Briñas School (1932–3),
accented with a tall, stylized tower. Emiliano Amann's severe Solocoeche
housing block (1932–3), the result of a national competition organized by
Tomás Bilbao for the city with Mercadal's help, was designed following the
Existenzminimum (minimal dwelling) standards approved at the Second
CIAM Congress in Frankfurt. In the province of Álava, Pablo Zabalo built
the Leza Tuberculosis Sanatorium (1934–5) at the feet of the Cantabrian
Range, a linear block composed of a grid of deep, square balcony openings
with broad glazing for the patient rooms.

The Canary Islands

Due to the geographic situation of the Canary Islands and their status as
a port of call along routes of international trade and elite tourism, architects there established direct contacts with European cultural trends
independently of mainland Spain, contributing to the islands' distinctive

architectural culture in the 1920s and '30s. The two main settlements, Las Palmas on the island of Gran Canaria and Santa Cruz on Tenerife, produced two independent groups that pursued a modern renovation of architecture in very different terms. In the first instance, architects based on both islands, working for a young and prosperous middle-class clientele, developed an early, prolific and well-informed modern style for residential and commercial projects, as well as a handful of public buildings. This group included the architects Miguel Martín-Fernández de la Torre, José Marrero Regalado and José Blasco Robles, together with the German architects Richard Oppel and Rudolf Schneider. At the same time, in Tenerife, a group of Surrealist poets and socialist activists led by the art critic Eduardo Westerdahl produced the journal *Gaceta de Arte* (1932–6), which championed, among other avant-garde movements, the more politicized architectural programmes of the CIAM and GATEPAC groups, often in a militant tone that reflected the increasing polarization of the times.

The leading figure of the first group was Miguel Martín (Madrid, class of 1920). Although he studied both in Barcelona and Madrid, and worked briefly for Zuazo, he returned to his native Las Palmas in 1922 (too early to share in the formative experience of the Generation of 1925). His exposure to the Modern Movement through travel and subscriptions to European journals was thus unfiltered by Madrid's cautious insularity. Following the usual regionalist Eclecticism of his early works, he began to evolve towards modern forms as early as 1927, working mainly on private houses and apartment buildings in the garden city of Las Palmas, where he eventually built more than six hundred projects.

By 1930, his work had evolved from the simplified, blocky masonry volumes of the 1927 Edificio Mulet into more abstract forms that showcased large horizontal openings and planes, as in the 1930 Edificio Straib. In his best works, he achieved a fluid, dynamic horizontality through contrasts of solids and voids using continuous terraces and deep balconies that wrap around the building volumes, in an attractive adaption of northern European modernism to the islands' idyllic climate. This is the case in the Cabildo Insular, or local government offices, in Las Palmas (1929–32, built 1937–42) and in such private works as the Casa Vega Pereira outside Las Palmas (1933–7) or the Casa Ayala in Santa Cruz de Tenerife (1933–6).

Martín received input on contemporary German modernism from his brother-in-law, the older architect Richard Ernst Oppel, who worked in Martín's studio from late 1932 until 1936. Oppel is considered to have contributed to Martín's stylistic development in these years, although his exact role has not been clearly established.[5] He is jointly credited with Martín on several projects, including the German School in Las Palmas (1933, demolished). Oppel was from Hamburg, where he built one of the modern public housing blocks in the Jarrestadt district (1928).

The role of Oppel is an example of the influence of the islands' German colony in promoting modernism, and the special relation with Hamburg, Germany's main port (images of the uncharacteristic brick housing settlements promoted by municipal architect Fritz Schumacher, including those of the Jarrestadt development, were published by Westerdahl in the *Gaceta de Arte*, for example).[6] The young architect Rudolf Schneider, also from Hamburg, came to the Canary Islands to design a modern building for the German School in Santa Cruz (built with José Blasco Robles, 1933–4, in the same years that the Nazis were attacking modernism in Germany itself). Schneider worked in the office of José Marrero Regalado from 1934 to 1941, where he rendered Marrero's works in sophisticated charcoal drawings that often surpassed the finished buildings in formal boldness and abstraction, recalling those of Mies van der Rohe, a master of the medium. Stylistic comparisons have also been made between modernism in the Canaries and the work of the Austrians Rudolph Schindler and Richard

Miguel Martín-Fernández de la Torre, Cabildo Insular (Island Council) Building, Las Palmas de Gran Canaria, 1929–32, built 1937–42.

96

José Blasco Robles, Casa Armas Marrero, Santa Cruz de Tenerife, 1932.

Neutra in Los Angeles a decade earlier, although Oppel and Schneider were economic refugees attracted to the islands' building boom rather than prophets of an exotic modern Arcadia. The local historian María Isabel Navarro Segura has also noted the influence of German economic interests in the islands and 'the aggressive efforts of the German colony to conquer the terrain formerly occupied by British and other European groups'. She points out that modernism was used in this effort as a means of promoting German technology and building products.[7]

José Blasco Robles and José Marrero Regalado arrived in Tenerife from the mainland in 1932 and 1933. A native of Almería, Blasco Robles studied in both Madrid and Barcelona (class of 1928), where he was a contemporary of Sert and Torres Clavé. He favoured jazzy curving soffits and corners over Martín's more severe geometric abstraction, though he made similar use of deep continuous terraces, as in the Casa Armas Marrero in Santa Cruz (1932). His prow-shaped Edificio Núñez (also 1932) was one of the first steel-frame structures in the islands.

But it was Marrero (Madrid, class of 1925) who developed the most active modern practice in Tenerife, occupying a position comparable to that of Martín in Las Palmas. Marrero was thoroughly eclectic, however, moving simultaneously among modern, regional and academic styles in the carefree spirit of a theatre director changing sets. He once declared that 'monumental classicism is the white tie and tails of good urbanism,' for example.[8] After working briefly in Madrid for Gutiérrez Soto, he began an independent practice there before returning permanently to his native Tenerife. He first came into direct contact with modernism on a visit to Stuttgart in 1930, which resulted in his Deco-Expressionist flavoured Siboney apartment block in Santander, in the north of Spain (1931–3). In his numerous modern works in Tenerife – mainly domestic designs – he failed to establish a consistent style or approach, producing buildings that one critic variously described as Loosian (his own house and studio, 1933), proto-rationalist (Casa Perera, 1934), near-Corbusian (Casa Palazón, 1934–5; Cine Baudet, 1933) and Expressionist (Lecuona Apartments, 1933).[9]

Together with Martín's brother, the painter Néstor Martín-Fernández de la Torre, Marrero was the main promoter of *Tipismo*, a civic movement that called for the superficial addition of 'typical' regional elements to island architecture, recycled from mainland regionalism, North Africa, the California Mission Style and the Canary Islands' British colonial architecture. Their aim was to create an exotic image for the tourist trade, complete with 'typical costumes' for service workers and the promotion of local crafts. Martín participated in the movement with his design for the Santa Cruz Casino (1929–35), and both built regionalist-style houses there. But Marrero's role took on a new dimension after the Civil War, when as General Housing Inspector he decreed a set of 'norms' imposing typical elements on all island construction (1939), and built the Our Lady of Africa Market (1941–6), a scenographic set piece for tourists and locals alike. Though no more serious in intention than the Hollywood-inspired nightclubs of Gutiérrez Soto, Marrero's mix of energetic frivolity and superficial populism and his arbitrary use of authority is a typical example of aesthetic and ethical shallowness on the part of the victors of the Civil War.

The *Gaceta de Arte*

The *Gaceta de Arte*'s collaborators took up the cause of modern architecture as both a social and an aesthetic crusade. Officially published by the literary section of the Santa Cruz Circle of Fine Arts and dedicated to 'contemporary expression' in the arts, the magazine had an international reach in terms of contents, collaborators and readership. It achieved a degree of fame in 1935 with the Surrealist Exhibition in the Tenerife Athenaeum, an event capped by the visit of André Breton and his entourage from Paris. The artists exhibited there, including Jean (Hans) Arp, De Chirico, Dalí, Óscar Domínguez, Marcel Duchamp, Max Ernst, Alberto Giacometti, René Magritte, Joan Miró, Man Ray and Yves Tanguy, were only a limited selection of the magazine's impressive range, which also covered the arts in Germany, the Soviet Union and elsewhere.

The *Gaceta*'s attention to architecture was due to the efforts of its editor, Eduardo Westerdahl (who was half Swedish and half Catalan), and the Surrealist poet and socialist Pedro García Cabrera. The two wrote a total of eleven 'Rationalist Manifestos' in its pages, taking positions on themes such as 'Architecture and Urbanism', 'The Formal Expression of the Republic', 'The Social Meaning of Architecture' and 'Rationalism as Biological Function'. García Cabrera applied the term 'rational' in place of 'abstract' to art, too, and was given to colourful declarations, as shown in his 1932 essay on workers' housing: 'Rational architecture is the first revindication achieved by art for a new civilization. The red blaze in which continents are burning, self-dispatched at great velocity towards integral egalitarian heights, has created the factor of repose.'[10] Westerdahl also published key texts by international figures dealing with the social dimension of architecture, including Ludwig Hilberseimer's 'The Minimal Dwelling', Le Corbusier's 'Architecture or Revolution', Ernst May's 'New Cities in the USSR' and Alberto Sartoris's 'Introduction to Monumental Architecture'.

Westerdahl and García Cabrera made several efforts to promote their social vision locally. As a member of the Santa Cruz City Council during the Republic, García Cabrera pushed forward a workers' housing colony designed by Marrero in 1936 but unrealized. In 1933, Westerdahl organized a Youth Congress in Las Palmas to campaign for 'a new city reflecting a new situation of social justice' and calling for functional urban planning, low-cost housing and public schools, baths and recreational facilities, echoing contemporary initiatives of the GATEPAC group in Barcelona. But the magazine's collaborators had no direct ties with the local architectural community or the conservative ruling elite they served, and their efforts were largely ineffectual. While García Cabrera's housing proposal languished in Tenerife, for example, Martín designed, financed and built a

INAUGURACION

EL 11 DE MAYO A LAS 6 DE LA TARDE

EXPOSICION
SURREALISTA

organizada en el Ateneo de Santa Cruz de Tenerife
por "Gaceta de Arte"

ABIERTA DE 11 A 12
Y DE 5 A 9 TODOS LOS DIAS
HASTA SU CLAUSURA EL 21 DE MAYO

Cover of the catalogue for the 21 Exposición Internacional del Surrealismo, Santa Cruz de Tenerife, 1935.

low-cost subsidized housing project in the garden city of Las Palmas, the Colonia ICOT (1937–9, during the Civil War). The *Gaceta* ceased publication with the outbreak of the war. Westerdahl was able to resume his promotion of contemporary art in the 1950s, but García Cabrera faced years of prison, forced labour and house arrest, and another collaborator, the Surrealist poet and socialist Domingo López Torres, was tortured and killed in July 1936, when pro-Franco forces seized the islands.[11]

The GATEPAC Adventure

The most important effort to carry out a programme of radical social reform through architecture, as advocated by the *Gaceta de Arte* and the international CIAM movement, was undertaken by the GATEPAC group. Following the contacts of García Mercadal with the organizers of the CIAM, GATEPAC was founded as the Spanish arm of the international movement in 1930. It was organized in three unequal divisions conceived as groups that would work and sign projects collectively. The Central Group, based in Madrid and led by Mercadal, failed in its attempt to attract established architects such as Arniches, Domínguez or Bergamín, and, with five younger recruits, never became an effective organization. The Northern Group, based in San Sebastián, was dominated by Aizpurúa, with the participation of his design partner Joaquín Labayen, as well as Luis Vallejo, Tomás Bilbao and a few others. But it was the Eastern Group in Barcelona, led by Sert and Torres Clavé, that formed the true heart of the movement, with a committed core of members who had known each other as rebellious students in the late 1920s and who found in the Catalan autonomous government a potentially receptive client. Key members included Sixte Illescas, Joan Baptista Subirana, Germán Rodríguez Arias, Francesc Fàbregas and Antoni Bonet.[12]

Like the CIAM congresses, which were dominated in their early years by the socialist architects of Weimer Germany and focused on the practical problems of workers' housing and city planning, the aims of GATEPAC were socialist in spirit. In a meeting between Sert, Aizpurúa and Mercadal after the founding of the Republic in 1931, for example, the three agreed to concentrate on publicizing projects of workers' housing and social clubs, popular cinemas, schools and the like, with 'the objective of interesting the Government in accepting radical solutions in favour of the proletariat'.[13] The group launched an ambitious programme of activities to promote its influence. These included participating in competitions and organizing exhibitions; the opening of a Barcelona storefront and meeting centre, prominently sited on the Passeig de Gràcia; and, most importantly, the publication of the quarterly journal AC. The journal was edited and published by the Barcelona chapter, under the direction of Torres Clavé and Sert, and funded by advertising and the members themselves.

The first issue of AC in March 1931 offered a concise, bold presentation of the group. It stood out for its modern typefaces, graphic design and straightforward, telegraphic prose, inspired by Ernst May's *Das Neue Frankfurt* and other modernist publications. Its contents included projects by Illescas and Aizpurúa, a critique of Barcelona urban planning, articles on the standardization of construction elements, on the design of hotels and on 'The Green City of Moscow', a review of 'Contemporary Photography and Cinematography and a report from the third CIAM meeting in Brussels. The front-page editorial concluded:

> Architecture corresponds to a utility, to an end. It should begin from elements, programmes, materials, space and light, and develop rationally from the interior (function) to the exterior (facade) in a simple and constructive manner, seeking beauty in proportion, order and balance. Suppress superfluous decoration. Struggle against the false use of materials . . . To bring architecture into its natural medium, that of the technical, social and economic, is the programme the GATEPAC group proposes to put into practice.[14]

Aizpurúa and the Lure of Political Extremism

GATEPAC was a high-risk adventure on which its members staked their careers, and the lacklustre performance of the Madrid group was not the only disappointment. In San Sebastián, Aizpurúa's discouragement with the scarce results of his collaboration and his gradual estrangement from the group coincided with his involvement in José Antonio Primo de Rivera's Falange Española, of which he became a founding member and Chief of Propaganda in 1933. With his conservative family background and religious faith, Aizpurúa was a typical candidate for Primo de Rivera's fascist movement, which drew on young 'men of action' mobilized by the weakness of the Republic in dealing with the violence of the revolutionary left and impatient with democratic process. Aizpurúa transferred his zeal for radical social change from GATEPAC to the fascists. This militancy cost him his life; at the outbreak of the war, he was arrested and executed by a Republican militia.

As a student, Aizpurúa (Madrid, class of 1927) frequented the Residencia de Estudiantes, where he became a friend of Lorca. He discovered Le Corbusier's *Vers une architecture* there in 1925 and immediately began experimenting with modernist ideas in student projects, to the astonishment of his classmates.[15] Fresh from a trip to the Netherlands, a highlight of which was a visit to Gerrit Rietveld's Schröder House (1924) in Utrecht, he and classmate Joaquín Labayen opened their San Sebastián studio with a Neoplasticist-inspired storefront in early 1928. Aizpurúa plunged into action, producing small interiors, unrealized projects and speculative designs, participating in a 1928 exhibition of local art and architecture and writing magazine articles in favour of the new architecture. His 1930 essay in Madrid's *La Gaceta Literaria* is steeped in the rhetoric of revolution:

José Manuel Aizpurúa
and Joaquín Labayen,
Royal Nautical Club,
San Sebastián, 1928–9.

Architecture in Spain doesn't exist; there are no architects, only pastry chefs. It's ridiculous to pretend that the new architecture is only for select minorities. The new architecture is for the masses, and it comes for them in order to redeem them. But when a serene spirit goes into the streets and finds buildings lacking tranquillity and full of sensualism, he loses his serenity and cries for revolution.[16]

Aizpurúa launched his career with the Royal Nautical Club of San Sebastián (with Labayen, 1928–9), his only significant completed work. Superficially, the project had all the characteristics of a frivolous stylistic adventure. It was sited like a docked yacht beside the seaside promenade, and in its open decks, ship railings, porthole window accents, mast and rounded bow relied on the ship metaphor in surprisingly literal terms. But the project also had many of the identifying attributes of orthodox modernism, including free-standing columns and pilotis, continuous ribbon windows with pivot openings, a non-axial, lateral path of entry and circulation and an overall asymmetry, composed with a rigour and sophistication seldom seen before in Spain. Its furnishings included Mies van der Rohe's tubular MR10 chairs and wood furniture by Robert Mallet-Stevens.[17]

Aizpurúa was introduced into the CIAM and the formation of GATEPAC by García Mercadal, and he became an enthusiastic participant in both. He attended the preparatory meeting for the Second CIAM Congress in Basel in 1929 and participated in Mercadal's competition on minimal housing for Frankfurt. In 1930, he and Labayen organized an exhibition of modern architecture and painting in San Sebastián that brought together most of the founding members of GATEPAC, immediately preceding the official establishment of the group in Zaragoza that October. As a result of these contacts, the Nautical Club was widely published in journals across Spain and abroad. Particularly important was the 1931 article by Sigfried Giedion in *Cahiers d'art* on the work of GATEPAC members as well as the visit of the ever-influential Le Corbusier to the work in 1930.[18] The club was the only Spanish building included in Philip Johnson and Henry-Russell Hitchcock's 1932 International Style show at the Museum of Modern Art in New York.

Working with Labayen and others – and signing projects with the collective initials 'GN' of the Northern Group – Aizpurúa entered a number of open competitions in the following years that took him into the heart of the Republic's social programmes. After his direct contact with CIAM members and their work, he abandoned the elaborate compositions of his first projects, such as the 1928 proposal for a restaurant on Mount Ulia in San Sebastián, where he manipulated Corbusian themes with a youthful extravagance. In their place, he took up a lean, functionalist simplicity inspired by the work of Swiss and German contemporaries such as Gropius and Hans Schmidt, whom he had met in Basel. He used programme elements to give character and orientation to a design, such as the trapezoidal auditorium that projects from the linear block of the 1935 Cartagena secondary school, or the curved backs of the lecture halls that bulge out from its upper storeys. (Designed with his cousin Eugenio María Aguinaga, the unrealized project was his only winning competition design, awarded during the right-wing government of Alejandro Lerroux.)

Together with the works of the Barcelona GATEPAC group, these projects were recognizably 'modern' to a degree seldom seen before in mainland Spain. They were free of lingering Art Deco or academic compositional habits, as well as the underlying tectonic characteristics of masonry construction, adhering instead to the formal logic of functional, asymmetrical layouts, skeletal structures and abstract, non-load-bearing enclosures that clearly identified them with international modernism.

However, by 1934 – and coinciding with his increasing involvement in the Falange – Aizpurúa had all but ended his relations with GATEPAC and began to sign projects with his own name. He was discouraged by the failure of the Northern Group to become a true functioning collective and by the general lack of positive results. He was particularly angered by the failure of an ambitious competition project for a new hospital in San Sebastián, designed with Manuel Sánchez Arcas, Labayen and Eduardo

Lagarde (1934), which was rejected by a jury that included Rafael Bergamín and Aizpurúa's former teacher Modesto López Otero.[19]

Aizpurúa was present at the two national councils of the Falange, for which he participated in drafting the '27 Points' of the movement and a paper on agricultural policy. With the artist Alfonso Ponce de León, he probably also designed the 'Curtain of the Fallen' that formed a backdrop to the meetings, commemorating the members murdered by gunmen of the radical left. Aizpurúa himself narrowly escaped assassination in 1934, when the local party leader was struck down in front of his studio. The following day a prominent local socialist was murdered, presumably by the Falangists.[20] With this increasing violence, the poet Gabriel Celaya, Aizpurúa's childhood friend, was shocked to find him with Lorca when he last saw the poet, in March 1936 in San Sebastián, months before the execution of both by opposing sides of the conflict at the outbreak of the war. He was further shocked when Lorca claimed that he dined regularly with Primo de Rivera and assured him that both were *buenos chicos* or 'nice boys'.[21] The literary critic José Carlos Mainer helps to clarify these apparent contradictions, and the underlying contradiction of Aizpurúa's trajectory, when he points out that fascism in the 1930s 'was not the negation of modernity but rather its pathology. The "modern" was still a place of encounter for those who, beyond their political convictions, were, above all, young. But this welcoming promiscuity did not cease to be a latent danger.'[22]

Mainer goes on to explain the seams of division latent in this common attraction:

> Inevitably, the search for the functional and the simple,
> the new and the radical, became politicized: the Left saw
> in the proposition a burning egalitarian ideal (simple, uniform
> goods, fresh in spirit, at the disposition of all), while fascism
> saw in the state that would supply these goods the collective
> expression of the force of a people definitively inserted in its
> destiny [a paraphrase of José Antonio Primo de Rivera] . . .
> This wasn't the same thing, and yet it was: all asked of art
> efficiency, simplicity and force, as well as the representation
> of the new values.[23]

Aizpurúa was ultimately unable to interest his fascist colleagues in modern architecture. In 1930, for example, he introduced his friend Ernesto Giménez Caballero to Le Corbusier in San Sebastián. Giménez was the editor of *La Gaceta Literaria* and by that time had become, in the words of Mainer, 'the intellectual creator of Spanish Fascism'.[24] But in his famous

1935 book on fascist aesthetics, *Arte y estado* (Art and State), Giménez blasted modern homes as 'an architecture for tuberculosis patients, of sanatorium dwellings, dental clinic salons and operating room bedchambers' derived from 'the Jewish, Socialist and pedagogic spirit of 1917'. He advocated in its place the 'order, classification, hierarchy and dignity' of the Roman villa.[25]

The Eruption of GATEPAC in Barcelona

The story of GATEPAC in Barcelona takes place against the backdrop of a conventional stylistic shift towards modernism protagonized by older architects who had begun their careers under the banner of Noucentisme. While Nicolau M. Rubió i Tudurí was designing the gardens of Montjuïc for the 1929 Exposition, for example, he built the city's first radio transmitter in a 'Rational' style that seemed appropriate for the new medium, based on his study of the works of Le Corbusier (Radio Barcelona, 1926–9). In 1931, he had a brief polemical success with his book *Actar*, an essay on the new 'architecture of the machine'.

Two other sophisticated stylists are worth mentioning. Francesc Folguera (Barcelona, class of 1917), alongside Raimon Reventós, was the author of the Spanish Village for the 1929 Expo, a pastiche of elements from Spanish regional architecture that would become the model for Marrero's Tenerife market. But soon after, he designed the Casal de Sant Jordi (1929–31), where he organized a seemingly styleless facade of unadorned window openings into a taut and complex composition that reflected the mixed programme of offices and residences. Raimon Duran i Reynals (Barcelona, class of 1926) was clearly influenced by the early residential buildings of Sert and other GATEPAC members in several refined modern projects, such as his Casa Cardenal apartment building (1935) with its simplified composition of continuous horizontal openings. However, in the same year, he designed another apartment building in the same block in full academic dress.

A case apart is Ramon Puig Gairalt (Barcelona, class of 1912), who, as municipal architect of L'Hospitalet, a Barcelona suburb, played a role comparable to Tomás Bilbao in Bilbao, promoting the construction of low-cost housing and modern urban design based on his study of the latest international developments. In his building projects he evolved from Noucentisme into a rather eccentric modernism, as in the so-called Skyscraper (Gratacel) of L'Hospitalet (1931–2), a diminutive residential tower with an assertive vertical run of corner balconies. Ramon's younger brother Antoni (class of 1918) was the author of another early modern project, the Myrurgia Perfume Factory (1928–30), which featured an exposed steel structure, horizontal lines and Deco details.

The force of the GATEPAC group dominated Barcelona's architectural scene from the moment it appeared. As students in the late 1920s, Sert and his classmates, impatient with the conventional academic education of the Barcelona school, began to work on modern designs – the 1928 Hotel on a Beach by Sert, Josep Torres Clavé and Joan Baptista Subirana was published in the local magazine *Gaseta de les arts* the same year. Sert travelled frequently to Paris, and on a 1926 visit he encountered *Vers une architecture* and other works by Le Corbusier. Hearing of Le Corbusier's 1928 visit to Madrid, the group hastily arranged two lectures in Barcelona to coincide with his return journey. Le Corbusier recalled, 'I received a telegram in Madrid signed by José Luis Sert (whom I then didn't know), to meet him at 10 p.m. in the Barcelona train station. Five or six young men received me, all short in stature but full of energy and fire.'[26]

Before finishing his studies in 1929, Sert worked in Le Corbusier's Paris office for several months, steeping himself in the Corbusian vocabulary. He returned regularly to Barcelona, where he was building two modern apartment blocks financed by his mother (Sert's father owned a tapestry factory, and his mother was a niece of the shipping magnate Antonio López; his uncle Josep María Sert was also a well-known muralist). In April, in open rejection of the retrograde architecture of the 1929 Exposition, Sert and half a dozen classmates and future GATEPAC members organized an exhibition titled 'New Architecture', held at the Dalmau Gallery on the Passeig de Gràcia, also the site of Salvador Dalí's first show a few years earlier. The exhibition featured modern projects by the group, most of which were collaborative designs, as well as a modernist manifesto inspired by Le Corbusier's writings. The show was widely covered in the local press. (Incredibly, Mies's German Pavilion at the Exposition had no recorded impact on the group, although it too received wide coverage.) Thus, on the eve of the formation of GATEPAC, Sert was already the leader of a functioning movement.

GATEPAC made its official entrance in Barcelona with the opening of its storefront and meeting centre on the Passeig de Gràcia, where models of buildings, examples of modern furniture and information about the group were displayed. In the same year, the first issue of the GATEPAC journal AC appeared, and Sert finished the most ambitious of his apartment buildings, which is located on a corner of the Carrer Muntaner (1929–31). Despite flaws such as poor lighting and ventilation in some units, the design stands out for its duplex apartments with double-height living rooms, and for the multilayered main facade, where Sert combined punctured voids, horizontal ribbon windows and shallow cantilevered balconies to create an abstract, weightless frontal plane.

Also worth noting from GATEPAC's early years are Sixte Illescas's Casa Vilaró (1929–30), with its ship-like covered deck or terrace, and the

abstract facade of Germàn Rodríguez Arias's apartment building on the Via Augusta (1930–31). Later in the decade, Rodríguez Arias and Ricard Churruca designed a large apartment complex on the Diagonal (1935–40), one of the most accomplished modern commercial designs of the period.

After these initial private projects that established the modernist credentials of the Barcelona group, their work stood out from their contemporaries for its public vocation and prototypical character. In the area of school building, for example, rather than simply submit modern designs in the competitions offered by national and local administrations, the group organized the International Exhibition of Modern Schools in Madrid and Barcelona in 1932, using material gathered by the Swiss delegation of CIAM, and dedicated two issues of AC to the problem.[27] Sert's unbuilt project for a school on the Avenida del Bogatell in Barcelona, with its square classrooms opening to continuous terraces for shade and cross-ventilation, was published in the second of these issues and was thus presented as an example of the ideas for school buildings outlined in the accompanying texts.

Characteristically, these texts frontally attacked the Ministry of Public Education's existing programme, as conceived by Flórez and run at the time by Bernardo Giner de los Ríos, in evident ignorance of the research and innovation behind it. GATEPAC rejected Flórez's regionalist prototypes as 'monumental, representative and useless', and suggested that 'those who direct this great school plan should not lose sight' of the 'norms of modern teaching' that replace 'rigid, inhuman principles' for 'an emphasis on the individual and human development of the child' – the essence of ILE teaching methods.[28] Similarly, their observations on the correct design of classrooms and the response of prototypes to climate and other factors offered little new, although their call to standardize elements and economize construction through modern technical means represented an advance.

GATEPAC's most ambitious plans for reform were directed towards the new Generalitat, or regional government of Catalunya, which, with the founding of the Republic, had wrested a degree of autonomy from the central government. The 1931 elections also resulted in the defeat of the conservative Lliga Regionalista by the leftist Republican Party (Esquerra Republicana de Catalunya, or ERC) under the leadership of Francesc Macià, who became the Generalitat's first president in 1932. All of GATEPAC's projects, from health centres and workers' housing to their proposed beachfront 'City of Repose and Vacations', were conceived and presented as part of a campaign to implement a comprehensive planning effort in Barcelona modelled on the emerging urban ideas of Le Corbusier and the CIAM group. The proposals coincided with the ERC's campaign pledges to address the needs for low-cost housing, healthcare and education and the reform of the dense and unsanitary slums of the Gothic Quarter, and they constituted

Josep Lluís Sert, Carrer Muntaner apartments, Barcelona, 1929–31.

a bid to replace the bourgeois Noucentista urbanity of the Lliga Regionalista with the revolutionary aesthetics of international modernism as the official Republican style.

GATEPAC's ambitious plans of urban reform coincided with the turn of the CIAM from questions of housing types, siting and massing to the more comprehensive issue of city planning, culminating with the fourth CIAM in 1933 and its theme, 'The Functional City'. This interest was sparked in part by the city-planning needs of the Soviet Union. In 1930, Ernst May took a brigade of German and Swiss architects and planners there with the objective of designing and building twenty new cities in three years. The promise of the Soviet Union contributed to Le Corbusier's return in these years to the city-planning issues that had occupied him in the early 1920s, culminating with his 1935 book *La Ville radieuse* (The Radiant City). With the direct collaboration of Sert and his GATEPAC colleagues, Le Corbusier began work in 1932 on his 'Plan Macià' for Barcelona. He presented the project at the Fourth CIAM Congress and included it in *Ville Radieuse*, together with plans for Algiers, Moscow, Rome, Stockholm and Rio de Janeiro, among others.

Le Corbusier and the GATEPAC group cultivated their contacts with President Macià and nursed hopes that their proposals would be officially accepted and realized, despite the Generalitat's political and financial limitations. In one of GATEPAC's greatest coups, the preparatory meetings for the Fourth CIAM Congress were held in Barcelona in May of 1932, and attended by Le Corbusier, Gropius, Breuer, Giedion, Cornelis van Eesteren and others. During this event, Sert arranged a meeting between President Macià and Le Corbusier to discuss urban-planning issues. No formal

GATEPAC, City of Repose and Vacations project, 1931–5. Original axonometric.

Le Corbusier with GATEPAC, Plan Macía for Barcelona, 1932–4. Detail of diorama drawing, port area.

contract for urban planning was ever offered by the Generalitat, however. Aside from facilitating public exhibitions of the Plan Macià and GATEPAC's City of Repose, the only concrete results of these efforts were GATEPAC commissions to build the Casa Bloc workers' housing complex and the Anti-Tuberculosis Dispensary, located in the Gothic Quarter. A 1936 commission to design the Regional Hospital of Valle de Hebrón was interrupted by the outbreak of the war.

The City of Repose and Vacations is significant as an exercise in zoned city planning as an example of GATEPAC's ideas on the relation of modernism and social health, and as testimony to the group's ambitions. Sert and his collaborators discovered the undeveloped beaches, located 24 kilometres (15 mi.) southwest of the city, in 1931. Inspired by Moscow's linear Green City (Moisei Ginzburg and Mikhail Barsch, 1930), which they published in the first issue of AC, they proposed to build a popular public resort on the site. It was to be organized through public subscription as a cooperative society of users, with the aid of public funding and expropriation of the land. They exhibited the completed plan in the public spaces under the Plaça de Catalunya in 1933, and gathered 800,000 potential subscribers. The group sent Joan Baptista Subirana to Madrid to seek the collaboration of Indalecio Prieto's Ministry of Public Works, which at the time was promoting a similar proposal for the San Juan Beach in Alicante

and studying plans for a popular resort along the Jarama river outside Madrid, one of the only known collective projects of GATEPAC's Central Group, under the direction of Mercadal and with Subirana's collaboration. The victory of Lerroux's right-wing coalition in 1933, however, put an end to these proposals.

The plan for the City of Repose called for four different zones of activity laid out parallel to the shore, comprising a mass bathing and entertainment area for day trips from Barcelona, a weekend camping area, an area for vacationers, including hotels, rental housing, sports facilities and boarding schools, and an area of hotel-sanatoriums for 'rest cures' and tuberculosis patients. The development was interspersed with parks and garden allotments and connected to Barcelona via a tram line and highway.

Unlike the City of Repose, Le Corbusier's Plan Macià proposed a radical restructuring of the city that could only have been realized through the mandate of an absolute authority, such as those he had encountered in Moscow and Rome, a possibility that Sert and his group did not discount in Spain's fast-changing political situation.[29] The plan called for the extension of the city via superblocks (measuring 400 by 400 metres (1,300 ft), or nine conventional Cerdà blocks with their corresponding streets), and occupied by the continuous, linear housing 'a redent' (like a simplified Greek key pattern) that he had developed for the Ville Radieuse. It also proposed the 'cleansing' or demolition of wide swathes of the Gothic Quarter, with three imposing administrative towers rising over the port. The plan's exhibition in July 1934, again in the Plaça de Catalunya, was widely seen and covered in the press, but its greatest influence can be found fifty years later in Oriol Bohigas's urban design for the 1992 Olympic

Village, where he took up its concepts of superblocks and landmark seaside towers.

The Casa Bloc (1932–6), located in the industrial district of Sant Andreu, was a test run for the housing prototypes of Le Corbusier's plan. Officially designed by GATEPAC, it is credited to Sert, Torres Clavé and Subirana. The block's linear massing takes the form of a large 'S' in plan, with two courtyards that open to opposing sides. With a steel-frame structure and raised on pilotis for much of its length, the building contains more than two hundred duplex apartments stacked on three levels, with access via continuous open galleries. The ground level and courts were to have included services and recreational facilities, though these were left incomplete at the outbreak of the Civil War and never realized. The modelling of solids and voids produced by the galleries on alternating floors creates an effective composition as a whole, although the project suffers from the poor quality of its materials and the awkward handling of its repetitive infill elements.

The Anti-Tuberculosis Dispensary (1933–7) is more assured in managing the new vocabulary of non-structural facades. On the southern exposure, infill panels of glass, stucco and glass block are framed by the exposed steel skeleton. On the northern street facade, continuous horizontal bands of glass run independently of the structural columns behind them. The L-shaped plan, with an interior court and open ground floor, creates a pocket of open space in the dense urban fabric. The centre was dedicated to the treatment of tuberculosis, as well as research and public education; today it is used as a public health clinic.

The Mediterranean versus the Machine

Parallel to GATEPAC's lobbying for social reform, the group began to make claims for a Mediterranean identity within the Modern Movement, distinct from the 'pure functionalism' of northern European architects and the 'machine for living', as Sert put it in a 1934 article, and more attendant to 'necessities of a spiritual and lyrical order'.[30] They found inspiration for this approach in the popular architecture of the Mediterranean, and particularly in the modest vernacular architecture of Ibiza, at the time an isolated, primitive outpost. GATEPAC featured the island's rural architecture in issue 6 of AC (1932), with photographs by Germàn Rodríguez Arias, and again in issue 21 (1936), with a text by Raoul Hausmann and photos by Erwin Broner, both members of the German arts colony there.

In a 1935 manifesto on the theme, 'The Mediterranean Roots of Modern Architecture', generally attributed to Sert, AC argued:

There has always been an architecture 'without style' (in the academic sense of the word), and generally without architects and plans. These Mediterranean structures are of a magnificent simplicity and dignity that we would like to see lavished on the large cities of today. Everything about them is natural, everything has been invented to serve man; all of its elements possess the just measure, the 'human' dimension. They don't try to impress with their monumentality, but they radiate light and optimism. Their elements are productions in series, polished and perfected century after century: doors of precise height and width, windows, pantries, furniture, ceramics.[31]

Invoking the same racial arguments on the 'Germanic' versus the 'Latin' that Giménez Caballero was using to discredit the Modern Movement,[32] the text also claimed a 'spiritual' affinity between modernism and Mediterranean architecture, a congruence they found lacking in the traditional architecture of Germany, with its 'steeply sloped roofs of slate', and which,

for racial reasons, breathes another spirit. Why then has modern architecture been called Germanic? Technically, it is in large part a discovery of the northern countries, but in spiritual terms, it is the Mediterranean's architecture without style that has influenced this new architecture. Modern architecture is a return to the pure

traditional forms of the Mediterranean. It is one more victory of
the Latin sea!

Though unacknowledged, it is likely that GATEPAC's interest in the vernacular was related to that of the Madrid architects of the ILE. It also recast
the Catalan nationalism of the Noucentistes in proletarian terms. But the
strategy was most strongly indebted to Le Corbusier's own evolution in
these years. We have previously noted reports on his attraction to the
vernacular architecture of Spain that he saw on his 1928 visit.[33] Historians
have also recounted his frustration with the overly technical approach of
his German and Swiss colleagues in the CIAM.[34] He began experimenting
with traditional construction systems in the 1930s, incorporating rubble
masonry walls in the Villa Le Sextant in Les Mathes (1935) and shallow
roof vaults in the 1935 weekend house in La Celle-Saint-Cloud and the
Maisons Jaoul in Paris, originally designed in 1937. Although realized in
concrete, the vaults were based on the traditional Catalan brick vaulting
that he and Sert had discussed at this time.[35]

In the same years, Sert and Torres Clavé employed rubble-stone retain-
ing walls and brick Catalan vaults in a group of weekend houses for a steep
site overlooking the coast of Garraf, just south of Barcelona (1934–5). The
clean lines of the exterior volumes were broken by the rounded forms of
chimneys and showers, as with the cisterns and ovens of rural houses in
Ibiza. In the interiors, which were published in issue 19 of AC (1935), the
tubular metal furniture of their early work was replaced by traditional
ceramics and modern versions of Ibiza's woven rope seating. A similar
change took place in the furniture on display in the GATEPAC storefront,
with many pieces designed and produced by Mobles i Decoració per la
Vivienda Actual (Furniture and Decoration for Today's Home), founded
by Sert, Torres Clavé and the student Antoni Bonet in 1935.

While the Generation of 1925 in Madrid situated their local, regionally adapted modernism in a rearguard position outside the Modern
Movement, GATEPAC's Mediterranean critique established one of the
themes that would be explored in modernism's post-war evolution, con-
necting the houses in Garraf to the first modern houses by José Antonio
Coderch and others in the 1950s.

GATEPAC during the Civil War

The outbreak of the Civil War sparked a popular uprising in Barcelona
that led to the enactment of radical social reforms like those GATEPAC
had been lobbying for, but GATEPAC itself was swept aside in the tumult
of revolution and war.

Josep Lluís Sert and Josep Torres Clavé, weekend houses, Garraf, Barcelona, 1934–5.

Anarchist workers' unions remained a powerful source of agitation during the Republic, as they had been since the turn of the century. The CNT (Confederación Nacional del Trabajo) and its allies organized general strikes against Macià's government, and armed uprisings broke out in 1932 and 1933. When Franco's coup reached Barcelona on 19 July 1936, armed militias organized by the CNT and other unions were crucial in defeating the rebels. They took over the streets of the city and led a fully fledged anarchist revolution, collectivizing factories and appropriating the abandoned properties of the rich. Lluís Companys, Macià's successor as president, brought the CNT into the government in September as part of a 'Popular Front' coalition of leftist and communist parties, and the new government continued the effort to implement a revolutionary agenda on the home front, despite the demands of the war.

For GATEPAC, these developments initially confirmed the promise of the Republic. Sert wrote to Le Corbusier in March 1936, following the election victory of the Popular Front in Madrid just before the outbreak of the war: 'The revolution that began on 14 April 1931 [the date of the Republic's proclamation] has not come to a halt after all.'[36] Sert himself soon left Barcelona for Paris, fearing for his life as uncontrolled bands of anarchist militias roamed the city carrying out summary executions of perceived class enemies. But Torres Clavé plunged into the revolutionary reform of architecture and building. He was a member of the PSUC (Unified Socialist Party of Catalunya), the Communist party that grew in influence with the Soviet Union's military aid to the Republic and which was instrumental in organizing the government and its war effort in the face of the anarchists' ineffective anti-institutional ideals. Working with his GATEPAC colleague Francesc Fàbregas, he transformed the College of Architects from a professional association into a workers' trade union, the Sindicat d'Arquitectes de Catalunya, which he directed. He participated in the collectivization of the building industry into a single collective enterprise, incorporating managers and workers on equal terms. He served on the commission overseeing the municipalization of urban property and the abolition of rents, and he joined students and anarchists in reorganizing architectural education.

Cover of the last issue of AC during the Civil War, 'Problemes de la revolució' (Problems of the Revolution), 1937.

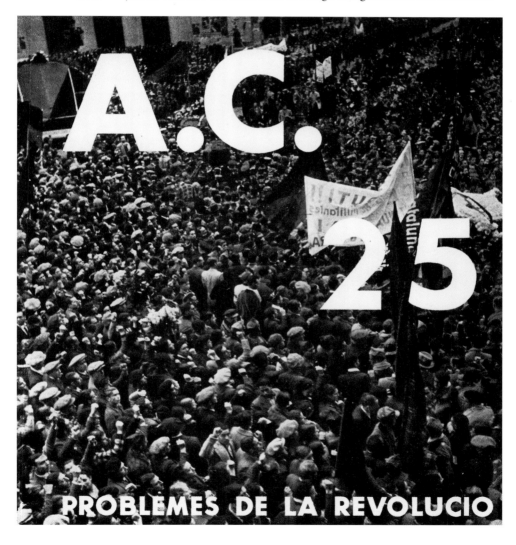

In Sert's absence, Torrés Clave continued directing AC, publishing two issues during the war. But the public role of GATEPAC had clearly been eclipsed by events. In a double issue that appeared late in 1936, an editorial declared, 'from our group, which is purely cultural, we limit ourselves now to advocating the triumph of rationalism in our profession, and a general and severe purification of the architecture of our time, as we are convinced that this is the best way to serve the cultural formation of the people.'[37] AC's last issue was dedicated to 'A plan of immediate action on the housing problem in the city's old quarter'. As with the dynamic poster art of Republican propaganda realized by Josep Renau and others, the issue was presented in an agitprop style, utilizing graphic images and bold headlines in Catalan, Spanish and French. It called attention to the direct relation between physical health and living conditions, citing mortality rates of up to 15 per cent in some buildings. It recommended the demolition of the worst blocks, their replacement with open spaces and low-rise social services and the relocation of residents to the abandoned apartments of the middle class in the Eixample.[38]

As with many other architects, Torres was sent to the war front as the Republic's situation worsened. He worked as a fortifications engineer, and was killed in the Battle of the Ebro in 1938. Following Aizpurúa, he was the profession's second prominent casualty in the war, and his mirror as a partisan for the most radical positions of the Republican period.

The Spanish Pavilion in Paris

The identification of modern architecture with the Republican cause was sealed with the Spanish Pavilion for the 1937 Exposition Internationale in Paris. Designed by Sert with the technical collaboration of Luis Lacasa (sent by the central government from its emergency capital in Valencia), the pavilion was mounted by the Republican government at the height of the war in an effort to attract international support. It is best remembered as the setting for Picasso's *Guernica*, which was exhibited together with works by Joan Miró, Julio González and Alberto Sánchez, and Alexander Calder's *Mercury Fountain*. Also on display were traditional ceramics and crafts, and photo panels on life in Spain in peace and war. Designed and built in only five months, the light, gracefully proportioned pavilion followed the basic scheme of the Anti-Tuberculosis Dispensary, featuring an exposed steel-frame structure raised on pilotis and framing a courtyard, its main facades enclosed with infill panels of glass and corrugated fibre-cement sheeting. A curving access ramp and angled exit stairs on the exterior added a dynamic, Corbusian sense of procession. The courtyard featured an outdoor auditorium and bar, protected by a retractable canvas

Josep Lluís Sert and Luis Lacasa, Spanish Pavilion, Exposition Internationale, Paris, 1937. View from outdoor stage, including Picasso's *Guernica* and Alexander Calder's *Mercury Fountain*, retractable roof shade over cane seating.

canopy, where films by Buñuel and others were shown, transplanting the outdoor nightlife of Spanish summers to the French capital.

The architecture of the Paris fair was dominated by the face-off between the belligerently overscaled Soviet and Nazi pavilions, designed by Boris Iofan and Albert Speer, respectively. Together with Alvar Aalto's Finnish Pavilion, which represented another small country that was about to be engulfed by world events, Sert's building might have seemed tragically anachronistic in its defence of modern architecture, but in fact the two buildings were also heralds of modernism's post-war evolution. In the case of Sert's design, it could be argued that the hastily improvised simplicity of its technical means, with its exposed framing and infill panels, pointed the way forward towards, for example, the light, steel-framed structures of California's Case Study Houses in the 1940s and '50s.

chapter five

Modernism Expunged: The Civil War and Its Aftermath, 1936–50

Petit was part of a group with backgrounds very similar to his own, above all in terms of careers cut short [by the war]: high school teachers who had been destined for brilliant university careers, historians obliged to work as antique dealers, poets working for technical publishers. Their company was cultivated and intelligent but quite depressed and displaced in time: dinners in which Gide and Proust were discussed as if recently published. Their bitterness and disappointment frightened me. At the time [the early 1950s], I didn't have much experience with the consequences of one or another exile on the intellectual spirit of what had been the brilliant youth of the last fifteen minutes of the Republic, and I couldn't imagine that most of those who found refuge in the Americas or in closer European capitals carried a similar burden.

Carlos Barral, 1978[1]

Franco's uprising and victory in the Civil War brought the first period of Spanish modernism to an abrupt end, its principal protagonists silenced or dispersed into exile. Fuelled by savagery on both sides, the war escalated into a clash of ideologies that consumed and transformed civil society, making any post-war reconciliation untenable. Among the most divisive acts of the war were the arbitrary executions of non-combatants on purely ideological grounds, carried out by uncontrolled militias on the Republican side and in systematic purges organized at the highest levels of Franco's 'Nationalist' uprising. The most notorious of these was the assassination of Federico García Lorca in Granada in August 1936, but even rural schoolteachers were rounded up and shot by right-wing Falangists.[2]

This ideological confrontation was heightened by the significant military support that Franco received from Hitler and Mussolini, and Stalin's equally essential military aid to the Republic, which brought the legitimate government increasingly under its influence. The war was thus seen by many as a dress rehearsal for the Second World War, with France and Great Britain watching from the sidelines.

Franco's victory brought no pardon or amnesty. Some 250,000 ordinary Republican soldiers and citizens were imprisoned and tens of thousands

Faculty of Philosophy and Letters, University City, Madrid, at the end of the Civil War. The campus was on the front line of the battle for Madrid throughout the conflict.

were executed. An ideological purge of Spain's universities, professional associations – including the Colleges of Architects – and ranks of intellectuals punished all those accused of secular liberal views or working on the Republican side during the war. Anyone associated with the Free Institution of Teaching (ILE), the Junta for Advanced Studies or the Residencia de Estudiantes was pursued with particular vehemence.

This persecution is seen in the file on Barcelona architects prepared by the local College of Architects on government orders after the war. Anyone listed as having served in the 'Red army' was under scrutiny, and those accused of occupying government positions under the 'Marxist domination', or of supporting the 'Marxist, Jewish, Anarchic cause', were subject to sanctions. Three lines on Francesc Fàbregas, who had worked on the municipalization of urban property in Barcelona for the Generalitat, were sufficient to bar him permanently from practising architecture in Spain: 'Fled abroad. Notable Leftist activist. Member of GATPAC [sic].'[3] Reports on the wartime conduct of 1,088 architects throughout Spain were prepared, and 81 were sentenced to varying degrees of sanctions, in a process begun by military courts and taken over by the new government's General Direction of Architecture, established as the governing organ of the profession.[4]

Many victims of these purges sought exile in the Americas or elsewhere, while those who remained suffered an internal exile of punishment, isolation and privation that generally ruined their careers. The destruction of Spain's intellectual elite and their replacement by the ideological apologists of Franco radically damaged the country's educational institutions and cultural life in ways that are still evident today.[5]

Architects in the War

During the war, young architects and students served on both sides. As with Torres Clavé, many worked as military engineers for defences and bridges. One of these was Ovidio Botella, who began his architectural studies in Madrid in 1933. He first worked on the Republican defences of Madrid, and later he devised an innovative system of floating bridges during the Battle of the Ebro in 1938 that even attracted the attention of the German High Command.[6] Several of Botella's classmates served as engineers on the Nationalist side, including two of the pioneering modern architects of the 1950s, Miguel Fisac and Alejandro de la Sota, the latter of whom was wounded in the eye in the Battle of Brunete outside Madrid.[7] After the war, the winning side counted 42 deaths among architect-combatants, and historians estimate that the profession's casualties on the Republican side were similar, although no official count has ever been made.[8]

Many architects were among the 450,000 Republican soldiers and civilians who fled on foot across the Pyrenees into France after the fall of Barcelona in January 1939. Among them were such well-known figures as Luis Lacasa and Manuel Sánchez Arcas, as well as young soldiers, such as Félix Candela, who would forge their careers in exile. They were interned by the French in the makeshift beachfront concentration camps such as Argelès-sur-Mer and Saint-Cyprien under very difficult conditions, suffering hunger, cold and disease. The horrors of the march and the camps were later recorded by the architect Jesús Martí from his exile in Mexico in a series of paintings, with titles that include *The Road to France, February 1939*; *Waiting for the Authorities to Open the Frontier*; *Walking to Argelès*; *Bonfires against the Deadly Cold*; and *Senegalese Guards Force Us to Put Out the Fires*.[9] Rescue operations organized by the remnants of the Republican government and its treasury, with the help of the leftist government of Lázaro Cárdenas in Mexico, arranged for the transport of many refugees to Mexico and countries in South America, or their resettlement in France. But as attested to by the sketchy personal stories collected in the 2007 Madrid exhibition 'Arquitecturas desplazadas', the voyage into exile was full of hazards and uncertainties, especially with the outbreak of the Second World War and the German occupation of France.

Tomás Bilbao, for example, had been Minister of Public Works in the wartime autonomous government of the Basque region until its fall in 1937. As the end of the war neared, he was named minister in the last Republican cabinet of Juan Negrín in Barcelona (1938–9). In France in 1939, he was detained by the Gestapo but managed to obtain refugee status. He settled first in Paris and then in Marseille but was not permitted to work; he finally left France with his family on board the *Nyassa* in 1942, in one of the last expeditions to Mexico organized by Republican refugee organizations.[10]

After France, Mexico received the largest number of Spanish refugees, some 20,000 families. Among them were 22 architects, by far the largest contingent in any country. Many of Spain's leading intellectuals also settled in Mexico, among them Luis Buñuel, the poets José Bergamín, José Moreno Villa, León Felipe, Luis Cernuda and Manuel Altolaguirre, the writer Max Aub, the philosopher María Zambrano and the composer Rodolfo Halffter. Other distinguished refugees from European conflicts included Hannes Meyer and Leon Trotsky. They found a vibrant cultural life in Mexico, encouraged by the progressive social policies of the Cárdenas government, in which modern architects designed state-sponsored schools, hospitals and housing, for example.

Spanish refugee organizations provided subsidies for many exiles in the early years, establishing schools and helping refugees find jobs and start businesses. We thus find Jesús Martí and Ovidio Botella working together in Mexico to build temporary schools for refugees before each went on to become an important builder and developer, giving work to many Spanish architects in the following decades.

Exile or Ostracism: The Fate of the Madrid School

Bernardo Giner de los Ríos was the first to document the location of 45 exiled architects in ten different countries, a list to which subsequent research has added very few names. He assembled the list for the inaugural congress of the International Union of Architects in 1947 and published it in his book *Fifty Years of Spanish Architecture*, the first history of Spanish modernism, published in Mexico in 1952.[11]

At the time, Giner was working as General Secretary of the Republican government in exile in Paris (he had served as a cabinet minister representing the Republican Union Party in all the Republican governments during the war). After a year in Santo Domingo, he settled in Mexico, where he helped to organize the Colegio Madrid, a school based on ILE principles, and where he designed cinemas, a theatre and other works. Giner was involved with the exiled government until 1965, as were Sánchez Arcas and Tomás Bilbao in the 1940s and '50s. With the end of the Second World War, Republican exiles hoped that the Allies would at least force Franco's isolated regime to accept democratic reforms. But Cold War politics put an end to these expectations when Eisenhower signed a treaty of cooperation with Franco in 1953.

Among the leading architects of the 1930s from Madrid, Giner found Luis Lacasa in Moscow, Manuel Sánchez Arcas in Warsaw, Rafael Bergamín in Venezuela and Martín Domínguez in Cuba. Many others stayed in Spain to face the temporary suspension of their architecture licences, economic fines and other sanctions. These included Carlos Arniches, Fernando García Mercadal and Vicente Eced, who also spent time in prison for having served as an officer in the Republican army.[12] Secundino Zuazo, who had returned to Madrid from his wartime refuge in Paris, was singled out with a sentence of three years' exile in the Canary Islands, in addition to other sanctions.[13]

Others such as Luis Gutiérrez Soto had sided with the Franco regime and emerged from the war with their careers intact, although they too had faced many dangers. Gutiérrez Soto sought protection from Republican militias in Madrid's Mexican Embassy in 1936. He was smuggled out of besieged Madrid to the Nationalist side and served in Franco's Air Force in Málaga for the rest of the war.[14]

Lacasa and Sánchez Arcas spent the Second World War working for the Soviet Academy of Architecture, first in Moscow and then during its wartime evacuation to the Urals. In 1954, Lacasa was transferred to Beijing, where he ran the Spanish section of the Foreign Languages Publishers. He briefly returned to Spain in 1960 but was forced to leave after a month (Franco's regime remained fiercely anti-Communist), and he died in Moscow in 1966. Sánchez Arcas built hospitals in the Soviet Union and Poland, retiring to East Berlin in 1958.

Rafael Bergamín was one of nine Spanish architects documented by Giner in Caracas. Like many architect exiles unable to revalidate their licences abroad, he established a successful construction and real-estate business working in partnership with local architects. His projects there include modern designs for cinemas, houses and commercial and residential buildings with the local architect Rafael Emilio Velutini, such as the Cine Hollywood (1940) and the Edificio Studebaker (1959). He returned to Madrid in 1958.

Martín Domínguez left Spain in 1938 and built a successful career in Cuba, designing, for example, the summer house of President Ramón Grau (1948, with local architect Honorato Colette), among other residential projects, and the 39-storey FOCSA apartment building in Havana (1953–6, with Ernesto Gómez Sampera and Bartolomé Bestard). Domínguez left Cuba for the United States after the Revolution, teaching architecture at Cornell University, where he and Colin Rowe sparred in amiable discussions. He died in 1970 at the age of 72 and was buried in his native San Sebastián, which he had revisited for the first time that same year. For José Ramón

Rafael Bergamín and Rafael Emilio Velutini, Cine Hollywood, Caracas, Venezuela, 1940.

Menéndez de Luarca, a Spanish student who became his teaching assistant in those last years, discovering 'the co-author of the Zarzuela Hippodrome' at Cornell, across the 'forced rupture' and 'amnesia' of the Franco regime, was like 'an unexpected apparition from the depths of history'. He was surprised to find not 'the revolutionary image of the Republican emigré' that he had expected, but an 'elegant gentleman' whose Madrid offices had been in the Palace Hotel, and who regaled him with 'fine cuisine' and stories of his friendships with Lorca, Buñuel and Dalí.[15]

Among the younger Madrid architects who made their careers in Mexico, Félix Candela (Madrid, class of 1935) won fame for his advances in the thin-shell concrete structures pioneered by Eduardo Torroja. Candela had worked as a student on the Hippodrome in the offices of Arniches and Domínguez, but his plans to further study thin-shell structures with the concrete pioneers Dischinger and Finsterwalder in Germany were cut short by the war. After working on Republican defences during the conflict, he first found stable work in Mexico with Jesús Martí before establishing his own engineering and construction firm, Cubiertas Ala (Wing Roofs), in 1948.

In the subsequent decades, Candela began experimenting with thin-shell forms on a trial-and-error basis. He specialized in hyperbolic paraboloid (hypar) vaults – double-curved planes in the shape of a saddle. In addition to their formal lyricism, the vaults could be built using straight boards for formwork, thus lowering costs. Notable examples include the restaurant Los Manantiales in Xochimilco, Mexico City (1958, with Joaquin and Fernando Álvarez Ordóñez), the Bacardi Bottling Plant (1959–60, with an administrative building by Mies van der Rohe) and the Lomas Chapel in Cuernavaca (1958). Candela also developed rectangular 'umbrella' hypar vaults with central columns and groin vaults, which he used for covering markets, subway stations, factories and warehouses. The firm built nearly nine hundred of these structures in Mexico before rising labour costs made them uneconomical in the 1960s.

There is no comprehensive study to date of the many architects who stayed in Madrid to face sanctions and other privations. Of the older generation, Teodoro de Anasagasti died of an infectious fever in besieged Madrid in 1938 at the age of 58.[16] Leopoldo Torres Balbás lost his position as Conservator of the Alhambra, but was permitted to remain at the Madrid School of Architecture, where he was fondly remembered by post-war students such as Francisco Sáenz de Oiza and was a decisive influence on Rafael Moneo's intellectual formation.[17] Zuazo, Mercadal and Eced built unremarkable works in the 1950s. Another victim of sanctions was Spain's first female architect, Mathilde Ucelay, a graduate of the Instituto-Escuela who finished her architecture studies in July 1936. For her wartime

Martín Domínguez, Ernesto Gómez Sampera and Bartolomé Bestard, FOCSA apartment building, Havana, Cuba, 1953–6.

participation on the governing board of the College of Architects under the Republic, she was heavily fined, her architectural licence was temporarily suspended, and she was permanently barred from public work. Nevertheless, she built a modest practice in domestic architecture in the following decades and experimented with the thin-shell structures of Candela, a friend and classmate. Her story came to light in 2006 when she was awarded Spain's National Architecture Prize at the age of 94.[18]

Carlos Arniches was also heavily fined and banned from public work for his association with the ILE, but he continued his practice with a number of small private commissions. One of these, in 1948, was to refurbish the Café Gijón, a famous haunt of the regime's outsider intellectuals, as portrayed in Camilo José Cela's 1951 novel *La colmena* (The Hive). The project included a kinetic sculpture by Ángel Ferrant, another survivor of the Republican era. The two were among the few pre-war figures who had direct contact with the upcoming generation of Spanish modernists in the 1950s. In the case of Arniches, José Luis Fernández del Amo, an architect of the regime who defiantly cultivated the pre-war avant-garde, invited him to design two new agricultural settlements, Algallarín in Córdoba (1953)

Félix Candela with Joaquin and Fernando Álvarez Ordóñez, Los Manantiales restaurant, Xochimilco, Mexico City, 1958.

Carlos Arniches,
Algallarín agricultural
colony, Córdoba, 1953.

and Gévora in Badajoz (1954), for the National Institute of Colonization, giving continuity to Arniches's pared-down vernacular modernism.

In 1948, after several years of teaching, Eduardo Torroja founded the Eduardo Torroja Institute, which became an important research centre. It was modelled on an institute that he had founded in the 1930s with López Otero, Sánchez Arcas and other engineers, but his efforts to continue in the more experimental spirit of the Republican era were met with opposition in official circles, according to the historian Carlos Sambricio. In 1949, the institute organized an international competition to develop mass-produced housing, but its results were effectively suppressed by the regime. After this disappointment, the institute's journal, *Informes de la construcción*, 'gradually ceased to publish news on California architecture, the work of Le Corbusier or other exceptional protagonists of the European reconstruction', Sambricio reports.[19]

Others were less compromised by their activities or political allegiances, or managed to navigate the hurdles of the post-war period more successfully, though concrete information is scarce. Luis Blanco-Soler, Bergamín's occasional partner, was exonerated by post-war tribunals and became the house designer for the Corte Inglés department store, which he converted into a point of modernity in post-war Spain in the 1950s.[20] At the end of his life, he served as president of the Royal Academy of Fine

Arts (1983–8) and was credited with revitalizing the institution in the first years of the democracy.[21]

Luis Feduchi, Eced's partner on the Edificio Capitol, narrowly escaped sanctions. Through pre-war commissions such as overseeing the furnishings of the first Parador in the Castle of Oropesa (1929–31), he had become an expert on period furniture. This had led to his recruitment during the war to work on the junta protecting artistic patrimony. After he was pardoned by a post-war tribunal, he found work designing film sets and teaching set design. One of these films was *Raza* (1941), scripted by Franco, where his knowledge of popular styles was put to use. In numerous commissions, including work on Franco's residence El Pardo, the restoration of various Spanish embassies abroad and the design and furnishing of the 1953 Madrid Hilton, he worked in both historical styles and a safe, modernized classicism. In the 1970s, he published a monumental five-volume work on the popular architecture of Spanish villages, *Itinerarios de arquitectura popular española*, before his death in 1975.

The Fate of Barcelona's Modernists

The story of the widely dispersed exile of leading names and the internal exile of others was repeated in Barcelona. Josep Lluís Sert used his contacts, energy and talent to build a brilliant career in the United States, becoming the most well known of the Spanish exiles. Germàn Rodríguez Arias settled in Santiago, Chile, and Fàbregas in Cuba, while Antoni Bonet launched a successful career in Argentina. The remaining members of GATEPAC who stayed in Barcelona, including Sixte Illescas and Joan Baptista Subirana, faced sanctions and social ostracism. Even Josep Puig i Cadafalch and Nicolau M. Rubió i Tudurí lost their licences to practise architecture. Puig retired to preside over the Institute of Catalan Studies, at a time when the use of Catalan in public was prohibited. In the face of the severity of the Francoist sanctions against leading modernists, architects such as Rubió i Tudurí and Raimon Duran i Reynals returned to the safer Neoclassical Eclecticism of their Noucentisme works.

With the aid of Sigfried Giedion and Walter Gropius, Sert travelled from Paris to New York via Cuba in 1939, joining the distinguished group of European refugees who brought modern architecture to the United States. At first, he set about using his CIAM experience to establish himself as an urban planner. With his friends' backing, he adapted the urban planning studies of the Fourth CIAM Congress for an American audience in *Can Our Cities Survive?*, a book published by Harvard University Press in 1942, the year after its publication of Giedion's *Space, Time and Architecture*. He was also the director of the CIAM from 1947 to 1957.

With an American partner, Paul Lester Wiener, Sert founded Town Planning Associates in 1941. Over the next eighteen years, he travelled frequently to South America for a number of CIAM-modelled planning efforts in Brazil, Peru, Colombia and Cuba, including a 1949 plan for Bogotá developed with Le Corbusier. The firm made use of Wiener's contacts at the U.S. State Department to facilitate many of these commissions, but none of the plans were implemented.

Sert's career took a new turn in 1953 when, at Gropius's urging, he was named dean of the Harvard Graduate School of Design, succeeding Gropius as the school's most prominent teacher. With a local partner, Huson Jackson, he designed several buildings for Harvard, notably the Holyoke Center (1958–65) and the Peabody Terrace apartments for married students (1962–4), inspired by Le Corbusier's Unité d'Habitation in Marseille. Sert also played an essential role in the commission and construction of Harvard's Carpenter Center for the Visual Arts, Le Corbusier's only building in the United States (1964). His American career spanned into the 1970s, when he built subsidized housing on New York's Roosevelt Island.

Pablo Neruda was instrumental in bringing Spanish refugees to Chile. Among them was Germàn Rodríguez Arias, who joined a large Catalan community in Santiago in December 1939. With the young Madrid architect Fernando Echeverría as his associate, he established a studio that, among

Josep Lluís Sert and Huson Jackson, Peabody Terrace apartments for married students, Cambridge, Massachusetts, 1962–4.

other projects, reformed various houses for Neruda, including his celebrated Casa de Isla Negra (1943), built around a tower inspired by the
popular architecture of Ibiza. The two architects also designed the Café
Miraflores (1942), a meeting place for Catalans in Santiago. With two other
exiles, Cristián Aguadé and the sculptor Claudio Tarragó, Rodríguez Arias
established Muebles Sur, a furniture company that mixed modern designs
with local craft techniques. He returned to Spain in 1957 and settled in
Ibiza, where he continued to design houses and other projects.

Francesc Fàbregas moved first to the Dominican Republic, where he
found work as a cabinetmaker through a Spanish refugee relief agency, and
then to Cuba, but his Communist militancy was an obstacle to his advance-
ment in both places. Ironically, he found common cause with the Cuban
revolution, the same uprising that forced Martín Domínguez into a second
exile in the United States. In 1959, Fàbregas designed housing and schools
for 20,000 displaced residents of the Sierra Maestra. He occupied various
official positions in Fidel Castro's government, including Chief of Housing
and Community Services in Havana, before retiring to Barcelona in 1978,
three years after Franco's death.

Antoni Bonet had entered the studio of Sert and Torres Clavé as a
student in 1932, and joined GATEPAC the following year, travelling to Athens
aboard the *Patras* with the group for the Fourth CIAM Congress. He spent
the first years of the Civil War in the office of Le Corbusier in Paris, and
assisted Sert on the Spanish Pavilion for the 1937 Exposition Internationale
there.[22] In Le Corbusier's office, he met the Argentines Juan Kurchan and

Jorge Ferrari Hardoy, who persuaded him to join them in Mar del Plata in 1938. The three founded the Grupo Austral, modelled on GATEPAC, and published three issues of a magazine with the same name, although their most well-known collaboration is the BKF chair, also known as the butterfly chair (1939).

In 1945, Antoni Bonet moved to Uruguay to design the seaside Punta Ballena resort, including the Solana del Mar Clubhouse, the clifftop house La Rinconada and the Casa Berlingieri, where he adapted the Catalan concrete vaulting of the Maisons Jaoul, which he had worked on with Le

Antoni Bonet, Casa La Rinconada, Punta Ballena, Uruguay, 1948.

Corbusier. Another of his houses, in Mar de Plata, was for the exiled poet Rafael Alberti (1945). Bonet returned to Barcelona in 1961 and over the next two decades built an abundance of interesting commercial projects in Barcelona, Madrid and various Mediterranean resorts. His best-known Barcelona works are the Catalan-vaulted Casa La Ricarda on the beach in Prat de Llobregat (1962) and the Meridiana Canodrome (1962–3).

For several former GATEPAC members, the odyssey of exile found a final point of return in Ibiza and the Mediterranean. Like Rodríguez Arias, Sert made his way back to the island in the late 1950s, and he built a vacation house for himself in the old town of Ibiza in 1961. Illescas summered there as well. The German Jewish architect and artist Erwin Broner, who had also written on Ibiza in AC, returned at the same time after a period in Richard Neutra's Los Angeles office. He built houses in the Ibizan vernacular and helped to establish the international arts colony Grupo Ibiza 59. The island had become a tourist destination, but the remnants of its Mediterranean vernacular culture and its relative isolation from mainland Spain made it an attractive refuge for the group.

Sert's return to the Mediterranean is marked in a series of projects beginning with the studio he designed for his old friend Joan Miró on the island of Mallorca (1953–7) and the Fondation Maeght in Saint-Paul-de-Vence, France (1958–65). In both, he adapted the sculptural concrete work of Le Corbusier's Chandigarh, with its sunscreens and rooftop light scoops, for a more intimate Mediterranean setting. His last work in Spain was the Miró Foundation in Barcelona (1968–74). He died in Barcelona in 1981, but his ashes are buried in Ibiza, under a simple stone marker with his name in Catalan.

The Architecture of Victory

Franco's Nationalist side began to elaborate an official architectural policy before the war had even ended. These plans were formed by a shadow government composed of right-wing intellectuals, political activists and military officers under the organizational and ideological umbrella of the Falange, in Burgos, their temporary capital during the conflict. The Falangists had been of minor political importance before the war, and the movement's founder, José Antonio Primo de Rivera, was executed by the Republic in November 1936. During the war, however, the Falangists and similar movements acquired thousands of new recruits, and they were quickly grouped together and appropriated by Franco and the Nationalists, who lacked a political base of their own. The Movement, as it came to be known, would become the official – and only – legal political party and workers' union of the dictatorship.

Josep Lluís Sert, Fondation Maeght, Saint-Paul-de-Vence, France, 1958–65. Detail of entry from Sert's archives.

The head of Franco's architecture policy was Pedro Muguruza, the architect of the 1920s Palacio de la Prensa on the Gran Vía who had apprenticed with Antonio Palacios. Muguruza found his way from Republican Madrid to Burgos early in the war and was named director of the architecture section of the Falange's Technical Services in 1937. From this position, he organized the future General Direction of Architecture under the Ministry of Governance. According to its founding decree, signed by Franco in September 1939, the new agency was to organize and direct all architects working for state, provincial and municipal services, as well as the 'colleges and syndicates' of the profession: 'In this way professionals will be representatives of architectonic-syndicalist-national criteria, previously established by the supreme organs that will be created to this end.'[23] The decree thus looked forward to a state-controlled corps of architects organized according to the Falangists' concept of vertical unions combining workers and managers.

Two other important state agencies were founded in Burgos in 1939: the National Housing Institute, under the Ministry of Work, and the General Direction of Devastated Regions, which was responsible for the post-war reconstruction effort and included the Junta for the Reconstruction of Madrid. A social housing agency, Obra Sindical del Hogar y de la Arquitectura (Syndicalist Work of the Home and Architecture, or OSHA), was established in Madrid in 1941.

To head the planning effort for the reconstruction and future growth of Madrid, Muguruza chose Pedro Bidagor (Madrid, class of 1931), who directed Madrid planning for the next two decades. Bidagor had spent the war in Madrid, where he met regularly with a group of architects in the headquarters of the CNT, the anarchist trade union, ostensibly to discuss urban issues. But the group also formed one of the Falangists' major clandestine spy networks in the capital, part of the Fifth Column that one of Franco's generals boasted about to the press.[24]

Bidagor had worked as a student on the technical preparations for the 1929 plan of Madrid competition, and under Zuazo on the New Ministries. His appointment thus assured a great degree of continuity between pre-war and post-war planning for the city. He published his 'Plan for Madrid' in 1941, and it was signed into law in 1946. It called for the continued growth of the city along the northern extension of the Paseo de la Castellana, with a major new stadium, a large commercial centre and hospitals and train stations, all of which were realized in succeeding decades. A green ring was to surround the nineteenth-century city limits, with satellite communities of workers' housing and industry beyond it.

The transformation of the conquered capital of the Republic into a fitting symbol of the new order was one of the chief preoccupations of

Muguruza and his colleagues, as was their desire to establish a suitable national style of architecture for the monuments they planned. The primary site for this proposed transformation was the northern heights of Moncloa, overlooking the Manzanares river, Madrid's battered line of defence throughout the war. In his 1941 plan, Bidagor proposed a symbolic centre there, with new monuments commemorating the conflict and the new regime that were designed to extend the historic city skyline above the river from the eighteenth-century Church of San Francisco el Grande, the Royal Palace and the unfinished Cathedral.

The question of establishing a suitable style for this effort revived the debate of the early 1900s on an appropriate national style, now inflamed by the exaggerated rhetoric and passions of the war and spurred by the examples of Hitler's Germany and Mussolini's Italy. The architectural historian Antón Capitel has argued that the modernism of the 1920s and '30s had only interested a minority of architects and was hated by Muguruza and his colleagues. They found it convenient to identify the Modern Movement with the Republican side, and thus clear the way for a return to academic practice, which they would package as a radical new imperial style.[25]

Addressing the First Assembly of Architects in a conquered Madrid in 1939, Muguruza called for 'the disappearance of the purely material concept of the "machine for living", which has been annihilating the concept of the home'. He condemned the urban concepts of modernism and its repetitive housing blocks, 'where the city loses its essential condition: that of a body integrating a series of organs that give vitality to the whole'.[26]

The debate over a new style had already begun during the war. Writing in *Vértice*, the sumptuous cultural magazine published by the Falange in Burgos, the philosopher José Luis Aranguren argued in favour of the Spanish Baroque. The architect Víctor D'Ors, influenced by Mussolini's Rome, called for the use of modern methods 'interpreted through the special idiosyncrasy of the Spanish soul'. Ernesto Giménez Caballero put in a word in favour of Salamanca's fifteenth-century Casa de las Conchas as a model, and Agustín de Foxá, echoing Albert Speer, wrote on the beauty of ruins.[27]

In the Assembly in Madrid, Muguruza took command of this debate by organizing group visits to Juan de Villanueva's Prado Museum and Juan de Herrera's Escorial. The visit to the Escorial was given special authority by the presence of two major Falangist intellectuals and leaders, Dionisio Ridruejo, National Head of Propaganda, and Rafael Sánchez Matas, Minister without Portfolio. Sánchez Mazas wrote of the visit in the Falangists' newspaper *Arriba* a few days later: 'The Escorial dictates the most important lesson for present and future Falanges. It resumes all our conscience, orders all our will and corrects, implacable, the slightest error in our style.'[28] Thus, a Neoclassicism inflected by 'the special Spanish idiosyncrasy' and the glories of the Spanish Empire under Felipe II was to be the new order – essentially a reinterpretation of the Neoclassicism of Zuazo's New Ministries, then still under construction.

Four Visions of the Escorial

Bidagor's plans for a symbolic centre of the regime on the heights of Moncloa included a 'Victory Avenue' with a 'Monument to the Fallen and to the Victory' set on a large open platform suitable for mass events, and 'framed by a grand Imperial facade'.[29] Nearby, he placed the headquarters of the Falange, never realized. While a Victory Arch and a modest Monument to the Fallen were eventually built in the 1950s, the most substantial and influential result of these ideas was Luis Gutiérrez Soto's Ministry of Air and its urban setting, the Plaza de la Moncloa (1940–51). Although built in Madrid's traditional red brick, rather than stone, the project is clearly modelled on the Escorial, with its multiple courtyards and plaza framed by secondary buildings, its large corner towers topped by pinnacles, its inclined slate roofs and its central portico. Before starting the design, Gutiérrez Soto travelled to Italy and Germany to visit similar projects, despite the ongoing world war. Though he was an outsider to Muguruza's group, he made the transition from his pre-war modernism to the new order with aplomb. He would go on to become a successful residential and commercial architect, whose high-end, conservatively modern buildings helped define the image of Madrid in the following two decades.

Bidagor's vision for the heights of the city was blurred by the overlapping effects of other initiatives. The nearby buildings of the University City, which bore the brunt of wartime fighting, were rebuilt to their original plans, including modernist designs such as Sánchez Arcas's Hospital and Aguirre's School of Philosophy. The head of the reconstruction was Modesto López Otero, who had led the planning of the original campus. The image of a pinnacled and domed skyline over the river was definitively broken by the construction of two commercial skyscrapers in the Plaza de España, at the end of the Gran Vía, not far from the Royal Palace. The first was the Edificio España (1947–53), with 25 storeys in a rather diluted neo-Baroque dress, followed by the Torre de Madrid (1954–8), in an equally diluted modern style, and at 36 storeys one of the tallest buildings in Europe at the time. Both were designed and built by the architect-developer Julián Otamendi and his brother, the engineer Joaquín Otamendi, despite Bidagor's opposition. Both had a greater impact on the public imagination than the Ministry of Air. They featured the mixed-use programmes of

Luis Gutiérrez Soto,
Ministry of Air, Madrid,
1940–51.

earlier buildings on the Gran Vía and marked the return to business-as-usual after the hiatus of the war.

Meanwhile, Franco had his own plans for a monument to the war, a project that could not help but capture public attention. The Valle de los Caídos (Valley of the Fallen), built outside the distractions of the city on a mountaintop near the Escorial, was envisioned by Franco in literal and perverse emulation of Felipe II's monastery-palace, with its basilica and royal burial crypt. It was designed by Muguruza (1940–50) and, after his illness and death in 1952, by Diego Méndez (1950–59) in a sober Herreran style, accompanied by an ambitious programme of monumental sculptures, artwork and decoration, including a concrete cross 150 metres (492 ft) high surmounting the mountaintop. The underground basilica, carved out of the 'living rock' by the slave labour of an estimated 20,000 Republican war prisoners, is the burial site for 34,847 of those killed on both sides, including José Antonio.[30] Franco himself would be buried there in 1975, until his exhumation in 2019.

Many of the architects uprooted by the war spent their idle days drawing fantastic imaginary projects. We have noted the fortified cities of Casto Fernández-Shaw in Chapter Three, and can mention Antonio

Julián Otamendi (architect) and Joaquín Otamendi (engineer), Edificio España, Madrid, 1947–53.

Palacios's imaginary remaking of Madrid in the extravagant image of his own architecture. But no vision captures the surreal logic of fascism as the response of the conservative middle class to the perceived threat of revolution better than Luis Moya in his project 'Architectonic Dream for a National Exaltation', conceived with the sculptor Manuel Álvarez-Laviada and the Viscount of Uzqueta during the war and published in *Vértice* in 1940.[31]

Moya (Madrid, class of 1927) was one of the spy-architects in Bidagor's circle at the CNT headquarters in besieged Madrid, although he is better described as a 'militant Catholic' rather than a Falangist.[32] The 'Dream' was, in Moya's words, the result of 'the necessity to fight for order in a spiritual way, to build an interior refuge where a higher thought could survive despite the medium (Red Madrid)'. It was both a visionary project in the spirit of Étienne-Louis Boullée and a serious preparation for Moya's future career, his peculiar and erudite examination of the possible conditions for what he called, in another essay, 'the resumption of a broken tradition'.[33]

The project envisioned a citadel on the heights of the battlefield in northern Madrid, a monumental cross-axis with a triumphal arch, a funerary pyramid with a burial crypt and basilica inside and other ceremonial and military buildings. The triumphal arch and pyramid are the most original elements of the design. In both, the naked geometric stone massing contrasts with Álvarez-mannered sculptural programmes of elongated, writhing, almost liquid figures and organic forms. Of the plan as a whole, Moya wrote:

Pedro Muguruza, Valle de los Caídos (Valley of the Fallen), San Lorenzo de El Escorial, Madrid, 1940–59.

the citadel is conceived as an efficient instrument of domination, head of the city, submission of revolts. Possession of water, electricity, radio, telephones, gasoline; what it does not possess,

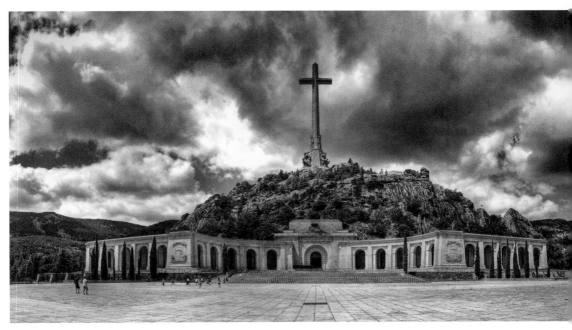

Luis Moya with Manuel Álvarez-Laviada (sculptor) and the Viscount of Uzqueta, 'Architectonic Dream for a National Exaltation', 1937–40. Rendering, section of the pyramidal basilica.

Francisco de Asís Cabrero, housing block, Virgin del Pilar Colony, Madrid, 1947. Built using Luis Moya's technique of unreinforced buttressed vaults.

it dominates. Other preoccupations: the reaction against anarchy is converted into the ordering of complicated circulations, the plaza conceived with every movement foreseen, like the chess-playing automation of Torres Quevedo, just as exact and fantastic.[34]

Muguruza recognized Moya's talent and appointed him to Bidagor's Junta for the Reconstruction of Madrid. Capitel maintains that, with his

'technical rigor and historical erudition', Moya was 'the only figure capable of coherently proposing a classical, traditional understanding of architecture, and probably the only one to seriously believe in its possible development'.[35] Moya's strategy was to overcome the superficial character of academic dress by basing the return to tradition on a return to traditional building methods. He cited the post-war shortage of iron and concrete to justify structures of unreinforced masonry vaults and domes, as in his brick Church of San Agustín in Madrid (1946–50). He applied this technique to public housing in a 1942 project in the Madrid suburb of Usera, in which the horizontal thrust created by a row of repeated shallow brick vaults was absorbed by masonry buttresses on the ends of the block. He published this construction system in the 1947 book *Bóvedas tabicadas* (Vaults between Walls), and the technique was taken up by others in public housing of the period, including a block of duplex apartments in Madrid's Virgin del Pilar Colony by Francisco de Asís Cabrero.

Moya shared his colleagues' taste for grandiloquence, however, and his work did not escape the glib scenographic qualities of the academy even when built in solid stone, as was the case with the Universidad Laboral (Labour University) of Gijón (1945–56, with his brother Ramiro Moya and Rodríguez Alonso de la Puente). A complex for 3,000 students built around

Luis Moya, Labour University of Gijón, 1945–56. Period aerial view of the chapel and tower.

a series of courtyards, it was said to be the largest building in Spain of its time. It was the first of several labour universities promoted by the Minister of Work, the Falangist José Antonio Girón, in a programme to educate the children of the poor in skilled trades. In a 1979 interview, Moya confessed that 'the Falangists wanted to do something very modern.' But he interpreted the supposed 'luxury' of the design as 'a monument to work'. He went on, 'those boys who came from shanty towns . . . should see what hard work can accomplish when it is made the fundamental instrument of a nation.'[36] With its 120-metre (393 ft) central tower and vaulted church, its ranks of classrooms and dormitories, its barrel-vaulted, clerestoried workshops and laboratories and its decorative programme copied from Greek and Roman sources, the Labour University is a curious counterpart to Franco's funereal Valle de los Caídos, an Escorial for the living project of Falangist social harmony, built not with slave labour but with the sweat of the defeated labouring class.

By the time Moya finished the Labour University in 1956, Spanish architecture had moved on to its post-war re-encounter with modernism. Moya remained surprisingly influential among students and peers as a teacher at the Madrid School of Architecture, where he served as director from 1963 to 1966. The impact of his emphasis on the constructive logic of building can be seen on architects as varied as Francisco Cabrero and Rafael Moneo, although we might also attribute the exaggerated austerity of some post-war architects, as in the case of Alejandro de la Sota, to a reaction against the excesses of formal rhetoric that his work exemplified.

chapter six

The Return to Modernism,
1949–60

There is a kind of silence in Spanish architecture, the silence of immobile space, figuratively older and foreign to the central European urge towards transparency and spatial movement in which the Modern Movement was born. The absence of the first European vanguard is clearly evident. In its place, the echo of the Surrealist experience can be recognized in the duplicity of meanings, the obscure sense of guilt and the obsession with the present moment.

Vittorio Gregotti, 1968[1]

The Franco dictatorship's destruction of Spain's cultural fabric following the Civil War meant that architecture – a realistic and therefore modern architecture – had to be virtually reinvented when the time came to put aside imperialist exaltations and return to the pragmatic tasks of rebuilding the country, reintegrating it in the international community and preparing it for technical and economic advance.

The first architects to begin this reinvention of modernism belonged to a generation of post-war graduates whose studies had been interrupted by the war and who therefore had some idea of the pre-war cultural situation. Miguel Fisac, Alejandro de la Sota, Francisco Cabrero in Madrid, José Antonio Coderch in Barcelona and others abandoned their early ventures in the official styles and began to search for ways to reintegrate Spanish architecture into the European and North American modern tradition as it was emerging after the Second World War.

The first new modernists had fought the war on the Nationalist side and were often enthusiasts of the Falangist or religious factions that gave ideological backing to the Franco regime. This situation not only afforded them ready opportunities for work but gave them a freedom of action unavailable to those formed before the conflict. As Miguel Fisac once declared, 'Since I had fought the war with Franco, I believed I had a right to say whatever I felt like.'[2] However, they were handicapped by their process of self-formation, which often resulted in unsystematic, intuitive design strategies and, consequently, uneven and eclectic formal development. Their suspicion of the pre-war Modern Movement, which they associated with the leftist politics of the Republic and the Civil War, often

José Luis Fernández del Amo, church tower at the Vegaviana agricultural settlement, Cáceres, 1954.

made their approach to modernism circuitous, though it also made them natural pioneers of its post-war critique.

Their political ideals, once fully invested in the modern cause, and combined with aesthetic austerity and the existential echo of the war, gave their best work a tragic, elegiac tone that found a broad range of expression, whether in evocations of a nostalgic and utopic rural vernacular (Coderch's Casa Ugalde on the Mediterranean coast), in the sublimated monumentality of official buildings (De la Sota's Civil Government Building, Tarragona) or in the investment of abstraction with spiritual feeling (Fisac's Parochial Church in Vitoria).

Among the second wave of graduates in the early 1950s, those too young to have fought in the war and thus less affected by its stark ideological choices, this aesthetic range extended to the disciplined, exhilarating formal complexity of the new 'Organicist' architecture (Ramón Vázquez Molezún and José A. Corrales's Spanish Pavilion at Expo 58 in Brussels), the rational, impoverished realism of emergency public housing (Caño Roto, Madrid, by Antonio Vázquez de Castro and José Luis Íñiguez de Onzoño), and a popular Miesian utopia of industrial abundance (the SEAT Vehicle Deposit in Barcelona by César Ortiz-Echagüe and Rafael Echaide).

Government commissions and national competitions gave the young modernists official recognition. Soon, culturally enlightened sectors of the Falangist party and the Church became patrons of the new architecture, as they did with the new movements in abstract art, led by figures such as Jorge Oteiza, Eduardo Chillida, Antoni Tàpies, Manuel Millares and Antonio Saura. Likewise, as occurred with many of these artists, a series of international prizes awarded throughout the decade gave Spanish modernism importance to the Franco regime as a means of gaining international legitimacy. This official support contrasts with the situation in other fields, where state censorship fought against the emergence of an increasingly critical social realism in literature (such as the novels of Camilo José Cela, Rafael Sánchez Ferlosio, Miguel Delibes and Juan García Hortelano) and Neorealism in film, as seen in the work of the directors Juan Antonio Bardem, Luis García Berlanga and Marco Ferreri, and the screenwriter Rafael Azcona.

Nevertheless, as the decade progressed, the distance widened between the young modernists and the official sphere that had initially supported them. Rather than succeeding their elders in positions of power, the Madrid modernists found themselves increasingly marginalized. By the 1960s, they were largely dependent on the private sphere. In Barcelona, ties to the regime were fewer while international contacts, particularly with Italy, were already influential in the late 1940s. A reliance on private commissions gave the Barcelonans a pragmatic, realistic outlook distant from the idealism of many of their Madrid counterparts, while implicating them in matters of interior and industrial design. By the end of the 1950s, two distinct currents had emerged, identified by later critics as the School of Madrid and the School of Barcelona.

The Eclipse of the Official Style

From the perspective of the 1940s, the possibilities for a modern revival seemed remote. As we have seen, the climate of fear created by official persecution coerced surviving architects of the Republican era into stylistic regression. All traces of modernism and the teaching methods of the Institución Libre de Enseñanza (ILE) were eliminated from the schools of architecture. Students were trained in the academic classicism of the nineteenth century, rendering the classical orders in large-scale drawings. The library of the Madrid school had been destroyed in the war, while Barcelona's was purged of modernist texts.[3] Federico Correa, a Barcelona graduate of 1953, recalled seeing as a student a photograph of the 1929 Barcelona Pavilion by an architect he had never heard of (Mies) and thinking that it must be in Venezuela.[4]

However, with the defeat of Germany and Mussolini's Italy, the Franco regime found itself in an isolated position. The dictatorship had been condemned by the victorious Allies at the Yalta Conference in 1945 and by the United Nations in 1946, in a resolution recommending the withdrawal of diplomatic relations and calling for democratic reforms. The country was also desperately poor. Food was rationed until 1952, and iron, concrete, machinery and other basic construction products were still scarce at the end of the decade. As the regime's claims to economic self-sufficiency, or autarchy, crumbled, reconnecting with the rest of the world became an imperative.

This opportunity came following the new international situation created by the Cold War and the outbreak of the Korean War in 1950. In 1951, Britain and the United States resumed diplomatic relations with Spain. In 1953, Franco signed a treaty with Eisenhower for the construction of American military bases on Spanish soil and a multi-million-dollar credit line, and in 1955, Spain was admitted to the United Nations. This recognition both legitimized the regime and encouraged its normalization, at least in appearance, while saving Franco from having to contemplate real political reforms. It also paved the way for economic growth and modernization in the country during the latter half of the 1950s.

In architecture, the regime's official opening to the outside world was announced at the Fifth Assembly of Architects in 1949, organized by

Muguruza's successor in the General Direction of Architecture, Francisco Prieto Moreno, and held in Barcelona, Palma de Mallorca and Valencia. By the end of the 1940s, it had become clear to state architects that the task of rebuilding and modernizing the country required modern building techniques and an accompanying stylistic realism. Especially pressing was the need for mass housing, as poor rural immigrants poured into Madrid, Barcelona and other cities, settling in makeshift shanty towns that housed tens of thousands.

In his opening address, Prieto Moreno told the assembly, 'The construction of housing, and especially modest housing requires all our effort.' He called for 'the industrial production of type elements', among other measures, and concluded: 'Spain cannot stand by impassively before the revolution in modern methods and their influence in the new forms. We must give national form to the new techniques so as to continue our history, reaffirming our national personality.'[5]

A more critical appraisal of official policy was made by Juan de Zavala, who told the assembly in an official address, 'The reaction against the forms used before our war has caused a conceptual confusion . . . It has produced an architecture completely isolated from the real problems that should inform it.' After reviewing the architecture of other countries, especially in the United States, he called for a 'new path': 'Now that the inevitable phase of reaction is over, we should dedicate our efforts to creating an architecture that is the product of our times.'[6]

Gio Ponti, the Italian architect and founding editor of *Domus*, was an official guest, and proved instrumental in the following months in orientating young Spanish architects and giving them their first international recognition, as we shall see in the case of Coderch. Ponti had successfully emerged from the Fascist period with his reputation and influence intact, and was invited by Prieto Moreno as a mentor and sponsor of the 'new path' Spain was about to embark on. He told the assembly in improvised remarks: 'In a time when so many things have changed, this voyage to Spain will prove to be one of the events that will most affect my future task. You Spanish architects can make a noble contribution to modern architecture without having to follow the style that prevails in the rest of the world.'[7]

The project that marked this official change in course was the 1949 competition for the Casa Sindical or Union House (1949–56), headquarters of the national trade union, today the Ministry of Health, located across the street from the Prado Museum. First prize was jointly awarded to the young architects Francisco de Asís Cabrero and Rafael Aburto (Madrid, classes of 1942, 1943). The two developed Cabrero's design together. Though monumental in scale, weight and symmetrical disposition, the project

Francisco de Asís Cabrero and Rafael Aburto, Casa Sindical (today the Ministry of Health), Madrid, 1949–56.

replaced ornamental detail for a clear expression of abstract geometry and constructive logic.

Cabrero had travelled to Italy in 1941 as the Second World War was getting underway, and he found inspiration in both the conservative and the radical lines of Italian architecture under Mussolini. He visited the Milan studio of Giorgio de Chirico, and in Rome the studios of Gaetano Minnucci and Adalberto Libera, leaders of the Italian Rationalist movement. For the Casa Sindical he turned to Giuseppe Terragni's Casa del Fascio in Como (1932–6) as a model. The central cubic block, sixteen storeys high and punctured by grids of square windows, is framed by low wings and set on an imposing granite portico. In contrast to Terragni, it is finely dressed in Roman brick, responding to the red brick of Villanueva's Prado Museum across the street and thus providing the local character Prieto Moreno had called for at the Fifth National Assembly.

Coderch and the Mediterranean Vernacular

A review of the formative years of Coderch and Fisac, two of Cabrero's contemporaries, aids the explanation of the complex mix of impulses behind the resurgence of modernism under Franco in Barcelona and Madrid, respectively. José Antonio Coderch's Mediterranean, vernacular-inspired modernism was influenced by both his conservative family background, monarchist and modestly aristocratic, and his contacts with international modernism through the auspices of Gio Ponti. Though he was familiar with the work of GATEPAC, his early houses in the seaside resort of Sitges were designed (with partner Manuel Valls) in the so-called Californiano or Spanish colonial style popular at the time. His contacts in Madrid, where he had briefly worked in 1941 with Pedro Muguruza, led to commissions for the public housing authority of the Falangist party's government ministry, the Obra Sindical del Hogar (OSH, Syndicalist Home Works). For these commissions, such as the Roses subsidized housing (1942), he began to rationalize his picturesque style towards a more

José Antonio Coderch and Manuel Valls, Casa Garriga Nogués, Sitges, Barcelona, 1947.

simplified vernacular. His private commissions underwent a similar evolution, as seen in the 1947 Casa Garriga Nogués in Sitges, the project that caught Ponti's eye in the exhibit of the Fifth National Assembly in Barcelona. Here Coderch introduced his now characteristic sliding, wooden exterior louvres and simplified balustrades, and rationally organized the plans, though today it would be difficult to recognize the project as an innovative work.

Coderch's relation with Ponti helps show how his attraction to the seacoast vernacular was rooted in Falangist ideas of cultural identity and a new society. Most revealing is his early enthusiasm for Ponti's and Bernard Rudofsky's unexecuted hotel project on Capri (Albergo di San Michele, 1938), which he had seen in the Italian journal *Architettura* in 1940 and which he proudly showed to Ponti when they met.[8] Coderch's unrealized Las Forcas development in Sitges of 1945 is inspired by this project, with its simple volumes terraced into the slope, while its programme proposed mixing middle- and upper-class homeowners with fishermen, artists and intellectuals in a model community of paternalistic social harmony. In his remarks to the Fifth Assembly, Ponti discussed the spiritual values that both projects implicitly share, which link them to the Mediterranean tradition that spans from Noucentisme to Sert: 'From our traditions and customs we have received an impalpable, immaterial heritage that is the origin of civilization . . . From the primitive Catalan house springs a spiritual fruit of the greatest and most sacred importance.'[9] Alejandro de la Sota said much the same thing – but with a more poetic sense of ambiguity – when he wrote in 1952: 'Coderch and Valls love the simplicity of the peasant and the fisherman in their work. There are a few of us who believe in this path, the path of whitewash and clay.'[10]

One suspects that Ponti had been called to Barcelona by Prieto Moreno to search for signs of renewal in Spanish architecture, and the modest innovations of the Casa Garriga Nogués presented the opportunity he had been looking for. He published Coderch's work extensively in *Domus* in 1949, leading to articles in *L'Architecture d'aujourd'hui* and elsewhere, and Coderch became *Domus*'s Spanish correspondent. Most importantly, he arranged for Coderch to design the Spanish Pavilion for the Ninth Milan Triennial of 1951. Coderch responded with his first openly modern design, which featured an amoeba-shaped display table, a wall incorporating his characteristic wooden louvres, and exhibits of contemporary artists, traditional crafts and photographs of works by Gaudí and popular Ibizan architecture. The reference to Ibiza established a connection with GATEPAC's publications on the island, while the mixture of contemporary art, traditional crafts and photography followed the recipe of the 1937 Spanish Pavilion in Paris.

José Antonio Coderch
and Manuel Valls,
Casa Ugalde, Caldes
d'Estrac, 1951–2.

Casa Ugalde,
upperfloor plan.

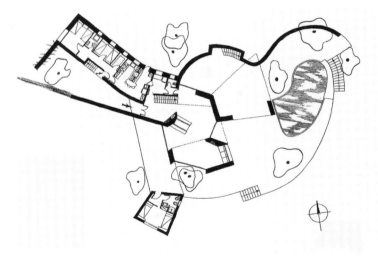

The weight of the moment can be sensed from the copy of the official rules for submissions in Coderch's files, where the requirement for work to be 'al gusto moderno' is underlined.[11] The pavilion received the Triennial's Grand Prize, and other top awards went to participants Joan Miró, Jorge Oteiza, Ángel Ferrant and others. In Milan, Coderch was introduced to Ernesto Rogers, Max Bill and Aldo van Eyck, who later invited him to join CIAM and Team X, the group that, from within CIAM, led a post-war renovation of its ideas. He emerged from this triumph a dedicated modernist, and in 1951 he designed the two most audacious and influential works of his career, which established him as at the forefront of Europe's post-war reinterpretation of modernism in regional and Organic terms.

The Casa Ugalde in Caldes d'Estrac (1951–2), with its abstract volumes extending into the landscape, pierced by voids, is one of the most original works of its time. Coderch took free inspiration from a primitive Mediterranean vernacular and its marriage to the landscape, developing an intuitive plan of curves, angles and knotty, cell-like spaces from the topography, the placement of existing pines and a radial embrace of the surrounding sea views. The Barceloneta apartment building (1951–4), a public housing project for fishermen, reinterprets Spain's traditional urban housing in its vertical strips of louvred balconies and its projecting cornice. The angled wall planes and interior plans, developed to maximize useable space, charge the building with a notable expressive complexity, though the work has obvious debts to contemporary Italian projects that reinterpreted traditional urban types, such as Franco Albini and Ignazio Gardella's Mangiagalli Quarter in Milan (1950–51).

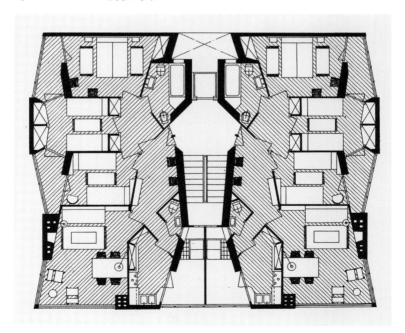

José Antonio Coderch and Manuel Valls, Barceloneta apartment building, Barcelona, 1951–4. Typical floor plan.

Fisac: Faith and Conscience

Miguel Fisac (Madrid, class of 1942), the son of a pharmacist, was born in a small town in La Mancha. While studying architecture in 1936, he became an early member of Opus Dei, the lay religious sect founded by José María Escrivá, which rose to influence under Franco. Fisac's reasons for joining reflect the reaction of many of his class to the reforms of the Republic, which he saw as 'a policy of frank religious persecution that created in believers a reaction of generous exaltation'. When the Civil War broke out, he escaped with Escrivá and others from Madrid to the Nationalist side, crossing the Pyrenees on foot with a guide paid for by Fisac's father. But he left the Opus in 1955 – at great cost to his career – due to his disagreements with Escrivá's conservative taste in religious art and architecture, and 'because [the Opus] had become a machine for producing power'. He recalled: 'I couldn't see how it could become the Christian medium for saving the world.'[12]

Like many of his contemporaries, Fisac noted that he learned nothing useful in school: 'I had to build my own personal understanding of architecture, without any masters other than the direct study of the buildings I came to know on my trips around the world.'[13] His journey towards modernism can be seen in the buildings he designed immediately after graduating for the Scientific Research Council (CSIC), the Franco-era

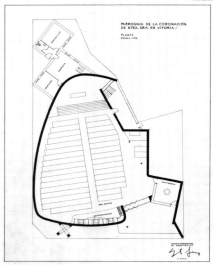

Miguel Fisac, Our Lady of the Coronation Parochial Church, Vitoria, 1958. *Right*: Interior view, *left*: plan.

successor to the Junta for Advanced Studies and Scientific Research on the Hill of the Poplars. As such, it was one of the chief prizes of war claimed by Escrivá, who situated one of his lieutenants at its head. As Alberto Moncada writes, 'Escrivá conceived Opus Dei as a sort of Catholic answer to the liberal, secularist ILE, which was blamed by the Spanish Church for the growing secularization of Republican Spain.'[14]

Fisac thus took part in the appropriation and, one might well say, mutilation of the ILE's main legacy in Madrid. He first rebuilt and unrecognizably transformed Arniches and Domínguez's auditorium into the overbearing Chapel of the Holy Spirit (1942–3), a simplified traditional design built entirely without iron due to wartime shortages. He then hemmed in Antonio Flórez's Residencia de Estudiantes with the granite-clad Central Building (1942–5), designed in what he called an Italian Novecento style, with a crudely detailed Corinthian portico emblazoned with tributes to Franco. Next, in the tall unadorned gateways and crisp brick volumes of the Institute of Edaphology (1944), he moved on to the stripped-down classicism of Marcello Piancentini and the 1942 EUR district, Mussolini's planned expansion of Rome.

In 1949, the year of the Fifth National Assembly, Fisac went on a European tour to take a direct look at modern precedents. 'Though I knew little about Rationalism,' he recalled, 'and though Spanish Rationalism didn't convince me at all, I decided that one must drink from the sources and see how to connect with this renovating current.'[15] He was disappointed by Le Corbusier's Swiss Pavilion in Paris, but found the alternative he was looking for in the Neoclassically derived modernism of Gunnar Asplund's Gothenburg Law Courts in Sweden, 'preferring Nordic Empiricism' to the 'dehumanizing postulates of the Modern Movement'.[16] On his return, in the CSIC's National Institute of Optics (1948–50), he maintained the simple, orderly openings and brick massing of his previous buildings but added a functional plan based on 'autonomous work units', and Scandinavian-inspired furnishings and details, such as the curving stone entry and the womb-shaped bar lounge with its nostril-shaped fireplace. With this work, Fisac's projects for the Hill of the Poplars had come full circle, establishing a line of continuity with the site's pre-war buildings.

Fisac's stylistic evolution continued with the abstracted rural vernacular of the Labour Institute in his hometown of Daimiel (1951–3), followed by a series of eloquently simple religious buildings that culminated in a parish church in Vitoria (Our Lady of the Coronation, 1958), with organically curving walls, the dramatic, indirect natural lighting of the altar from one side, and a plan that reduced its Scandinavian models to their essence.

The Grup R in Barcelona

Barcelona's first post-war modernists began to organize themselves at the Fifth Assembly in 1949, when a group including Francesc Mitjans, Antoni de Moragas, Josep María Sostres and others decided to work together on a competition for subsidized housing, in emulation of GATEPAC. After the collective won the competition, its members continued to meet, forming the nucleus of the Grup R, founded in Coderch's studio in 1951, with the addition of others including Joaquim Gili and Oriol Bohigas. Likewise inspired by GATEPAC, Grup R modelled itself as a platform for self-education and mutual support, and for the public promotion of modernism through exhibitions, student competitions and articles in local and international journals. Its members assumed the role of official representatives of modernism in Barcelona, receiving the international figures whom Moragas invited to speak at the Barcelona College of Architects, including Alberto Sartoris, Alvar Aalto, Bruno Zevi and Nikolaus Pevsner.

Sostres (class of 1946) was the best informed of the group and assumed the role of scholar and teacher, organizing topics for discussion. He devised the group's name, evocative of the Italian Rationalists' Gruppo 7. 'It has to seem to say a lot without saying anything,' Moragas remembers him reasoning, given the evident dangers of an overtly political stance under Franco.[17] Sostres's architectural designs sought to establish a daring, though sometimes over-studied, re-encounter with the most rigorous formal strains of pre-war modernism. Of his Casa Agustí in Sitges

(1953–5, demolished), he wrote, 'the house is treated like a sculpture, a relatively complicated abstract volume unified by the Suprematist finish of whitewash.'[18]

Bohigas, together with his friend and partner Josep Martorell (both class of 1951), was the youngest of the group, and he became one of its driving forces. He had been raised in the late Noucentiste atmosphere of Barcelona in the 1930s, in the progressive circles of middle-class Catalanism. In his memoirs, he recalls the distress that the popular sacking and burning of churches and convents produced in his family with the outbreak of the war, and later, his shock at the rude language of the first fascist general he heard on the radio.[19] Grup R gave him a platform from which to defend the Noucentiste civic values of his childhood, but now in the guise of GATEPAC's radical modernism, whose works he emulated in his first projects with Martorell, such as the Casa Guardiola (Argentona, 1954–5).

Joaquim Gili (class of 1947) had been a student member of GATEPAC before the war, and with his partner Francesc Bassó (class of 1949) produced one of the better-known works of the group for the publishers Gustavo Gili (Barcelona, 1954–61). This family commission is a late exercise in the International Style of the 1920s, with red-painted pilotis, a vertical slatted brise-soleil and a handsome double-height interior space with an

Josep María Sostres, Casa Agustí, Sitges, Barcelona, 1953–5.

exposed structure, balconies and piano curves. Gili joined the family business in 1964 and helped to transform it into Spain's leading publisher on modern architecture.

Grup R's first public exhibition, held in the Layetanas Galleries in 1953, was a major cultural event. Twenty projects by members were presented as the culmination of Catalan architecture from the Gothic period onwards, with special emphasis on Modernisme and GATEPAC. Coderch abandoned the group after this first show, uncomfortable with the publicity it attracted, and he warned of the dangers of politicization.[20] Nevertheless, activist members, including Bohigas, Gili and Moragas, pushed for a broader public engagement with issues beyond the merely formal. These tensions culminated in 1958, when a series of lectures on 'Economy and Urbanism' precipitated the group's dissolution.

Grup R's mild activism took place against the backdrop of the first visible signs of opposition to the regime in Barcelona, beginning in 1951 with a boycott of streetcars after a fare increase, followed by a general strike. Barcelona students returned from France in the same years with outlawed books on Marxism, Sartre and the Civil War hidden in their luggage.[21] With its republican legacy of Catalan nationalism and radical labour movements, the city marked its distance from Madrid, as the Madrid-based architect Carlos Flores noted on his first visit in the mid-1950s: 'Barcelona was "something else," with a new air, closer to Europe.'[22]

The First Post-War Generation in Madrid

Madrid lacked a visible pressure group to unite architects around the cause of modernism. Just as before the Civil War, Madrid's architects had come to the capital to study from the far-flung regions of Spain and lacked the common social connections that defined Barcelona architecture and Barcelona society in general. Though this began to change as the 1950s progressed, the early history of post-war modernism in Madrid – of Cabrero, Fisac and their peers – is a story of individual talents and struggles.

The conflicts inherent in the position of defending modernism from within the regime mark the career and personality of José Luis Fernández del Amo (class of 1942). Deeply religious, he joined a right-wing Catholic group in the 1930s that brought him into the orbit of the Falangists. Nevertheless, he professed a fascination for the proscribed intellectual movements of the pre-war era. He spent the 1940s rebuilding towns in rural areas all over Spain for the Devastated Regions programme, an experience that impressed upon him the power of rural vernacular architecture:

José Luis Fernández del Amo, Vegaviana agricultural settlement, Cáceres, 1954.

In everything I found the supreme lesson of the essential, the primary, produced by the immediate generation of existence. When architecture reacted to the First World War with a rigorous rationalist manifesto, it moved along this path cleaned of the accumulated debris of historicist styles.[23]

In 1947, he was appointed architect of the National Institute of Colonization and designed agricultural settlements such as San Isidro de Albatera in Albacete (1953), Vegaviana in Cáceres (1954) and Villalba de Calatrava in Talavera de la Reina (1955), developing a vernacular modernism based on the culture and landscape of each region. Town layouts were rationally organized, with houses incorporating agricultural dependencies and arranged around a church, town hall and Trade Union Brotherhood building. As mentioned earlier, he was influenced in this approach by Carlos Arniches, one of the proscribed pre-war figures to which he found himself drawn. Arniches's two settlements, Algallarín and Gévora, represent a direct – and rare – connection between the pre-war and post-war interest in popular architecture.

In the same years, Fernández del Amo became a leading defender of contemporary art. His settlement churches incorporate works by the young artistic vanguard, such as Manuel Mompó's mosaic facade and Pablo Serrano's abstract altarpiece and Vía Crucis for the church in Villalba. In 1952, Fernández del Amo was named the first director of the Museum of Contemporary Art in Madrid and organized the influential competition for its unrealized home. He may have been forced out of the directorship in 1958 due to his repeated insistence that Picasso and other artists of the Republican era deserved a place in the museum's collections, as Serrano suggests.[24] In 1953, Fernández del Amo organized the First Congress of Abstract Art in Santander. Together with similar events, the congress proved decisive in the regime's eventual acceptance of abstract art. Fernández del Amo was aided in this cause by the New York Museum of Modern Art's exhibition 'Modern Art in the United States', including works of Abstract Expressionism and contemporary architecture, which passed through Barcelona on its European tour in 1955. The show was financed by the U.S. State Department as an advertisement for American values of individualism during the Cold War. The art historian Gabriel Ureña notes that its message was not lost on the Franco regime: 'More than once, when rigid recalcitrants called for a Crusade against Abstraction, they were answered with mocking disdain that that was exactly the fashion in the USSR and they called it "Socialist Realism".'[25]

Alejandro de la Sota (class of 1941) is one of the key figures of this period owing to his impact on future generations as a teacher and mentor, and the enduring resonance of his work, which is built around his lifelong effort to purge expression from architecture and reduce it to an essential, almost invisible state. He began his career with the distilled vernacular details of the Esquivel settlement for Fernández del Amo's National Institute of Colonization in the province of Sevilla (1948–52). The visceral force of his rejection of expression can be glimpsed in his description of the Casa Arvesú in Madrid (1954–5, demolished), when he describes his aim to eliminate the representative role of the facade: 'If we could enter our houses like the Comendador [of Don Giovanni], passing through the walls, we could do away with that other stupid word: *the entry!*'[26] Characteristically, none of this vehemence is evident in the concise elegance of the design, with glass walls overlooking the garden and a protective, curving brick facade to the street, its open plan is set into motion by the spiral of the entry stair that penetrates a fold in the facade.

This ascending movement is a prelude to the descending, spiralling cascade of balconies of the Gobierno Civil or Civil Government Building in Tarragona (1956–63), the winner of a state competition and the first frankly modern official building in post-war Spain, where De la Sota confronted the issue of representation head-on. Its balconies form sculptural voids in the solid marble mass of the facade, and their asymmetrical movement is as radically modern and violent as a Constructivist sequence of jump-cut film stills, tensing around the authoritarian symmetry of the central balcony on which this movement comes to rest. The sense of the

Alejandro de la Sota, Casa Arvesú, Calle Doctor Arce, Madrid, 1954–5, demolished.

tragic with which the work addresses the ceremony of civic authority flickers just below the surface, as the visual command of the traditional axis, extending horizontally into the territory, is replaced by the swerving vertical cut of the balconies, like the arc of a dive bomber or a burst of artillery shells impacting the facade. The remaining elevations and plans, which are organized around a 6-metre (20 ft) grid of steel columns, are emphatically functionalist and non-monumental, eschewing symmetry and any trace of hierarchy or clear, repetitive order.

This radical representation of authority establishes the work in a key position between Terragni's Casa del Fascio and Breuer's 1966 Whitney Museum in New York, and in the contemporary debate raised by Sigfried Giedion, Fernand Leger and Josep Lluís Sert's 'Nine Points on Monumentality', presented at the Eighth CIAM Congress in 1952. With affinities to the contemporary abstract sculpture of Eduardo Chillida or Jorge Oteiza and their interest in spatial voids, the cryptic expressionism of the Civil Government Building is unique in De la Sota's career. In his subsequent work, emotion is only intuitively sensed, if at all. But the impact of Tarragona would echo through Spanish architecture, particularly in the first decades of democracy (1980s–90s).

Francisco J. Sáenz de Oiza (class of 1946) is another of the outstanding figures to emerge in Madrid in this period. His varied and dynamic career converted the erratic eclecticism of the self-taught into an extravagant philosophy of design. Oiza approached every commission as a problem of creative self-reinvention, a strategy that permitted him to seize the initiative in several of the formal revolutions of the coming decades. A charismatic teacher, he attracted a wide circle of collaborators, disciples and students over the years, who broadened his impact on Spanish architecture.

Oiza visited the United States on a grant in 1948–9, when visas were still hard to come by.[27] On his return, as a young adjunct professor of building hygiene and salubrity, he was the first to talk to students about modernism, using this unlikely position to take a militant stance.[28] In one oft-told incident, at a public presentation of Luis Gutiérrez Soto's quietly modern work for the army's High Command (Madrid, 1949–53), Gutiérrez Soto explained that he had neither the budget nor the technical resources to permit air conditioning; Oiza famously stood up and said, 'Well, in the next project, less stone and more BTUs!' (British Thermal Units, a measure of cooling power).[29]

Despite this radical stance, an early competition victory, the Basílica of Arantzazu in the Basque region (1949–55, with Luis Laorga), found Oiza struggling to reconcile a renovated formal language with the representational demands of religious architecture. The architect and critic Juan Daniel Fullaondo later suggested that Oiza may simply have been calculating the

degree of his break with traditionalism, so as to shock but not entirely repel the public of the time, as indeed it did, in a strategy of gradual conquest.[30] The basilica's traditional plan is composed of an unclassifiable hybrid of forms: a pair of heavily rusticated towers; a curving top-lit apse; asymmetrical vaults in the transept windows recalling Barcelona Modernisme; and a nave with curving balconies evoking some of the milder Expressionist works of the 1930s. More provocative perhaps were the works of contemporary art incorporated in the design, including geometric bronze doors

Above: Francisco J. Sáenz de Oiza with Luis Laorga, Basílica of Arantzazu, 1949–55.

Right: Francisco J. Sáenz de Oiza, Jorge Oteiza and José Luis Romany, chapel project, Camino de Santiago de Compostela, 1954.

Left: Alejandro de la Sota, Civil Government Building, Tarragona, 1956–63.

by Chillida and an altarpiece of burned, rasped and polychromed wood by Lucio Muñoz. A frieze of abstracted apostles by Oteiza was initially vetoed by Church authorities, but it was eventually installed in the late 1960s.

The spirit of technical knowhow and advance that impressed Oiza in the United States is registered as pure spirit in his proposal for a chapel on the Camino de Santiago pilgrimage route (1954, with Jorge Oteiza and José Luis Romany). An empty structural cage, prefiguring a space frame, is raised over the sculpted base enclosure like a modern Greek temple. Here, Oiza radically addresses the representational questions raised by the critique of the Modern Movement from the Right by adding an idealized functionalist technique to the repertoire of expressive form.

Oiza had his first opportunity to realize this exalted Miesian rationalism in the down-to-earth circumstances of Madrid's emergency public housing in Fuencarral A (1954–6) and the Directed Settlement of Entrevías (1956–8, with Manuel Sierra and Jaime de Alvear), which we will examine below. In these projects, the utopian promise of modernism collided with the difficult reality of the urban housing crisis.

Mid-Decade: The Second Generation in Madrid

Madrid's architectural graduates of the late 1940s and early 1950s belonged to a generation that, in the words of Rafael de La-Hoz, 'suffered the war but didn't make it'.[31] For this group, the debate between representation and functionalism was of little concern; they pioneered in its stead an intense formal 'Organicism' of complex geometries, inspired in large part by Bruno Zevi's revisionist *History of Modern Architecture* (1950). Using the work and ideas of Aalto and Frank Lloyd Wright as its main models, Zevi's concept of an 'Organic architecture' proposed a formal evolution from pre-war functionalism to a 'humanist maturation', a 'new poetic' attendant to psychological and social concerns.[32]

One of the first to come into contact with Zevi's ideas was Ramón Vázquez Molezún (class of 1948), who received the Rome Prize and used the Spanish Academy there from 1949 to 1952 as a base for wider European travels. He regularly sent drawings and models back to Madrid, including his winning competition entry for Fernández del Amo's Museum of Contemporary Art in 1953, a compositional tour-de-force that marked the course of Organicism for the next fifteen years. The museum project introduced a cellular modular plan like that of Wright's Usonian houses, but based on squares joined on the diagonal in an elongated, ribbon-like configuration. The projecting angles of the diagonal runs of modules across the facade are staggered from floor to floor to create a syncopated spatial weave. Molezún would return to this strategy with his frequent partner José A. Corrales (class of 1948) in the angled roofscapes of projects such as their school in Herrera de Pisuerga, Palencia (1954–6, demolished).

The formal potential of the unrealized museum was developed by José María García de Paredes and Rafael de La-Hoz (both Andalusians and graduates of Madrid's class of 1950) in the St Thomas of Aquinas Residential College at Madrid's University City (1953–7). The elongated Wrightian plan incorporates a chapel that exploits the 45-degree zigzag of its side walls to direct views and light towards the altar. The profile of the residential tower recalls Aalto's Paimio Sanatorium in Finland (1929–33), but here the diagonally set rooms form a jazzy rhythm across the unifying horizontal lines of the open-air circulation galleries, which cast dramatic shadows over their faceted walls.

Paredes spent two years at the Rome Academy in the late 1950s alongside Javier Carvajal, and they collaborated on several projects. Carvajal had begun his studies in Bohigas's class in Barcelona and finished in Madrid in 1953. He had already designed (with Rafael García de Castro) a functionalist residential tower in the Plaza de Cristo Rey in Madrid (1954–8) and the School of Higher Mercantile Studies at the new campus of the University of Barcelona (1955–61). With its elongated office block of gridded square openings (inspired by Terragni and the Casa Sindical) and its dense, carpet-like spread of ground-floor classrooms and public spaces, the work set the standard for a formally precise functionalism in Barcelona.

In Rome, under the influence of Organicism, Carvajal moved towards more complex formal compositions. His collaboration with Paredes on the Spanish Pavilion for the Milan Triennial of 1957 won the Grand Prize, Spain's third consecutive triumph in Milan (Coderch's win was followed by Molezún's in 1954). The two also designed the Panteón de los Españoles (Spaniards' Pantheon, 1957) in a Roman cemetery, a strikingly abstract, expressive work of board-formed concrete cut with horizontal slashes, which foreshadows Carvajal's formal compositions in exposed concrete of the 1960s. Back in Spain, the two joined Corrales and Molezún to design the Directed Settlement of Almendrales (1958–64), part of Madrid's emergency housing programme, discussed below.

The most outstanding work of this period was Corrales and Molezún's Spanish Pavilion for the 1958 Brussels World's Fair, winner of the exposition's Grand Prize. Their design adapts a Wrightian honeycomb plan, in which each hexagonal module is an independent constructive unit supported by a central column that doubles as a rainwater drain. But unlike Wright, the cellular module is the building's maximum scalar division; the structure is articulated at a larger scale by breaks in the floor level and ceilings that follow the site terrain, and by adjustable interior partitions.

José A. Corrales and Ramón Vázquez Molezún, Spanish Pavilion, Brussels World's Fair, 1958.

The irregular perimeter is enclosed in large planes of glass framed in steel, like the facets of a crystal. The forest-like interior is animated by the rhythmic play of the ingenious structure, which anticipates the space frame in the geometric complexity and logic of its prefabricated elements and connections. The building presented to the world an image of a technologically advanced and sophisticated Spain that was highly misleading. Like Sáenz de Oiza's chapel on the road to Santiago, the Spanish Pavilion is an ecstatic, youthful dream of modernism set against the more complex reality of the time.

José María García de Paredes and Rafael de La-Hoz, St Thomas of Aquinas Residential College, Madrid, 1953–7.

The End of the Decade: Mass Housing and the SEAT 600

From early in the 1940s, the shortage of housing forced masses of rural immigrants into large shanty towns that sprang up around Madrid, Barcelona and Bilbao, a situation portrayed in films such as José Antonio Nieves Conde's *Surcos* (1951) and the black comedy *El Pisito* (1958), directed by Marco Ferreri with a screenplay by Rafael Azcona. From 1940 to 1960, Madrid's population doubled from 1.1 to 2.1 million, and Barcelona's rose 50 per cent, from 1 million to more than 1.5 million. The private sector was dedicated to building profitable housing for the middle and upper classes. Public action lagged far behind the problem until the 1960s, when governmental incentives for developers made public housing profitable as well, although often at the cost of basic public services and elementary principles of site preparation and urban planning. In the period leading up to this change in policy, public authorities and the Church embraced mass-housing prototypes and principles of the Modern Movement in a number of initiatives.

The approach to the housing problem began in fits and starts in the 1940s. A Housing Institute (INV) programme of 1944 that promised to build 130,000 housing units a year collapsed due to the lack of industrial capacity and inadequate financing.[33] As we have seen, housing was one of the main themes at the Fifth Assembly in 1949. As one of the assembly's activities, idea competitions for standardized housing were organized by the Colleges of Architects of Madrid and Barcelona. In Madrid, Fisac studied European models of expandable units for his widely published proposal. Architects and public planners travelled to Germany, England, Italy and the Netherlands to housing fairs and to visit contemporary developments. However, different proposals for industrially produced, prefabricated housing by García de Paredes and La-Hoz, the Eduardo Torroja Institute and Alejandro Goicoechea, the inventor of the contemporary Talgo pendular train, were discounted by public officials, as the need to create work and the low cost of unskilled labour made mass production neither practical nor cost-effective.

Several projects in Madrid and Barcelona in the early 1950s drew on modernist prototypes to address the housing crisis. One of the largest was the Congress of the Eucharist development on the Can Ros site in Barcelona (1952–61), organized by the Church and financed by the central government and semi-public savings banks, on the occasion of a Vatican congress held in Barcelona in 1952. Architects Carlos Marques Maristany, Antoni Pineda and Josep Soteras built 2,700 units for the working and middle classes in a Ville Radieuse-type plan of cross-shaped towers, eight-storey linear volumes and public spaces and services.

Another example in Barcelona, the Montbau development in Vall d'Hebron, which was sponsored by the Municipal Housing Board, followed CIAM planning precepts with lineal south-oriented blocks (first phase 1953–61). The architects were Guillermo Giráldez (a member of Grup R), Pedro López Íñigo and Xavier Subías.

A second major attack on the housing problem was launched in 1954–5 with the Law of Limited Rents, which authorized the INV to build 550,000 units over five years, a campaign that began and ended in Madrid with the 35,000 units of the Directed Settlements (1956–9). The law's technical standards included maximum unit sizes, construction quality norms and provisions for standardized building elements and fixtures. It also incorporated measures reflecting the socialistic paternalism of the Falangists then heading the INV, including state supply of scarce construction materials and a provision for 'auto-construction', in which families built their own homes by working on Sundays, their one day off, in lieu of down payments for low-interest government loans, thereby converting resident families into homeowners.[34]

As at Madrid's University City in the late 1920s, young architects were tapped for the design of the Directed Settlements by Julián Laguna, the Commissioner of Urban Planning of Madrid, who encouraged their innovative ideas. The settlements are notable for the functionalist rigour and austerity of their typological investigations, carried out in the spirit of the pre-war Modern Movement but with great material limitations. Replacing shanty towns on Madrid's periphery, they established a suburban scale of rowhouses and low blocks generally oriented in relation to sunlight amid ample open spaces, breaking with traditional street grids.

The Directed Settlement of Entrevías (1956–8) was the site of the Pozo del Tío Raimundo shanty town (Uncle Raimundo's Well), where a populist Jesuit priest, José María de Llanos, took up residence and led the fight for housing in the pages of the Falangist newspaper *Arriba*. By the 1960s, Padre Llanos had been converted by the poor rural immigrants of the Pozo into an ardent Communist. His demands were tolerated only because of his right-wing origins, and they forced Franco to become personally involved in the housing question. Franco visited Oiza's and De la Sota's Directed Settlement prototypes in Fuencarral in 1956 and gave his nod of approval to the programme.[35]

At Entrevías, Oiza developed a variation on his building type for Fuencarral A based in part on the American work of Ludwig Hilberseimer and Mies, a block of brick rowhouses with horizontal slot windows on the upper floor. The plans were so rigorously studied that Oiza assigned the project to his students for years, challenging them to improve them.[36] Residents, however, were not always so pleased. They often substituted the

slot windows for conventional openings, and struggled to fit their country furniture into bedrooms measuring less than 2 metres (6½ ft) wide.

Caño Roto, or 'Broken Spigot' (1956–9; second phase 1959–63), was the first built project by Antonio Vázquez de Castro and José Luis Íñiguez de Onzoño (Madrid, class of 1955, 1957). Its innovative unit types include a walled patio-house and apartment blocks with staggered duplexes. Its pin-wheel layout of communal gardens and plazas was adapted to the sloping terrain, with a commercial and civic centre and an abstract playground by the sculptor Ángel Ferrant. Vázquez moved his family into one of the patio houses, for which he designed simple tubular furniture. Other settlements include the functionalist Canillas (Luis Cubillo), Fuencarral (José Luis Romany), Orcasitas (Rafael Leoz and Joaquín Ruiz Hervás), and the more Nordic-influenced Almendrales mentioned above (Corrales, Molezún, García de Paredes and Carvajal).

The settlement programme was cut short by Franco's change in government in 1957, which replaced the Falangists and their socialist experiments with the pragmatic 'technocrats' of Opus Dei, led by López Rodó, who guided the economy out of inflation and into the sustained economic expansion of the 1960s. In late 1957, the new government instituted the

Antonio Vázquez de Castro and José Luis Íñiguez de Onzoño, Directed Settlement of Caño Roto, Madrid, 1956–9.

Social Emergency Plan, which first introduced subsidies to private developers for mass housing. The first quota of 60,000 units over two years in Madrid was surpassed by more than 24,000 units.[37] Housing initiated under this plan was denser, more repetitive and homogeneous, such as Barcelona's Besòs development, with its chequerboard of twelve-storey linear blocks in alternating orientations (López Íñigo, Subias and others, 1958–60). Nevertheless, the functional formal vocabulary and the rupture with regular street grids of the Directed Settlements became the norm. In Madrid, large operators created entire new districts using a single architect, as was the case with the URBIS developments of Moratalaz and La Estrella by Domínguez Salazar.

While the housing crisis was one of the main factors that led to official approval of modern design on pragmatic grounds, it also tested the limits of an architecture modelled on the pre-war Modern Movement, as Oriol Bohigas observed in his 1962 manifesto 'Towards a Realist Architecture',[38] where he took up the anti-Positivist arguments of Bruno Zevi for the first time. In the context of Spain's poverty and underdevelopment, Bohigas questioned the use of a formal language conceived for mass industrial production based on prototypes, standardization and machined precision. He proposed instead a 'Realist' alternative that would acknowledge the primitive artisan conditions of building in Spain. The limitations of what Bohigas called an idealistic, technical and utopian formalism might be seen in the Miesian aspirations of Oiza's Entrevías settlement, for example, while the crude exposed concrete and muddy brick walls of Caño Roto introduced a poetic, Realist texture to the settlement, in which the evident pathos of the conditions under which it was built contribute to its expressive and critical force.

Bohigas's own example of a Realist architecture was his housing project for metallurgic workers in Carrer Pallars, Barcelona, composed of austere brick blocks with sloped tiled roofs and slightly angled exterior walls (1958–9, with Martorell). The design sought to continue Coderch's vernacular Organicism on a larger scale and adapt the precepts of Italian Neorealism as seen in Mario Ridolfi's Tiburtino quarter of Rome (1950), with its nostalgia for the vernacular and the undertone of social criticism it shared with Italy's Neorealist film-makers.

Oriol Bohigas and Josep Martorell, housing for metallurgic workers, Carrer Pallars, Barcelona, 1958–9.

César Ortiz-Echagüe and Rafael Echiade, Vehicle Deposit, SEAT complex, Barcelona, 1955–65.

Bohigas's manifesto is part of a curious ideological flip of positions at the end of the decade. On the one hand, we find him swapping his early enthusiasm for the leftist agitations of GATEPAC for a position closer to the post-war critique of orthodox modernism from the right, as in the vernacular modernism of Coderch or Fernández del Amo, now transformed into a position of leftist critique. On the other hand, the build-up to Spain's economic take-off of the 1960s brought a new interest in American-style functionalism to the architecture of those aligned with the regime. The targets of Bohigas's criticism included Miesian buildings such as Cabrero's glass-and-steel tower for the Falangist newspaper *Arriba* in Madrid (1960–62), and a series of buildings for the SEAT automobile company by César Ortiz-Echagüe and Rafael Echaide. Amid the poverty of the 1950s, the SEAT automobile was the first harbinger of the coming economic expansion and was emblematic of its popular character. SEAT was a joint venture between the Spanish state, Fiat and private investors.

In 1957, it launched the SEAT 600, a small two-door model designed for the average family and budget and based on the Fiat 600. Only some 120,000 had been produced by 1962, but its impact on popular expectations was great. For Ortiz-Echagüe and Echaide (Madrid, class of 1952, 1954), the American work of Mies van der Rohe offered an appealing image for the representative buildings of this new industry, and for its promise of a new era of industrialized abundance. However, as Bohigas suggests, the hand-craft techniques used to create this image betrayed a modesty of available means evident also in the modest attributes of the SEAT 600 itself.

SEAT's first president was Ortiz-Echagüe's father, José, a military engineer who had founded CASA, Spain's first important aircraft manufacturer, in 1923. Ortiz's first project for SEAT was the factory canteen in the Zona Franca of Barcelona (1954–6, with Manuel Barbero and Rafael de la Joya). The design, a series of diaphanous glazed pavilions set amid gardens, was inspired by the melding of landscape and architecture of Richard Neutra, whom Ortiz had accompanied as a German translator during the latter's 1954 visit to Spain. At his father's suggestion, the structural skeleton and cladding were of aluminium, a material then unknown to Spanish architecture but supplied in abundance to CASA. Owing to the site's poor soil conditions, this lightweight solution proved cheaper than a steel structure despite the material's high cost. CASA engineers worked with the architects on the details, which were developed from aircraft industry parts, including moveable sun louvres operated by wing-flap mechanisms. The project won the 1957 Reynolds Aluminum Prize, and the architects were invited to the United States, where they were received by Mies, one of the prize jury members.[39]

On his return and in association with Rafael Echaide, Ortiz designed a Miesian complex for SEAT on Barcelona's Gran Vía (1955–65, disfigured) inspired by Mies' Chicago works of the period, including a crown-hall-type showroom, an office tower inspired in the Lake Shore Drive apartments (its crude curtain wall included spandrel panels of brick finished in miniature tiles) and a multi-storey vehicle deposit, where newly minted SEAT 600s were displayed behind sheer glass walls. The architects designed a similar complex for SEAT in Madrid (also altered). Like Fisac, with whom he had apprenticed, Ortiz had been recruited by Opus Dei as a student, and he eventually abandoned architecture for the lay order.

It is tempting to find parallels between, on one hand, the apparent functional neutrality of the Miesian formal language and its roots in German Romantic classicism, and on the other, the strange mixture of pragmatism and religious zeal that made up Opus Dei's particular brand of positivism, which set the tone for the economic boom engineered by its government technocrats. Bohigas makes reference to this subtle ideological undertone in his Realist manifesto when he attacks 'the abstract Idealism of those who believe themselves to work in a utopian industrialized society'.[40] With the SEAT buildings and other contemporary projects that shared their spirit, the last surviving strains of the Franco era's right-wing, visionary idealism found a perfect camouflage in the language of post-war functionalism.

chapter seven

The Organicist Eden, 1960–75

Young architects worked in the shadows, in a country closed in on itself. Spanish architecture, despite being among the best of those years, paid a high price for the wariness with which the entire world looked on the country's leaders. Sáenz de Oiza, Oteiza, Chillida, Alba or Higueras defended a modern architecture of emotion, in vivid contrast to an officially conservative France, which was choking in its all-too-strict Rationalism.

Claude Parent, 1994[1]

Seen from the perspective of Caño Roto and the other Directed Settlements of the 1950s, by 1968, the year Sáenz de Oiza's exuberant 'Organicist' Torres Blancas (White Towers) was completed, Spain was all but unrecognizable. The technocrats who took charge of Franco's economic policy at the end of the 1950s triggered a classic economic take-off based on industrialization, construction and tourism. As a result, Spain's average growth rate in the 1960s was second only to Japan's. But as the historian Stanley Payne writes, the 'cultural and religious counterrevolution carried out in Spain during the late 1930s and '40s was totally undermined by the social, cultural and economic changes wrought by development, as in the long run were the basic institutions and values of the regime itself.'[2] By 1968, the country enjoyed a robust consumer economy. At the same time, a growing anti-Francoist movement openly contested the regime in the streets. Its protagonists were members of the underground Communist Party, leftist students and professors in the newly massified universities, workers organized by clandestine trade unions in the thriving industrial sector, progressive priests and the terrorists of ETA, the Basque independence movement that launched its violent opposition to the regime that year. The revolution in social mores, fashion and culture sweeping the rest of Europe and the United States was embraced by a dissident cultural elite and popular culture alike. By 1968, Spanish society had clearly outgrown the repressive cultural and political corset of the dictatorship.

Fernando Higueras in the lobby of the Hotel Las Salinas, Lanzarote, mid-1970s.

Architecture was also transformed by prosperity. While public commissions dominated architectural debate in the 1950s, in the following two decades this protagonism was ceded to the booming private sector through commercial building, private houses and the new tourist industry. Modern architecture formed part of the popular imagery of prosperity, progress and consumer culture. This can be seen in popular film comedies such as *Los Tramposos* (1959), directed by Pedro Lazaga, where Carvajal's recently completed tower in the Plaza de Cristo Rey played a prominent role, alongside modern interiors, fashions, domestic appliances and automobiles.

While many firms dedicated to commercial work and housing continued to practise conventional functionalism, a new generation of Madrid architects led by Fernando Higueras (class of 1959) pushed the Organic option to a new level of geometric inventiveness. The results were often comparable to contemporary neo-Brutalism in Great Britain and the United States, although the Madrid architects generally combined abstract structural expression with regional elements and qualities that responded to Spain's climate, landscape and culture. The formal richness and idealism of this generation proved contagious for many of its elders, including Oiza and José Antonio Coderch. But by the end of the decade the initiative had exhausted itself through its own complexity and impracticality.

Building on the examples of Fernández del Amo, Sáenz de Oiza and Fisac, the Organicists forged strong ties between architecture and the other arts to a degree unseen even during the years of the Republic. Higueras was an accomplished artist and classical guitarist; he was a disciple of Andrés Segovia, and he collaborated with the artist César Manrique on several architectural projects for the Canary Island of Lanzarote. Likewise, Antonio Fernández Alba was already close to the artists of the El Paso group in his student days, and group members Antonio Saura and Manolo Millares moved into a Madrid apartment building that he had designed (1958–61), where he also installed his own studio.

Most importantly, under the direction of the architect Fullaondo, *Nueva forma*, the leading journal of the movement (1966–75), brought contemporary art, literature and music together in its pages, reflecting the wide cultural interests of its sponsor, Juan Huarte, the great patron of the arts of the period and Oiza's client for Torres Blancas. The magazine interspersed quotes from the likes of Beckett, Kafka, Mayakovsky and Alberti through its features on art and architecture. One of its favourite sources was Joyce's *Ulysses*, previously censored in Spain, as elsewhere, and still in legal limbo under the limited freedom of the press conceded in 1966 by Manuel Fraga, Franco's Minister of Information and Tourism. Fullaondo dedicated issues to contemporary artists such as Jorge Oteiza, Eduardo Chillida, Lucio Muñoz and Pablo Palazuelo, and to composers such as Luis de Pablo.

Despite its formalism and the political conservatism of most of its practitioners, Organicism represented an implicitly critical stance against the exploitive, unplanned character of speculative development in the 1960s, both in Spanish cities and on Spain's once pristine coastlines. A handful of collective housing projects from the period, in which conventional city blocks were replaced by intricate, interwoven public spaces, have generally escaped the social failure of their Brutalist counterparts in Britain and offer an interesting alternative to the formulas of contemporary urban planning. In resort architecture, another handful of projects proposed models of development in harmony with the existing landscape, another road not taken.

Beginnings: From a Modern Regionalism to the 'Essential Forest' of Fernando Higueras

Antonio Fernández Alba (Madrid, class of 1957), one of the first of this new generation, grew up in Salamanca, and he brought to his works the digni-fied sobriety of northern Castilla. Shortly after finishing his studies, he designed his seminal work, the Convent del Rollo in Salamanca (1958–62). Exactingly built in the city's famous yellow sandstone, the convent combines elements of popular architecture – a traditional cloister, sloping clay-tile roofs and Luis Moya's *bóvedas tabicadas* (unreinforced masonry vaults) – with radically Rational elements, such as the orientation of the nuns' cells in parallel stepped tiers for continuous southern exposure. The curving walls of the chapel are inspired by Aalto, but more specifically, as the archi-tect Vittorio Gregotti observed in 1968, the sculptural massing 'returns, with the closed geometry and the mono-material hardness of the fortifi-cation, to central Spain's tradition of monumental eloquence.'[3] Fernández Alba established himself as an influential teacher and writer and went on to produce works of an eclectic variety in succeeding years.

Fernando Higueras (Madrid, class of 1959) won early fame as the *enfant terrible* of Organicism in a series of brilliant student competition projects. In a 1960 competition design for ten spiralling artists' residences, with folded thin-shell roofs inspired by the vaults of Eduardo Torroja, he declared his principles: 'when making a work of architecture, we shouldn't always follow the easy, comfortable and oft-repeated aesthetics of Mondrian . . . the economics of pre-existing industries don't always have to impose sys-tematic, repetitive and elemental solutions . . . [and] it is not a crime to deliberately search for architectonic expression in singular buildings.'[4]

In 1961, he won the competition to build the state's Centre for Fine Arts Restoration in Madrid's University City. He worked on the design with a fellow classmate seven years his junior, Rafael Moneo (Madrid, class of 1961), who left Spain for Denmark in the same year to work on the Sydney Opera with the studio of Jørn Utzon. The elegant but rather undefined competition design – a circle of stepped, angular forms – suggested an

Fernando Higueras
with Antonio Miró,
Centre for Fine Arts
Restoration, University
City, Madrid, 1965–84.

Centre for Fine Arts
Restoration plan, entry
level.

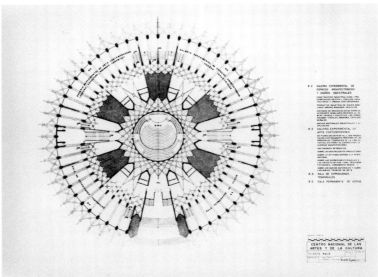

artificial topography, such as a crater. For the definitive project of 1965, Higueras and his associate Antonio Miró systematized the design in constructive terms with the help of two of the period's leading engineers, José A. Fernández Ordóñez and Julio Martínez Calzón. Nevertheless, its complex formwork proved extremely difficult to build, and the project was not completed until the 1980s, following many budget crises and delays. The circular building is popularly known as the 'Crown of Thorns' for the ring of spiky triangular skylights on its roof. The structure is a filigree of exposed concrete elements derived, as the architect Iñaki Ábalos points out, from Higueras's study of Gothic and Renaissance domes and vaults, and with evident associations to vegetal and crystalline forms in its centred composition.[5] However, despite the project's brilliance and influence, the doubts raised by its uncertain completion cast a shadow over Higueras's career and marked the 1960s Organicist movement for a short life.

The centre proved to be the Organicists' only important public commission. In succeeding competitions, the more adventurous designs of the Madrid School – projects by Higueras himself, Fernández Alba, Fullaondo, Sáenz de Oiza, García de Paredes, Corrales and Molezún and others – were consistently rejected in favour of more conventional designs. These defeats included competitions for the Spanish Pavilion at the New York World's Fair (1963), the Congress Centre and a new opera in Madrid (both 1964, the latter unrealized), and new university campuses for Madrid, Barcelona and Bilbao (1969).

In several more modest projects built in the same years, Higueras created a domestically scaled interweaving of architecture and nature, partially inspired by Wright's Prairie houses, that extends into the landscape to create an adaptable organic framework for an idealized concept of social community. His first completed building, a house for the artist Lucio Muñoz, north of Madrid in Torrelodones (1961–3, with Miró), established the basic ingredients of this vision, which was subsequently developed in the emergency public housing of Hortaleza (Madrid, 1962–3, with Miró, Lucas Espinosa and Arturo Weber) and the Colegio Estudio, a private school in Aravaca, Madrid (1962–4).

Terraced into a granite outcropping, the Muñoz house features layers of low, hovering hipped roofs finished in traditional 'Arab' clay tiles and supported on exposed joists and close-set pairs of pretensioned concrete beams, a motif that reaches back through Wright to Japan (the paired beams of Kenzo Tange's Kagawa Prefectural Government Office, 1958), as well as to vernacular Spanish construction. In Hortaleza, Higueras transformed the sheltering overhangs of the house into continuous circulation galleries that surround the simple low blocks, creating plant-filled intermediate zones of shaded social spaces, like the galleries of traditional *corralas* in Madrid's older districts that housed the poor. Comprising 1,100 housing units, schools and a church, the project was designed and built in only four months.

The Colegio Estudio was founded in 1940 by former teachers of the Instituto-Escuela (including Ángeles Gasset, the niece of the philosopher José Ortega y Gasset) and continued its innovative teaching methods. It was tolerated by the regime, it seems, because the curriculum included religious education. Higueras himself was a graduate, and many of the political leaders of the future democracy were educated in the suburban campus he built. The Wrightian elements of his design – the low, hipped roofs, shaded cloisters and patios, the warm brick and natural wood, the built-in planters, low ceilings, wide corridors and shadowy but diaphanous interiors, illuminated indirectly by natural light – conspire to create a singular atmosphere particularly suited to Madrid's harsh climate.

This 'essential forest', as the critic Luis Fernández-Galiano calls it, appears in many domestic projects of the Organicist movement and could be considered one of the period's most innovative creations, a modern update of the dark, almost windowless interiors of Spain's popular

Fernando Higueras with Antonio Miró, Casa Lucio Muñoz, Torrelodones, 1961–3.

Fernando Higueras, cooperative apartments for military officers, Glorieta de San Bernardo, Madrid, 1967–75. View of interior court.

architecture.[6] Higueras made another contribution to defining this ambient type for urban buildings in his large apartment block for military officers in Madrid's Ensanche (Glorieta of San Bernardo, 1967–75), where the window wall is pushed back from the street behind deep balconies and continuous concrete parapets with generous planters.

The White Cities of Sáenz de Oiza and Juan Huarte

Sáenz de Oiza set out to outdo Higueras with his Torres Blancas apartments in Madrid, creating in the process a dazzling one-off prototype, the most emblematic and unrepeatable work of the decade. The commission, together with that for the Ciudad Blanca (White City) resort in Alcudia, Mallorca, came from Juan Huarte. Félix Huarte and his three sons, Juan, Jesús and Felipe, built the Huarte Group into a major construction firm and industrial conglomerate based in their native Pamplona and Madrid, starting in the 1930s and expanding after the Civil War. Significant projects of the firm include the concrete work for the School of Philosophy at the

University City, the thin-shell vaults of the Fronton Recoletos and, after the war, the Air Ministry, the cross of the Valley of the Fallen and Real Madrid's original Santiago Bernabéu football stadium. The firm's furniture company, H Muebles, began producing modern industrialized designs in the mid-1950s under the direction of Juan, and one of its patents, a universal joint, was used to assemble the structure of the Spanish Pavilion in Brussels in 1958.

Félix's offspring began financing ambitious cultural ventures in the 1950s, with special attention to creators from the Basque region and Navarra, including Fullaondo and Sáenz de Oiza. Juan lent one of the first exhibition spaces, on Madrid's Paseo de Recoletos, for Fernández del Amo's Museum of Contemporary Art, known as the Sala Negra (Black Room). He financed Jorge Oteiza's prize-winning sculptures for the 1957 Biennial of São Paulo and his controversial abstract frieze of apostles for Oiza's Basílica of Arantzazu. Other ventures in patronage include Luis de Pablo's Alea, a contemporary music group founded in 1964, and X Films (1961), which produced experimental films by artists such as Oteiza and José Antonio Sistiaga. Juan's brother Jesús was behind the literary publisher Alfaguara, founded in 1964 by the novelist and future Nobel Prize-winner Camilo José Cela.

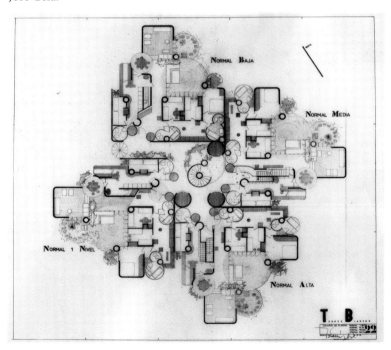

Francisco J. Sáenz de Oiza, Torres Blancas, Madrid, 1959–68. Typical floor plan.

Juan Huarte was not one to put aside his interests in artistic experimentation when he turned his attention to real-estate development. He conceived Torres Blancas and Alcudia as projects that would redefine the reigning models of luxury urban and resort living, an ambition that demonstrates his confidence in the commercial appeal of the avant-garde and its utopian aspirations.

The design process for Torres Blancas (1959–68) was exhaustive, passing through a series of different concepts and variations until construction began in 1965. Oiza's first idea was a plug-in tower in which each client would buy a slot on a floor slab and build his own architect-designed home, but Huarte said no. The presence of Fullaondo and Moneo in his studio as young assistants at different times may have helped turn his attention to Organicism, as seen in his next proposals, a series of pinwheel plans with duplex units arranged along deep arms. Oiza developed these plans through a number of geometric iterations based on circles, rectangles, curves and an extraordinary Wrightian hexagonal grid, although these precise geometries were diluted in the final plans. Oiza established the basic concept of the tower as a 'tree rising from the ground', a trunk of apartments with deep terraces, crowned by overhanging roof gardens and pods containing social spaces.[7] On the recommendation of his structural engineers, he concentrated the load-bearing concrete walls on the exterior, with ducts, stairs and elevators in individual circular structural tubes, a comparatively economical solution that allowed for free interior plans.

The massing of the final design is a brilliant mixture of verticality, density and compression. Rectangular piers rise 22 storeys to support the deep overhangs of the circular roof pods. Between the piers, tiers of balconies in circular segments project outwards and overlap, their rhythms changing with the different apartment types. Affinities with Baroque architecture (a constant reference in the writings and work of Fullaondo at the time) are evident in the building's alternation of swelling circles and restraining piers.

Francisco J. Sáenz de Oiza, Ciudad Blanca (White City), Alcudia, Mallorca, 1961–4.

The hundred-unit Ciudad Blanca in Alcudia (1961–4) was one of the first projects to introduce vacation apartments on the Spanish coast. The development's master plan, only partially realized, was designed by Oiza and Fullaondo. Picking up ideas introduced by Coderch in his unbuilt Torre Valentina complex on the Costa Brava (1959), Oiza designed the basic apartment unit as a deep line of rooms between parallel bearing walls, with a staggered horizontal layout to assure privacy. The floors of each unit step down in section towards the sea, ending in a large terrace, which features an interlocking prefabricated concrete parapet and planter that adds expressive punch to the massing. Stacked up on four levels in progressive setbacks, the units form an open-ended cellular assembly that zigzags across the site, creating, as the critic Lluís Domènech pointed out, a kind of artificial landscape.[8]

The Living Cell: Houses, Housing and Hotels

While Sáenz de Oiza, ever restless, took up the role of fervent convert to Organicism, pioneers of the movement in the 1950s, among them Corrales and Molezún in Madrid and Coderch in Barcelona, continued to develop a more sustainable and less 'exacerbated' Organicism, to use the expression of Antón Capitel.[9] A number of projects by these figures and others enriched Organicist concepts and ambient types for the single-family house, collective housing and vacation resorts.

Corrales and Molezún developed the social dimensions of Organic space in their works of the 1960s, as well as an interest in inventive constructive detail. Their sprawling house for Jesús Huarte in Puerta de Hierro, Madrid (1962–6) is typical of the dwellings of large families of the elite during this period, with separate zones for the parents, their many children and the live-in servants. Their design interweaves indoors and outdoors, organizing flexible, multi-use spaces into zones of increasing intimacy around three patios, which merge along the southern lot line into a series of stepping plant-filled terraces with service areas under them, shielding the precinct from a noisy street. The long line of the central living area is covered by a single rising slope, as in Aalto's Maison Louis Carré in France (1959), here handsomely built in brick with tile roofing.

The project's jumble of sloping roofs, Corrales explained later, was 'very popular, like a village'.[10] He repeated this effect in his *parador nacional* (state-owned hotel) in the privileged natural setting of Sotogrande, in the province of Cádiz, where the maze of crisscrossing slopes is centred by an overscaled chimney (1963–5).

In multi-storey projects, the two architects switched from popular references to crisp, modern blocks of great technical sophistication that extend

José A. Corrales
and Ramón Vázquez
Molezún, Casa Jesús
Huarte, Puerta de
Hierro, Madrid, 1962–6.
View of main living
room volume.

across their sites like the contemporary network structures of Team X. In their Oasis Hotel in Maspalomas, Gran Canaria (1965–7, with Manuel de la Peña), an open network of interrelated buildings, courtyards and gardens is organized in a hierarchy of social and private spaces. Working alone on subsidized housing in the Polígono de Elviña in A Coruña (1965–7), Corrales used elevated glazed public corridors in lieu of conventional streets at ground level. The passages are connected between the linear building blocks by bridges and include commercial spaces. He used a similar scheme in the competition for the Autonomous University of Madrid in 1969 (with Estanislao Pérez Pita).

Javier Carvajal created a rather 'exacerbated' variation on the 'essential forest' of the Organicist interior in a series of large houses realized in exposed concrete, including his own residence in Somosaguas, north of Madrid (1964–5). Here, instead of Higueras's overhanging tile roofs, we find abstract, hovering horizontal masses, counterbalanced vertically with high chimneys. His Torre de Valencia apartments (1968–72), a tour-de-force in white concrete that overlooks Madrid's Retiro Park, reflects the impact of Torres Blancas. The unit plans are models of the Organic motif of staggered cellular conglomerations, although the result can seem overly formal and heavy, as in his houses. As a new appreciation for the traditional city began to take hold, the project was criticized in the press for the intrusion of its profile on the park and the visual axis of the Calle de Alcalá.

Coderch's only work in Madrid, the Girasol (Sunflower) apartments (1965–7), offers another original interpretation of Organicist space. Its layout is like a comb, with a row of multi-storey wings separated by deep narrow patios, both extending from the street wall to the circulation spine at the back of the site. The wings are only a single unit wide, with living areas that flow out into terraces overlooking the shaded patios.

In Catalunya, Coderch repeatedly turned to plans of staggered setbacks with corner windows, as in his Casa Rozes in Girona (1961–4), a strategy that introduced light indirectly into the rooms. In multi-family housing, the setbacks often resulted in symmetrical, diamond-shaped buildings that pulled away from the street, as in his apartment complex for the Urquijo Bank in Barcelona (1968–73), with a massing of corrugated concrete reminiscent of Paul Rudolph's work. Coderch devised a variation of the approach for office buildings in the four towers of the Edificios Trade (1966–9), substituting a continuous undulating curtain wall for the setbacks, with echoes of Mies's 1922 Glass Skyscraper project.

José A. Corrales and Ramón Vázquez Molezún with Manuel de la Peña, Oasis Hotel, Maspalomas, Gran Canaria, 1965–7. Entry pavilion.

Federico Correa and
Alfons Milà, Flash Flash
restaurant, Barcelona,
1970; graphics,
Leopoldo Pomés.

There were few other Organicists in Barcelona in the 1960s. Federico Correa and Alfons Milà (both Barcelona, class of 1953) worked for Coderch after they finished their studies and considered themselves his disciples. They built a few houses that could be described as Organicist; the Casa Julià (1956–60) and the Casa Rumeu (1961–2), both in the coastal town of Cadaqués, were inspired by the free plan of the Casa Ugalde, with non-orthogonal geometries, walls of local stone and overhanging tile roofs. The two architects began working in Cadaqués in the 1950s, when they modernized one of the old fishermen's houses in the port (Casa Villavecchia, 1955), setting an example for similar interventions, including a house Correa reformed for himself (1962) and works by Coderch and the American–Italian team of Peter Harnden and Lanfranco Bombelli. These respectful interventions set a model that helped to save the picturesque fishing village from the fate of other coastal towns disfigured by development.

Javier Carvajal,
architect's residence,
Somosaguas, Madrid,
1964–5.

Correa was close to the Italian architects of the neo-Liberty movement, and the influence of Ignazio Gardella's Casa alle Zatere in Venice of 1957 can be seen in the team's most precociously mimetic work, an addition to the Godó i Trias Factory (Barcelona, 1963–4), where the elaborate brickwork emulates that of the original factory buildings, a strategy that provoked controversy at the time. They were also known for the interiors of the restaurants Reno (1961) and Flash Flash (1970), which featured Pop graphics by Leopoldo Pomés. But their lightly Organicist Torre Atalaya (1966–70) on Barcelona's Diagonal was no match in formal excitement for the contemporary towers of Sáenz de Oiza or Carvajal in Madrid.

Like Corrales in Elviña, the architects of other housing developments applied Organicist ideas on an urban scale, replacing conventional city streets and massing for an approach closer to Caño Roto. For the Ciudad

Antonio Perpiñá, Luis Iglesias and Carlos de Miguel, Ciudad de los Poetas (City of Poets) development, Madrid, first phase 1964–70.

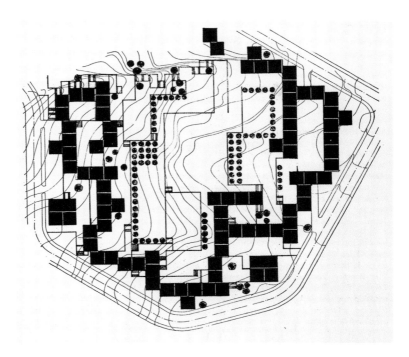

Ciudad de los Poetas, diagram of partial master plan.

de los Poetas (City of Poets) development in northern Madrid, for example, irregular patterns of interlocking housing blocks define an appealing landscape of interconnected terraces and gardens over a sloping site (first phase Antonio Perpiñá, Luis Iglesias and Carlos de Miguel, 1964–70).

The Organicist Resort

Coderch's unrealized Torre Valentina project on the Costa Brava, Girona (1959), mentioned previously, set the standard for integrating resort development into handsome natural settings: its low blocks of linear apartments stepped down in section alongside the topography, nestling under the site's Mediterranean pines. Schemes using setbacks from floor to floor, as seen in Oiza's Ciudad Blanca, were particularly suited to steeply sloping sites, where building and landscape could merge into a terraced topography. Examples include the Mediterranean fisherman's settlement of Almuñécar by Rafael de La-Hoz (1963), or Rubens Henríquez's Ifara housing cooperative on the steep volcanic slopes of Tenerife in the Canary Islands (with Félix Sáenz, Fernando Isidro and Felipe Amaral, 1969).

While these projects also introduced setbacks in plan for a village-like massing of repetitive units, a more monumental scale could be obtained by maintaining each setback floor in a continuous horizontal line, creating the profile of a stepped pyramid and recalling the ancient agricultural terraces cut into some of the Canary Islands' precipitous volcanic slopes. An interesting example is the Maravilla Aparthotel, one of twelve projects in the Ten-Bel resort development on the Costa del Silencio, Tenerife (1967–70), designed by local architects Javier Díaz-Llanos and Vicente Saavedra (class of 1960 in Madrid and Barcelona, respectively). The building stands on a cliff at the edge of the ocean, in a lush natural setting that the architects conserved.

As was the case before the war, architects in the Canary Islands were isolated from their mainland peers and had independent contact with foreign trends. Díaz-Llanos and Saavedra's College of Architects in Tenerife (1966–72, with Fernando Isidro Hernández) is as much Brutalist as it is Organic, showing the influence of British and Italian design, with a textured concrete volume articulated as a stack of floor trays slung through an expressed structural frame.

Javier Díaz-Llanos and Vicente Saavedra, Maravilla Aparthotel, Ten-Bel resort, Costa del Silencio, Tenerife, 1967–70. Partial view.

Fernando Higueras, Hotel Las Salinas, Lanzarote, 1973–7.

César Manrique's home (now the César Manrique Foundation), 1966. Lava bubble with pool, dance floor, bar and barbeque.

The most dramatic pyramidal structure of the period was built by Fernando Higueras. For the Salinas Hotel on Lanzarote (1973–7), he distributed a six-storey structure in two symmetrical snaking arms creating a variety of different landscape forms. Viewed from the water, the terraced floors resemble an artificial promontory, with rooms hidden behind deep balconies and large planters and vegetation. Moving inland, the arms come together around steep shaded valleys and grottos. Higueras designed the lush grounds and swimming pool in collaboration with local artist César Manrique, who had brought him to the island.

Returning to Lanzarote from New York in 1964, Manrique dedicated the rest of his life to protecting the island's dramatic landscapes of exposed black lava against insensitive development. He personally oversaw a number of projects that exemplify this aim, as seen in his own house (1966), now the César Manrique Foundation. Here he combined the simple, whitewashed vernacular of the island with a series of living spaces occupying natural air bubbles in the solidified lava, including a grotto-like swimming pool with an adjacent barbeque and dance floor, situated in a roofless cavity.

Manrique's and Higueras's work on the island marks a point of encounter between the Organicist movement and the social upheavals that swept

Luis Peña Ganchegui, Plaza del Tenis, San Sebastián, 1975–6; with Eduardo Chillida, *El Peine del Viento* (The Comb of the Wind), 1976, steel.

José María García de Paredes, Almendrales parish church, Madrid, 1962–5.

José María García de Paredes, Manuel de Falla Auditorium, Granada, 1973–8.

across Europe in the late 1960s and early 1970s, which reached places like Lanzarote and Ibiza, more isolated from the reach of the Franco regime on the mainland. In the words of Iñaki Ábalos, the two men transformed Lanzarote from 'that hell where Franco sent the disaffected [a place of forced exile] into one of the centres of an imaginary map of liberty, incipient environmental values and the hedonistic beauty of the period'.[11]

Organicism and Place

In the work of Luis Peña Ganchegui and José María García de Paredes, the formal preoccupations of Organicism begin to mix with a greater awareness of place, and of local tradition and character. Peña, another graduate of Madrid's class of 1959, reintroduced modern architecture to the Basque region, blending modern and traditional elements in response to the rainy local climate and abrupt topography. In the Aizetzu housing complex in his native Motrico (today Mutriku, 1964–5), three housing blocks raised on pilotis with pitched slate roofs spill down the hillside in a picturesque tumble, their open ground floors functioning like the region's porticoed plazas.

Alejandro de la Sota,
Maravillas School
Gymnasium, Madrid,
1960–62.

Peña designed the Plaza del Tenis in San Sebastián (1975–6) as the setting for Eduardo Chillida's seaside sculptural group *El Peine del Viento* (The Comb of the Wind). Here, the cellular unit returns in the form of the solid granite pavers that make up the plaza's surface. These adapt to the rocky promontory in the low, angled lines of steps, translating the pyramidal landscape forms of Las Salinas into a gentle flow of habitable horizontal space extending between the rocks and the sea.

In his parish church in the Directed Settlement of Almendrales (1962–5), Paredes adapted the multi-columned, skylit organization of Corrales and Molezún's 1958 Spanish Pavilion to create what he called a 'multi-polar' space, like that seen in the Mosque at Córdoba, which he contrasted to the 'polarization towards the altar' of a traditional church. Paredes's intent was to promote the sense of community among worshippers, a stance

Alejandro de la Sota,
Casa Domínguez,
A Caeira, Pontevedra,
1976.

that anticipated the liturgical reforms of the ongoing Second Vatican Council.[12]

Paredes's career culminated with the Manuel de Falla Auditorium in Granada (1973–8). The bulk of the brick-clad concert hall is cut into a steep slope and staggered in massing, deferring to the scale of the Alhambra, not far away. The large trusses spanning the hall are covered with a broken profile of traditionally tiled pitched roofs, and inside, the stage is asymmetrically placed between large and smaller seating areas. Clearly of its time and yet in harmony with its historic setting, the building marks a transition towards what the critic and historian Kenneth Frampton would soon call Critical Regionalism, absorbing and recasting the old atavistic search for a national style in new, more nuanced terms.[13]

On the Fringes of Organicism

Alejandro de la Sota was unmoved by the siren song of the Organicist moment, as seen in his masterpiece of the period, the Maravillas School Gymnasium in Madrid (1960–62), and its brilliant section in which classrooms are suspended between deep exposed trusses that span the gymnasium below. This technical approach, although radically unadorned, nevertheless conveys an understated poetic force. In the compact section, De la Sota used the angled bottom chords of the trusses to pull the floor above them away from the longitudinal walls, opening space underneath it for a steep grandstand on one side and clerestory windows on the other. The floor of the classrooms above is consequentially raked and literally cradled between the trusses. Its angled underside, finished in exposed insulating panels, bathes the space in received natural light.

De la Sota completed other intriguing works of enigmatic significance in these years. In the César Carlos Residential College at Madrid's University City (1967), for example, the glazed gallery of the gymnasium bridges the roofs of two small, independent residential towers, for men and women

Miguel Fisac, Centre for Hydrographic Studies, Madrid, 1959–60.

respectively. In the Casa Domínguez in A Caeira, Pontevedra, in De la Sota's native Galicia (1976), a semi-buried plinth containing bedrooms and services is separated by an open-air void from the upper level of living areas, raised to capture views. A metal terrace with glass block paving added to the exterior hovers uneasily between the two levels, in an unresolved, almost parodic hybrid of two elevated homes, both Modern classics: Le Corbusier's Villa Savoye (1931) and Mies's Farnsworth House (1951).

The difficulty of reading De la Sota's late works is coupled with his almost fetishistic attention to construction technique, be it custom details such as stair railings or his equally studied use of off-the-shelf industrial products, as in the insulated metal panels that clad the Postal Savings Bank's computer centre in Madrid (1973–4), recalling Lu is Lacasa's fascination with American product catalogues in the 1920s (another reflection of the aspirations of Spain as it emerged from a position of scarcity and industrial underdevelopment). Similarly, when writing in 1984 on Maravillas, De la Sota echoed Rafael Bergamín, stating with characteristically subtle, ironic vehemence, 'I think that not making architecture is one path towards making it.'[14] In essence, he was translating the tectonic basis of form developed by Zuazo and Moya to the more purely technical means of modern construction. This focus on technique, in turn, left a door open to more intuitive formal decisions, with results that were sometimes whimsical, sometimes poetic.

In the context of the 1960s, this position of strict technical honesty, with all its renunciations, eliminated a lot of nonsense, but it also dismissed any concern for the impact of architecture outside the limited purview of the profession. While the Organicist movement represented one of the last hurrahs of the avant-garde impulse to remake the world, as improbable a proposition as it ever was, De la Sota's stance was to turn away from an indifferent world, where architecture meant nothing, and take refuge in the esoteric, secret pleasures of the architect's craft.

Miguel Fisac also stood back from the exacerbations of high Organicism, focusing instead on exploring the structural and formal potential of concrete. Most notably, he invented a system of precast roofing beams that he called 'huesos', or bones. These post-tensioned hollow beams, cast in metal moulds with unusual rounded sections, overlap one another as they span a roof. In the Centre for Hydrographic Studies in Madrid (1959–60), the beams span 22 metres (72 ft), alternating with clerestory skylights integrated in their profiles. The wave-like patterns of shadow and light on their undersides in the interior can be seen as an iteration on the Organicist interest in repetitive pattern, albeit in an atrophied, concentrated form.

Fisac also developed new textures for poured concrete. His 'flexible formwork' used polyethylene film restrained with ties. The film gave the concrete

a soft, smooth finish and was filled out with the liquid concrete like stuffed upholstery. His stated aim was 'to give reinforced concrete a texture and finish that reflect its properties as a bland and flexible material'.[15] In Madrid's MUPAG Rehabilitation Centre (1969), the surface appears quilted and inflated. In a small apartment building in his hometown of Daimiel (1978), the poured concrete takes the form of irregular vertical tubing.

One curious exception to this preoccupation with surface texture is the 'pagoda' (1965–8), an administrative tower for the Jorba Laboratories, which Fisac built beside the highway that links Madrid to its airport. Fisac rotated each floor 45 degrees with respect to the floor below, and spanned the twisting gaps between the continuous ribbon windows on each floor with hyperbolic paraboloids in board-formed concrete. Built as an advertising ploy, the spiky, curvaceous tower was his most popularly known building until its controversial demolition in 1999.

As we have mentioned, after Higueras's Crown of Thorns, state clients avoided the more extreme Organicist designs. The contested competition for the Spanish Pavilion at the 1964 New York World's Fair, for example, went to Javier Carvajal with a sober, windowless volume floating over low walls. Within this relative caution, some of the most formally ambitious works for the state were realized for the labour universities built across the country in the 1960s and early 1970s, modernist successors to Luis Moya's mega-fantasy in Gijón. The best-known is a campus for 5,000 students at Cheste, outside Valencia (1967–70), by Fernando Moreno Barberá (Madrid, class of 1940). Moreno built its twenty-odd buildings entirely of exposed concrete, with expressive systems of brise-soleil and exposed structural elements directly inspired by the work of Le Corbusier, such as the unrealized Palace of the Soviets in Moscow.

Near the end of the regime, a team led by Julio Cano Lasso (Madrid, class of 1949), and including a young Alberto Campo Baeza, built a tightly grouped complex of blocks and patios for 1,200 female students in Almería (1971–5). The design takes Organic monumentality down the same path of sculptural abstraction as the contemporary work of American architects such as Edward Larrabee Barnes or I. M. Pei. The project also included commissioned artworks by members of the El Paso group. While the design would prove indicative of future developments, its immediate impact was muted due to its status as an official government commission.

The Rebirth of the Political Left

Julio Cano Lasso, Labour University, Almería, 1971–5.

Cano Lasso's Labour University appeared at a time of growing political upheaval that culminated with the death of Franco in 1975 and was followed by the 'Transition', as the period was called, to a democratic, constitutional monarchy. In this interval, architectural concerns took a back seat, both within the profession and in society as a whole, although the climate of protest and resistance produced a handful of radical experimental proposals that captured the imagination of a younger generation.

Illegal demonstrations, strikes and underground political organizations first appeared on university campuses and in the factories of the industrialized north in the mid-1950s, and grew through the following two decades in escalating cycles of protest and repression. The trajectory of Spanish architecture was particularly affected by student mobilizations at the universities of Madrid and Barcelona in the mid-1960s. The reawakening of openly leftist thinking among both students and professors divided architecture schools into opposing ideological camps.

The radicalization of campus life went hand in hand with its massification, as universities opened their doors to post-war baby boomers and the children of the new middle classes. Incoming students at Madrid's School of Architecture jumped from little more than a dozen to more than four hundred in 1957, and a thousand in 1964.[16] As head of studies, Javier Carvajal led efforts to modernize teaching, promoting Sáenz de Oiza and appointing new professors such as Fernández Alba, Fullaondo and Moneo, who had returned to Madrid in 1965 following his period with Utzon and two years at the Spanish Academy in Rome.

However, in 1968, student protests came to a head in a strike that paralysed the school for the entire autumn term, with students abandoning classes for popular assemblies, echoing protest actions at other university departments. The regime responded with the declaration of a state of exception and police control of the building. The school's director was replaced, and Fernández Alba, Sáenz de Oiza and other reform teachers left the school for several years in protest.

Student demands focused on pedagogic issues, with political revindications still off-limits, but in the background. Antón Capitel, a student at the time, explains: 'It wasn't enough for us that the professors were modern. We wanted to know how to design, what was the methodology. All kinds of questions were in the air. On the one hand, the neo-hyper-avant-gardes: Archigram, Haus-Rucker, Superstudio, the Metabolists. On the other, semiotics, Structuralism, cybernetics, sophisticated technologies.' Students demanded 'scientific certainty' in place of teaching methods based on 'intuition, creative will and the example of the masters'.[17]

Oriol Bohigas describes a similar atmosphere at the Barcelona school, where he recalls conversations on Marxism and Existentialism with his students in the halls, and attending semi-clandestine meetings for diverse committees and causes. He credits Federico Correa, who had joined the faculty in 1959, with modernizing the teaching programme, 'But Correa couldn't overcome the disruptions of the students' political protests, the only phenomenon of real interest in university life.'[18] Unrest climaxed in 1966 with the 'Caputxinada', when police surrounded a Capuchin monastery in the city where some five hundred students, professors and intellectuals had secretly gathered to establish the Democratic Student Union. The stand-off lasted for days until police stormed the monastery and arrested everyone. Bohigas and two other architecture professors were arrested and expelled from the school, as was Correa soon after.

Barcelona architects were also distracted by the seductive allure of the Gauche Divine, or 'divine left'. Figures associated with this elite, progressive social movement included Correa, Bohigas and younger architects such as Óscar Tusquets, together with writers, editors, actresses, models, photographers and other hangers-on. Their main hangouts were the Barcelona dance bar Bocaccio, bars like Correa and Milà's Flash Flash and the town of Cadaqués (where Salvador Dalí lived and international figures such as Marcel Duchamp and Man Ray summered). The critic Llàtzer Moix describes the Gauche Divine as an elite 'that decided not to wait for the end of the Franco dictatorship to begin acting with complete freedom'.[19] They claimed for themselves the revolution in social and sexual mores, fashion, music, pop culture and political militancy that they had seen on trips to London and Paris.

The most interesting architect to emerge from the ambience of the Gauche Divine was Ricardo Bofill. His resort developments and working-class housing projects of the 1960s and '70s, designed with his multi-disciplinary collective studio, Taller de Arquitectura, infused late Organicism with the utopian spirit and hip social mores of the moment, and attracted broad international attention to Spanish architecture for the first time since Aizpurúa or Sert in the 1930s.

Bofill was a precocious political activist. He was arrested as a student in 1957 for his involvement in a campus chapter of the Partit Socialista Unificat de Catalunya (Unified Socialist Party of Catalunya, or PSUC), one of the historic leftist parties of the Republic. Fewer than ten years before, arrested leaders of the party had been executed, and in the 1950s several received long prison terms. Bofill got off with expulsion from the Barcelona School of Architecture and finished his studies in Geneva, Switzerland, in 1960.[20]

In his first works he took on Organicist themes with a dramatic flair, as in the fanning plan and faceted facades of an apartment building in Barcelona's Carrer Nicaragua (1962–4). In the same years he began assembling the Taller, widening his horizons to city planning, sociology, economics and the arts. Key members over the years included his sister Anna Bofill, a composer, architect and mathematician; the philosopher and politician Xavier Rubert de Ventós; Salvador Clotas, a writer and activist later involved in the Socialist Party; and the poet José Agustín Goytisolo, who wrote texts and poems about the Taller and proposed 'the largest amount of images for each project'.[21] The Italian actress Serena Vergano, Bofill's wife, starred in *Esquizo*, a full-length experimental film that Bofill financed and directed in 1970. The Taller's leading architects were Ramón Collado, Xavier Bagué, Manuel Núñez Yanowsky and Peter Hodgkinson, who joined the group in 1966 after studying at London's Architectural Association and working for Peter Cook of Archigram.

The group first attracted attention with their exotic vacation apartments on the Mediterranean: Kafka's Castle in Sitges (1966–8) and La Manzanera in Calpe, Alicante, including Xanadú (1966–71) and La Muralla Roja or the Red Wall (1969–73). Inspired in part by Archigram and Anna Bofill's studies of open geometric growth patterns, the Taller developed these projects as conglomerations of living units plugged into service structures. Their method transformed the more intuitive cellular compositions of Organicism into geometric systems produced by mathematical formulas, which they manipulated to create picturesque effects. They proudly noted, for example, that Kafka's Castle was designed on a single sheet of paper, with many details developed on site.[22] With the saturated colours of their stucco finishes, exotic names and oneiric visual metaphors and fantasies, the projects left behind Organicism's more subtle evocations of clustered villages and land forms, turning instead to the bright Pop imagery of contemporary music and culture.

With its deep green walls and stack of dollhouse-like cellular units, Xanadú was said to evoke an inhabited tree, a pagoda, a castle or the abrupt outcropping known as the Peñón de Ifach, visible across Calpe's bay. In the Red Wall, metaphoric evocations include references to the kasbahs and adobe fortresses of North Africa, or M. C. Escher's obsessive drawings of impossible staircases. In the themes of the inhabited wall – the labyrinthine interior realm of patios, passageways, bridges and stairs, or the oneiric sequences of open-air rooms of the roof terraces – the Taller explored ideas about the phenomenology of spatial experience that had begun to circulate internationally, as in Gaston Bachelard's *Poetics of Space* (published in Spanish in 1965). This turn to metaphor and scenographic settings prefigured the postmodern classicism of Bofill's subsequent career, exemplified by his large social-housing projects in France, beginning with Les Arcades du Lac in Saint-Quentin-en-Yvelines (1980).

The ambitions of the Taller were not limited to building dreamscapes for the weekend getaways of the Gauche Divine. Their Barrio Gaudí (1964–8) planned 2,000 units of subsidized housing in the industrial town of Reus, where Gaudí was born (five hundred were actually built). The Taller sought to create an authentic neighbourhood, reintroducing conventional streets

Ricardo Bofill Taller de Arquitectura, Xanadú, 1966–71, and La Muralla Roja (the Red Wall), Calpe, Alicante, 1969–73.

that grouped commercial and recreational spaces. The eight-storey brick blocks are connected by raised plazas and feature a faceted geometry of overlapping solids and voids, accented with brightly coloured patios and balconies.

More ambitious still, for the Ciudad en el Espacio (City in Space) they proposed to cover a large parcel in the working-class Madrid suburb of Moratalaz with a modular system of cubic volumes, 'developed organically in space, following defined geometric laws'.[23] The system combined 1,500 units of varying sizes with a network of public spaces, gardens and circulation in the air, freeing the ground for services and parking. After presenting the project in a 1968 manifesto,[24] they sought to realize it as a self-managed cooperative without bank financing. The venture attracted wide media attention and hundreds of subscribers but was stymied in bureaucratic red tape. A breaking point for the patience of the regime came with a promotional programme consisting of a band led by the bluesman Taj Mahal that jammed for several evenings on the construction site in the summer of 1970, attracting a crowd of thousands that was eventually broken up by the police.[25]

Walden 7 (1970–75), built in the Barcelona suburb of Sant Just Desvern, is the culmination of these experiments and the Taller's best-known project of this period, featured on the cover of *Architectural Design* in July 1975. The Taller packed 446 apartments into a sixteen-storey megastructure, another step in their monumentalization of low-cost housing. Units are again composed of multiple unprogrammed modules, arranged around five vertiginous courtyards, with access via passageways and bridges that string around the courtyards and the exterior. The nearly solid brick massing is staggered vertically, opening and closing as it rises to form multi-storey

Ricardo Bofill Taller de Arquitectura, Walden 7, Sant Just Desvern, Barcelona, 1970–75.

openings that break through into the patios. Windows are undersized and few in number, with many partially hidden behind rounded balconies grouped in irregular vertical runs across the continuous, almost reptilian brick exterior skin.

The Taller presented the project as a response to the modern city's 'lack of a sense of community, of collective activity, of public space at the disposition of the individual'.[26] But as part of a residential suburb, Walden 7 could not overcome the larger structures of social and territorial organization that underlay these problems, and served only as a one-off utopian proposal. Barcelona could thus finally boast a tower that measured up to the ambition, vision and folly of Torres Blancas.

Next door to Walden, Bofill and the Taller transformed the concrete silos and spaces of an abandoned cement plant into a sprawling communal studio, home and garden (1973–5). Inspired by the 'surreal' and 'magical' quality of the complex, the Taller transformed it into a seductive expression of its own collective organization.[27] But the result was to confine their radical social experiment to a privileged private sphere, as isolated in its own right as Walden was in the suburbs. The studio contributed to a public perception of the group as a kind of eccentric cult organized around Bofill.

An Evanescent Utopia

In Madrid and elsewhere in Spain, the radical Left did not so readily find the economic means or political space for such extravagant self-realization. Radical experimentation was mainly confined to formal ideas about structural systems and technology, inspired by Buckminster Fuller and other advocates of technological utopia, but it was temporary in nature, with limited applications. Worthy of mention, however, are the brilliant folding and geodesic structures of Emilio Pérez Piñero and the inflatable pavilions of José Miguel de Prada Poole.

Pérez Piñero (Madrid, class of 1962) began developing his folding structures in the early 1960s, before the politicization of architecture schools, and his inventions were actively promoted by Franco's regime. Working in isolation in his hometown of Calasparra, Murcia, and with limited means, he based his structures on networks of articulated struts that expanded like unfolding umbrellas or accordions. He first attracted attention in 1961, when he won a student competition for an ambulant theatre at the Sixth Congress of the International Union of Architects in London, with Félix Candela and Fuller on the jury. In 1964, he built a 'Transportable Pavilion' in front of Zuazo's New Ministries for Franco's celebration of 'Twenty-Five Years of Peace'. The large-span horizontal space truss was deployed on wheels to facilitate its unfurling and raised into position on telescoping vertical supports. In 1966, he designed a geodesic dome for a portable theatre seating 1,800, commissioned by Manuel Fraga's Ministry of Information and Tourism, which travelled throughout Spain. His last completed project was a dome for Salvador Dalí's Theatre-Museum in Figueras. A reckless driver, he was killed in a traffic accident in 1972.

Prada Poole (Madrid, class of 1965) belongs to a later, thoroughly politicized generation. He conceived his experiments in pneumatic structures as a radical rejection of permanence in architecture, asking instead, 'Why not build with air?' In his 1968 manifesto 'The Ephemeral Architecture of Soap Bubbles', he echoed the visionary utopianism of Yona Friedman or Constant, proclaiming 'three stages of non-existent architecture: urbanistic dematerialization, the constitution of a planetary city and society, and the development of the magic city, evanescent and immaterial, crisscrossed by stimulating, energetic waves, like solar ebullition'.[28]

To create his pneumatic pavilions, he used fans to slightly pressurize the air inside 'bubbles' of 3 mm pvc film, without any other structural armature. He developed his first prototypes at the Madrid School of Architecture in the late 1960s, working with students, though he lacked a teaching position at the time. In 1971, a group of Barcelona students (including future architect Carlos Ferrater) invited him to help create an encampment on the beach in Ibiza for students attending an international congress on industrial design. The result was Instant City, a month-long social and cultural experiment that brought together the revolutionary impulses of the period, from communal living and non-hierarchical decision-making to art happenings and a wild opening-night party. Prada Poole's colourful structures,

Emilio Pérez Piñero, Ambulant Theatre, 1961.

José Miguel de Prada Poole, Instant City, Ibiza, 1971. Interior detail.

produced from material designed for inflatable swimming pools, provided an appropriately ludic setting.

Residents built their own housing units, interpreting Prada Poole's spherical and cylindrical prototypes, and plugged them into tubular corridors around a central meeting space. The team found that staples worked best to seal joints in the film, and Prada Poole devised valve-like doors made of overlapping flaps of inflated plastic, which he compared to vaginas and sphincters. The complex housed three hundred 'Instant Citizens', according to one eyewitness account, and seven hundred according to the organizers.[29]

Though they stood for less than three days, the pneumatic domes that Prada Poole built for the 1972 Encounters of Pamplona were probably the most elegant synthesis of his system. This week-long avant-garde artistic happening, involving some 350 artists, was the first and last of its kind in Spain, and the last – and perhaps most ambitious – of the cultural projects sponsored by the Huarte family. After many problems and revisions, Prada Poole's final design comprised eleven interconnected vaults, each 25 metres (82 ft) in diameter and 12 metres (40 ft) high. In this case, the joints in the plastic were factory-welded, and the film was scented with vanilla to cover

the smell of the plastic. The artist Isidoro Valcárcel Medina recalls: 'The
space was rather magical, so immense, with the light filtering through the
arches, which gave it an orangish effect, and the continuous sound of the
ventilators.'[30] The domes were used as an event space and for exhibitions,
including videos and artworks hung on clotheslines.

The Encounters occupied the entire city for a week in late June. The chief
organizers were the composer Luis de Pablo and the artist José Luis Alexanco,
who worked under the exclusive patronage of the Huarte family. Aiming
to situate the event on a par with the concurrent Spoleto Festival, docu-
menta 5 in Kassel and the Venice Biennale, they cast a wide net, bringing in
the most radical artistic tendencies of the moment, from Conceptual and
Minimal art to performance, sound installations, video, computer art, electronic music and experimental cinema. The participants included several
international figures, among them John Cage, Steve Reich and Dennis
Oppenheim.

Prada Poole's domes, and his underlying vision of an evanescent architecture, were in perfect consonance with the spirit of the Encounters, in
which participants tended to reject the objecthood of art in favour of the
ephemeral and immaterial, an art of public acts and events. Such works
activated in turn the public spaces in which they were realized, with the
city as a whole as their ultimate scenario, transforming the public realm
into a space of encounter. But Pamplona was not Lanzarote or Ibiza, and
the event was contested on all fronts, although it attracted a large and enthusiastic public. Barely tolerated by local authorities and infiltrated by flocks
of plainclothes police, it was also boycotted by the powerful underground

Communist Party, which saw it as reinforcing the image of the regime. It was also greeted by ETA's terrorists, with the detonation of two small bombs.

The political tension extended to the events of the Encounters and led to the early demise of Prada Poole's installation, as well as the early closure of the festival. Two days after the domes were finished, an unauthorized public discussion on the question 'What Is Art?' devolved into a debate on political repression. According to the journalist Pepa Bueno, Juan Huarte felt compelled to intervene, dissolving the crowd of some three hundred people by playing composer Josep Maria Mestres's electronic music at an unbearable volume. According to José Luis Alexanco, someone slashed the plastic film with a knife during the ensuing chaos, and the organizers turned off the ventilators as a safety measure. The police removed all traces of the structure that night.[31]

The organizers of a 2009 retrospective of the Encounters at the Reina Sofía Museum in Madrid note that the event marked both the culmination of the artistic experimentation of the 1960s and its demise, in which the utopian 'collective myth of a "new beginning" found its real-world limits'. The Encounters, they concluded, 'forced into question the misleading accommodation between the artistic and the political vanguard, that explicit association between art and political commitment that the forces of resistance to the dictatorship had embraced.'[32]

However, both the ephemeral utopias of Prada Poole and the Encounters and the political agitation that eclipsed them – that is, the myriad radical leftist parties that channelled the political activism of the time (including, ultimately, the Communist Party itself) – belonged to a world that was about to disappear. With the death of Franco in 1975, events overcame ideologies, although they were accompanied, via mass demonstrations and mobilizations, by a constant public pressure for change. The first free general elections were held in 1977, a new constitution was approved by popular vote in 1978 and finally, after a botched military coup attempt in 1981, Felipe González was elected in 1982 to head a relatively moderate socialist government. With his victory, voters pushed aside both the heirs to the Franco regime and its historic opponents in the formerly outlawed Communist Party, both of whom had risked and sacrificed so much to bring about a democratic reconciliation. The historian Santos Juliá wryly describes the Socialists as 'a revolutionary party that doesn't do revolutions'. The party was elected instead, he writes, 'to launch the typical left-wing policies of social democracy. As Karl Kautsky famously pronounced, the new was better than the old, and those that promised a future, rather than those who came burdened with the past.'[33]

chapter eight

Building Democracy, 1975–92

In the early 1980s, men like [fashion designers] Francis Montesinos, Manuel Piña or Antonio Alvarado sought to dress us for a society that had to reinvent itself. And then there was Jesús del Pozo. [In his] workshop on Calle Almirante, we could dream that perhaps we no longer lived in a dark and retrograde country. We too could get all dressed up and imagine ourselves, see ourselves differently, and learn to be Europeans while still remaining Spaniards. This was one of the first steps towards entering democracy, to be able to be different and accept difference. To enjoy what was called 'elegance' and dress in accordance with the codes of each occasion without being retrograde or reactionary.

Ángeles González-Sinde, 2011[1]

The Transition was a difficult time for both public and private architecture. The economic uncertainty provoked by the uncertainties of the political process coincided with the effects of the 1973 oil crisis and the decline of Spain's industrial base. Despite its recent consolidation, Spain's industry proved as vulnerable as those of other developed countries in the face of new, cheaper competitors. The country's growth rate plummeted for the first time since 1959. Unemployment reached record levels and rising inflation threatened to spiral out of control.

The crisis caught commercial building in an expansive phase, and it took years for the sector to recover. By the 1980s, when new democratic institutions began to function, public projects offered architects the best opportunities for innovative design, while private commissions definitively lost their previous protagonism. Cutting-edge architecture had been a natural interest for an elite of visionary industrialists who had helped create the economic miracle, as exemplified by the Huarte family discussed in the previous chapter. Now a new generation of idealistic political leaders found in architecture a means to give palpable form to the new political era.

Responding to the demands of Basques, Catalans and other regions that sought a degree of self-rule, the 1978 constitution organized Spain's 52 historic provinces into a decentralized network of seventeen 'autonomies', or regional governments, each with legislative, executive and judicial

Antonio Cruz and Antonio Ortiz, Santa Justa train station, Sevilla, 1987–91.

branches. The autonomies acquired wide jurisdiction in areas such as education, healthcare, housing and culture. Much of the new architectural work came from these administrations, as well as from the central government and local municipalities. All sought to bring public services up to the standards of a modern European state, as well as stimulate economic recovery and establish new institutional identities. In 1986, Spain joined the European Union, and by the end of the decade European development grants for infrastructures, including highways, rail networks and airports, helped to integrate and open these regions to one another and to the rest of Europe. Public architecture became one of the most visible symbols of this political and economic rejuvenation. This representative role culminated in 1992, when Spain simultaneously hosted two major world events, the Summer Olympics in Barcelona and the Universal Exposition of Sevilla.

The system of autonomies promoted the consolidation of regional centres of architecture, focused on the cultural activities of the professional colleges and new local architecture schools. The colleges published magazines, organized exhibitions, lectures and awards programmes and oversaw local competitions. New architecture schools were established with the expansion of university education in the 1960s and '70s. For example, schools opened in Sevilla, Valencia, A Coruña, Valladolid and Pamplona (part of the private University of Navarra, run by Opus Dei). Near Barcelona, a second school opened in suburban Vallès.

The tectonic realignments of political power also transformed the profession, sweeping aside long-standing client–architect relationships and provoking a generational renewal. Figures such as Fernando Moreno Barberá, who had made his career within the Franco administration, found themselves shunned, replaced by younger colleagues and those who, for political reasons, had not sought or found public work under Franco. Architects were appointed to several key political positions and were instrumental in this process in many cases. Oriol Bohigas was the most outstanding example. He became the director of urban planning in the first democratically elected municipal government of Barcelona in 1980, under the socialist mayor Narcís Serra, and launched a far-reaching renewal of architecture and urban planning in the city. Other figures played similar roles in Madrid's central ministries and in other local and regional administrations.

While architects had to resituate their work and thinking within the new political landscape, they also had to come to terms with the upheavals in international architecture provoked by the different ramifications of postmodernism. These ideas circulated widely through new journals such as *Arquitecturas bis* and *2C*, the translation into Spanish of key texts by the publisher Gustavo Gili and others, and direct contact, both abroad and in Spain, with many of the principal international protagonists of the new movement.

The coincidence of these two moments of rupture was propitious, offering a ready architectural paradigm for the new era. However, with only a few exceptions, Spanish architects resisted the most extreme formal expressions of postmodernism, whether in the historicist and Pop modes of its Anglo-Saxon varieties or in the severe rationalism of Aldo Rossi and the Italian Tendenza movement, whose ideas had their strongest impact on urban planning.

The architecture of the 1980s in Spain stands out clearly from its functionalist and Organicist predecessors. Architects incorporated the critical insights of postmodern theory – in terms of building tectonics and craft, contextual thinking, urbanism, preservation, iconic reference, type forms and so on – and these insights transformed their work. However, they tended to adopt these concepts in a spirit of continuity rather than rupture with the Modern Movement, without necessarily rejecting its basic compositional strategies or principles, or even many of its formal characteristics. In the rest of Europe and the United States, postmodernism arrived with a sense of the exhaustion of the modern project, which, in the Marxist analysis of the Italian critic Manfredo Tafuri, was cast as an instrument of capitalist domination and dehumanization.[2] But in Spain, after decades of constructing a small, self-referential architectural culture in relative isolation, architects tended to see the profession as something akin to a guild, with a body of technical knowledge proven in a continuum over time. This inclusive postmodernism gave the young Spanish democracy a distinctive new style. It also offered, once the revisionist moment had exhausted its formal appeal, one way forward towards a renewed, contextual modernism.

By 1992, Spanish architecture had become a point of interest for the rest of the world. Two Madrid journals founded in the mid-1980s marked this international reach: *Arquitectura Viva*, directed by the critic Luis Fernández-Galiano, and *El Croquis*, whose lavish format and in-depth coverage earned an international prestige that far transcended its Spanish base. Like the weighty tomes of *El Croquis*, with their dark covers and innovative graphic design, the best architecture of these years had a monumental heft and seriousness. The solid brick massing and concrete vaults of the Santa Justa train station in Sevilla, designed by Antonio Cruz and Antonio Ortiz for the 1992 Expo, is a noteworthy example. But this solemnity should not be misunderstood. It was the formal, dress-up attire of a country bursting with optimism, youthful energy and faith in the immediate arrival of a brighter future.

Organicism's Last Stand

Some of the most interesting works of the Organicist period were completed well into the 1970s, as we have seen. The decade also saw the first stirrings of what might have become a Spanish variant of British High-Tech architecture, a last twist in the Organicist impulse to reinvigorate modernism, focusing on an 'exacerbated' technical refinement of functionalism rather than on formal complexity. But this initiative was quickly swept aside by the postmodern critical agenda, as championed by a new generation.

Three ambitious projects illustrate this moment of radical change. They were all for bank headquarters located on Madrid's central artery, the Paseo de la Castellana: Corrales and Molezún's Bankunión (1970–75), Sáenz de Oiza's Bilbao Bank (1971–81) and Rafael Moneo's Bankinter (1972–7, with Ramón Bescós). The first two designs, both winners of hotly contested limited competitions, explored different approaches to a technically inspired formalism, while the third completely changed the rules of the game.

For Bankunión, a modest eleven-storey tower, the veteran Organicists shifted into something a bit more Pop, employing an exotic coppery finish of anodized aluminium and a series of wilful formal moves: a barrel-vault

José A. Corrales and Ramón Vázquez Molezún, Bankunión, Madrid, 1970–75.

Francisco J. Sáenz
de Oiza, Bilbao Bank,
Madrid, 1971–81.

roof, a semi-circular 'prow' projecting from the narrow end of the tower for signage and a horizontal rail for the window-cleaning basket, hoisted above the curtain walls like a nautical cornice – very James Stirling. The architects pushed the structure, vertical circulation and services to the perimeter and ran air-handling ducts up the exterior, just as in the contemporary Centre Pompidou (1977).

Although Sáenz de Oiza's extraordinary Bilbao Bank remains Organicist in conception, here he replaced the concrete of Torres Blancas with an exquisitely crafted Corten-steel curtain wall, a material he selected, in part, in homage to the steel works of Bilbao, although these were soon to close. The project thus shared British High-Tech's nostalgia for a fading industrial era. The thirty-storey tower stands north of Zuazo's New Ministries complex on a prominent corner of the 19-hectare (46 ac) AZCA development, a superblock of office buildings, shopping concourses and apartments built during the 1970s. Oiza and his engineers developed a unique structural solution for the building: like a pair of tree trunks, the two central cores, situated on either side of the train tunnels passing under the site, support a series of cantilevered concrete platforms at five-storey intervals. These

in turn support stacks of four conventional steel-framed floors. The excuse for this exotic solution was that it required fewer interior columns, and every fifth floor was column-free. The thicker floor sections of the cantilevered platforms create an irregular rhythm of spans from floor to floor. Oiza accentuates this on the facades with projecting maintenance catwalks that double as shading visors, thickening the curtain wall and giving it contrasts of shadow, material and colour. The beautifully proportioned minimalist detailing includes rounded corners, evoking Wright's laboratory tower (1950) for the Johnson Wax Building.

Moneo's Bankinter marked the arrival of the postmodern agenda championed by a new generation. Here the building as a physical artefact was no longer the centre of attention, becoming instead the nexus of a network of relations: contextual, urban and historic. Moneo's most radical decision was to preserve the existing late nineteenth-century *palacete* (mansion) on the site. He squeezed the new building behind it, as a backdrop, when the practice of the time would have been to clear the site. The Castellana's turn-of-the-century mansions were disappearing in these years in favour of new developments, a loss that was widely protested.

A second major decision was to clad the building not in steel and glass but in brick. The fine-pressed brick matched that of the *palacete*, but more broadly it was the brick of Madrid, of Villanueva, Flores and Zuazo. In particular, as the critic Antón Capitel pointed out at the time, the facade provocatively recalled Cabrero and Aburto's brick-and-glass cube for the Casa Sindical (1949–56), a work situated on the cusp of the modern and the monumental retro-classicism of Mussolini's Rome.[3]

Moneo lavished on the work the uncompromising attention to detail and craftsmanship that he had learned during his apprenticeship with Oiza. Indeed, much of the design's innovative critical position is carried by the detailing. For example, the window jambs are staggered in depth, showing off the thickness of the masonry in progressive setbacks. The bronze lintels, in contrast, read as thin lines underscored by reveals, a thoroughly contemporary treatment that emphasizes the contradictory non-load-bearing condition of the thick masonry.

In preserving the site and subjecting the project to its restrictions, Moneo converted the design problem into a series of contextual responses to existing conditions. He sculpted the massing with a curve on one side and crisscrossing angles on the other that mark the entry and emphasize the quality of the tower as a screen. These moves recall the work of Robert Venturi, in particular his competition design for the Yale Mathematics Building (1970), where, as in Moneo's design, regular rows of horizontal windows are crowned by taller openings on upper floors. However, these contemporary formal themes, with their origins in Asplund and Aalto, are combined here with more archaic building craft, such as the bronze bas-reliefs in the spandrels between the windows of the upper floors by the sculptor Francisco López Hernández. These confirm the retro, almost Deco resonances of the facade and proclaim the return of history to contemporary architecture.

Moneo: Towards a Tectonic Postmodernism

Bankinter was the result of Moneo's long, peripatetic preparation for the profession, during which he elaborated on his formation in Organicism to establish a position of his own within postmodernism, transforming himself in the process into an international figure. As a student, he had been drawn to Leopoldo Torres Balbás, the historian and curator of the Alhambra during the Second Republic, who became a model for his broad intellectual formation. After his apprenticeships with Oiza (1956–61) and Utzon (1961–2), he won the Rome Fellowship (1963–5), and in these years he travelled widely, studying contemporary and historic works, meeting important figures in architecture and sending articles back to Spanish journals detailing what he had seen. On his return, he won a coveted professorship in Barcelona (1971–81) and became a founding member of the editorial board of *Arquitecturas bis* (1974–85). The venture was organized by Bohigas and the publisher Rosa Regàs, who gathered younger collaborators including Helio

Piñón and the brothers Manuel and Ignasi de Solà-Morales. Among other articles, Moneo wrote the introduction to the November 1974 issue on Aldo Rossi and Vittorio Gregotti.

Moneo's first contact with the United States came in 1968, when he travelled with a group (which included Bohigas) to the International Design Conference in Aspen, Colorado; there they met, among others, Peter Eisenman, who had just established the Institute for Architecture and Urban Studies (IAUS) in New York. This encounter was succeeded by others, including a 1974 meeting in Cadaqués of the editorial boards of *Arquitecturas bis*, the Italian journal *Lotus* and the IAUS's *Oppositions*. Eisenman invited Moneo to spend the 1976–7 academic year in New York, where he was a visiting fellow at the IAUS and taught at Cooper Union and Syracuse University. In the summer of 1976, *Oppositions* published his article on Rossi's *Architecture of the City* and Modena Cemetery, introducing Rossi to American readers for the first time.[4] Another influential essay, 'On Typology', appeared in 1978.[5] In the following decade, as his practice thrived, Moneo was appointed chairman of Harvard's Department of Architecture (1985–90) and was named the first Josep Lluís Sert Professor of Architecture in 1991. The symbolism of the chair's title was unmistakable, closing the circle around the years of Spain's isolation under Franco and welcoming the new architects of the young democracy back into the international community.

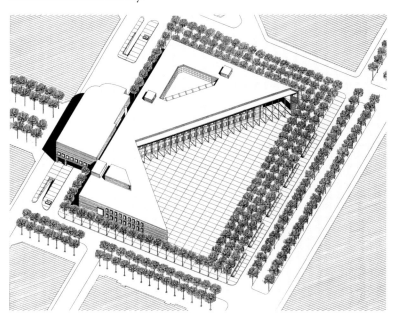

Rafael Moneo, Logroño City Hall, 1973–80. Axonometric.

Logroño City Hall, view
of plaza.

In his public buildings of this period, the Logroño City Hall (1973–80) and the Museum of Roman Art in Mérida (1979–85), Moneo applied the formal strategies unveiled in Bankinter to redefine civic architecture. The commission for Logroño, capital of La Rioja, came as Franco's regime tottered towards an uncertain future, Moneo's project is a manifesto for a non-authoritarian concept of civil government. He wrote, 'People should understand the city hall, even through its formal elements, as a public building at their service,' and he vowed to 'achieve the degree of dignity sought by an institution of this nature without resorting to empty rhetoric and false monumentality'.[6]

He took as his starting point the Baroque and Neoclassical *plazas mayores* of cities such as nearby Vitoria (built, it should be remembered, by Enlightenment liberals), where the town hall is part of an ensemble of otherwise uniform buildings that enclose a public square. He broke the closed form of the plaza type and its surrounding arcades into a two-armed fragment and set it at a 45-degree angle with respect to the surrounding streets. The fragmentation converts the closed plaza into a more conventionally modern, amorphous space. At the same time, the diagonal skew neutralizes the two facades' frontal, and thus potentially monumental relation to the plaza, converting them instead into oblique, dynamic planes that open to approaching visitors. Similarly, the skew transforms the contained rhythms of the plaza's arcades into dynamic diagonal vectors. Moneo accentuates this effect, opening the corner where they would otherwise have met to create continuous sight lines that pass through to the back of the building. He studiously avoids any indications of hierarchy, with uniformly egalitarian openings and entry doors that are tucked around a corner on each side of the meeting point of the arcades, with a discretion worthy of De la Sota. The parallels with Colin Rowe's contemporary interest in figure–ground studies and urban collage are evident, but with the composition's modern, open spatial flow, so too are the differences.

Mérida, capital of the western region of Extremadura, was a major Roman city, and it contains the largest trove of Roman remains in Spain. Moneo's museum was the first important cultural undertaking of the new democracy and established a crucial precedent for architecture's role in shaping the public image of the new era. The project was backed by the conservative central government of President Adolfo Suárez, confirmed at the polls only months before the commission. Its chief promoter was the architect Dionisio Hernández Gil, an Extremadura native who oversaw historic monuments and patrimony in the Ministry of Culture. He had met Moneo at the academy in Rome and had recommended him for the job (laws on the competitive adjudication of public commissions were not yet in place). Another key figure was Hernández Gil's boss at the ministry, Javier Tusell, a noted historian who, in the same years, was negotiating the return of Picasso's *Guernica* from the Museum of Modern Art in New York (1983), closing another symbolic circle with the past.

Moneo used an approximation of Roman building techniques for his design, utilizing load-bearing brick walls filled with poured concrete that rise around openings spanned by spectacular brick arches, creating a monumental interior space to suggest 'what Roman Mérida might have been', as he recalled in 2011.[7] He crosscut the traditional masonry with modern spatial and structural devices, as in Bankinter but with greater drama. The main nave is a virtual rather than a literal space, defined indirectly by the nine successive arched openings that pierce the structure's massive parallel walls, an abstract spatial device comparable to Colin Rowe's analysis of phenomenal transparency in modern architecture.[8] In contrast, the two mezzanine levels that stretch between the walls in the resulting alcoves are not supported by vaults, as in Roman construction, but instead are flat, skeletal, modern concrete slabs, with pipe-railing balustrades that expose their thin edges. Walls and floors are thus a dialogue of vertical and horizontal planes in opposing constructive systems.

228

The design was Moneo's clearest statement of a trans-historical, tectonic postmodernism, a synthesis that won the project international acclaim. He elaborated a theoretical argument for this approach in a 1977 essay in *Arquitecturas bis*, where he proposed an understanding of history in terms of constructive systems, emphasizing that 'the construction of architecture has always supposed the invention of form.'[9] This is, in many respects, the approach to tradition advocated by Luis Moya, one of Moneo's teachers in the 1950s, as well as that of Secundino Zuazo before him and, ultimately, Viollet-le-Duc, which demonstrates the strength of Spain's architectural teaching tradition across various generations.

Other Postmodernisms

Moneo was not the only architect to take on Venturi and Rossi, of course, although he proved to be the most influential. Others took up the challenge, graduates from the tumultuous school years of the late 1960s, but they were held back at first by the economic crisis of the late 1970s. They positioned themselves with a small private commission or two and had to wait for the first public works of the 1980s to demonstrate their full potential.

In Barcelona, an early foray into postmodernism came out of the trendy social milieu of the Gauche Divine. The Georgina Belvedere in Llofriu, Girona (1971–2), by Óscar Tusquets and Lluís Clotet of Studio PER (both Barcelona, class of 1965), was built for Georgina Regàs – sister of Rosa Regàs, the publisher of *Arquitecturas bis* – and Oriol, the owner of the dance bar Bocaccio. The design was ironically historicist: an arcadian lookout on a hillside, with a tiny vacation residence inside its base. The upper belvedere featured a traditional order of simple square piers supporting an open wood trellis with a railing of classically turned balustrades. Most provocatively for the time, this apparent bucolic retreat was actually designed for parking, as is made clear by the SEAT sedan portrayed in plans and photos. The work is the only Spanish project featured in Charles Jencks's *The Language of Post-Modern Architecture* (1977, an early primer on the movement).[10]

A similar approach – albeit pared to its essentials – for a summer house on the Italian island of Pantelleria (1972–5) eloquently embodied the sun-drenched, primal hedonism pursued on Mediterranean islands from Ibiza to the Aegean in those years. Here, Tusquets and Clotet built two long terraces into the volcanic slope, with a small residence hidden under the upper terrace, as if a cave. The edge of each terrace is lined with a row of unadorned concrete columns, which can support removable cane shading matts. They described the house as like a 'newly built ruin', capable of evoking ancient Greece or the ageless agricultural constructions celebrated in Bernard Rudofsky's *Architecture without Architects* (1964).[11]

Flanking Moneo on the Left were the more orthodox followers of the Tendenza represented by the Barcelona magazine *2C: construcción de la ciudad* (Building the City; 1972–85). The journal was the 'organ' of the Grupo 2C architectural collective and was directed by Salvador Tarragó, who translated Rossi's *Architecture of the City* into Spanish in 1971. The venture recalled GATEPAC in its leftist zeal and collective action, replacing Le Corbusier and CIAM for the Tendenza and Rossi, who was a direct and frequent collaborator.

The magazine dedicated three monographic issues to Rossi, who participated in an exhibition of the group's work in Barcelona in 1977. The exhibit drew on work from the different centres of the group: the Basque Country, the northwestern region of Galicia, Sevilla and Barcelona. Rossi made personal contact with these centres through lecturing and teaching. The group's contacts extended to Josef Paul Kleihues, director of the ICA housing programme in Berlin, and to Rob and Léon Krier.

The strongest architectural projects published in 2C came from peripheral provinces. In San Sebastián, a small group led by Miguel Garay and José Ignacio Linazasoro (Barcelona, class of 1970, 1972) organized a series of seminars with figures such as Rossi, Tafuri and the Krier brothers (1973–6). The two designed one of the first constructed buildings of the European

César Portela, Casa Xosé Muruzábal, Cambre, 1992–6.

movement, the *ikastola* (private schools with classes in the Basque language) in Hondarribia, Gipuzkoa (1974–8), which received international attention. The school adapted the square openings and simplified Beaux-Arts plans of the Tendenza with axes, symmetries and a central courtyard, while the architects' renderings recall the style of eighteenth-century French architectural engravings. Architecture here was called on to participate in the reconstruction of a once prohibited regional identity and language. Later, however, the *ikastolas*, with their indoctrination of schoolchildren in the ideological narratives of Basque nationalism, would become symbols, for many, of the coercive social atmosphere created by both local supporters of ETA's terrorists and the more 'benign' pressures of nationalist regional governments. Linazasoro himself, like others, ultimately left the region for Madrid in the 1990s.

In Galicia, César Portela (Madrid, class of 1968) and Pascuala Campos (Barcelona, 1966) were recognized early for a group of public houses for *Gitano* (Romani) families near Pontevedra (1971–4). The project evokes a *Gitano* encampment, suggesting a populism that might seem patronizing today: long, narrow houses raised off the ground, with barrel roofs, gathered in an arc like a circle of wagons. Portela subsequently separated from Campos, and in the following years he developed a regionalism based on local type forms and materials, in contrast to Linazasoro and Garay's more international outlook. His private houses of the 1980s updated the granite walls and large glazed galleries of traditional Galician buildings. He based his public works on the canneries and port structures found along Galicia's seacoasts, utilizing simple, elongated volumes with pitched roofs and exposed interior trusses, as in his waterside cultural centre in Cangas, Pontevedra (1984–9).

Moneo himself influenced several younger followers. Their work made an impact in their time through its embrace of traditional urban forms, although they seem less remarkable today. In 1976, Gabriel Ruiz Cabrero and Enrique Perea (both Madrid, class of 1971) won a closely watched competition for the College of Architects in Sevilla (1976–82), with a jury that included Moneo and Rossi. The design respected existing street lines, with openings whose vertical proportions roughly recalled traditional balcony windows. As in Bankinter, the finish was brick, and the ground floor featured angled cuts into the massing. Another influential debut was made by the Sevillians Antonio Cruz and Antonio Ortiz (Madrid, class of 1971, 1974; Ortiz apprenticed in Moneo's Madrid studio). Their apartment building in Sevilla's Calle de Doña María Coronel (1974–6) was again noted for its brick fabric, balcony windows and a kidney-shaped central patio.

Among the older figures drawn into the movement, Oiza's feisty variations on postmodern themes stand out in this final phase of his career. The Palacio de Festivales in Santander, a concert hall overlooking the bay (1984–90), with its colourful striped masonry and toy-like towers, mixes formal ideas from Stirling, Mario Botta and Rossi. His M-30 public housing in Madrid (1986–90) coils around an open-ended central space, with its back to the nearby highway. The facades around the central space are painted with colourful Euclidian forms, mixing late Le Corbusier and Venturian Pop.

Generic versions of a rationalist postmodernism continued to appear into the 1990s, especially in isolated provinces, despite the movement's evident signs of fatigue. Rossi, writing for his joint exhibition with 2C in 1977, had approvingly declared: 'We tend towards a popular architecture, comprehensible to the masses.'[12] But this simplicity quickly made the model tedious, and it became a mindless bureaucratic instrument in the hands of unambitious architects and municipal technicians.

The Persistence of Modernism

This panorama of Spanish architecture during the early years of democracy is completed by the surprising resilience, and even resurgence, of various modernist options. These ranged from a rather formalist functionalism inspired by early modern models – dedicated as much to rejecting Organicism as to ignoring postmodernism – to the first manifestations of a more poetic minimalism, as well as hybrids of modern and postmodern ideas that ultimately help to consolidate the position established by Moneo. Almost all of these approaches, whether conservative or radical, were nevertheless influenced by postmodern values. The most obvious was that of contextual design, with all its implications for urbanism and history. More subtly, many architects found a reflection of the expressive or poetic aura of postmodern type forms and semiotics – as seen in Aldo Rossi's hypnotic drawings – in the canonical forms of modernism itself. The taut, enigmatic work of Alejandro de la Sota proved to be a touchstone for this renewed poetic sensibility. In particular, references to the sculptural cascade of balconies of his Civil Government Building in Tarragona became a leitmotif in works of these years and later.

We have seen how De la Sota had been left on the sidelines by the Organicist moment in the 1960s. He was further marginalized in 1971, when he left his teaching post at the Madrid School of Architecture after losing his bid for a *cátedra* (full professorship) in the same competition for three coveted posts that sent Rafael Moneo to Barcelona. Nevertheless, De la Sota attracted a loyal cadre of former students, apprentices and admirers who formed the core of his modernist resistance.

Of this group, mention should be made of Víctor López Cotelo and Carlos Puente (Madrid, class of 1969, 1974), whose early work together includes the sprawling functionalist Pharmacy School at the new campus of the University of Alcalá de Henares (1979–85), and an elemental, vernacularly inspired town hall for the village of Valdelaguna, outside Madrid (1983–6).

Manuel Gallego (Madrid, class of 1963) developed this approach further with a strong regional focus. He worked in De la Sota's studio before returning to his native Galicia in 1967. His designs are as regionalist in their own terms as those of César Portela, but he arrives at this sense of place by fine-tuning modernist concepts of space, light, formal simplicity and abstraction in order to incorporate the new issues of context, history, local traditions, landscape and climate. His early houses are simple volumes set within a larger zone of domesticated outdoor space, integrated in the landscape with extended stone walls, terraces and *parras* (climbing grape arbours), as in his own beach house in Corrubedo (1969–70). His public buildings were among the first to integrate modern designs into historic urban settings, as in the Museum of Sacred Art for the Colegiata of Santa María in A Coruña (1982–5), where the narrow facade is divided into well-proportioned stucco panels framed in granite trim, using local materials with a spare, almost Japanese elegance. In A Coruña's Museum of Fine Arts (1988–95), he unapologetically inserted modern elements in the remains of a partially demolished Baroque convent. But the quiet simplicity of these interventions cedes protagonism to the dynamic spatial development of the interiors. The main stair rises through a succession of shifting spatial voids towards the natural light that descends from rooftop skylights. As it rises, the stair loses density,

Manuel Gallego, Museum of Fine Arts, A Coruña, 1988–95. Detail of main stair and lobby.

shifting from a sculptural block of granite on the ground floor to bridge-like spans of wood and steel.

The work of Juan Navarro Baldeweg (Madrid, class of 1967), another alumnus of De la Sota's studio, shows a similar sensitivity to the experiential qualities of architecture. His first built project was the Casa de la Lluvia (House of Rain, 1977–82), a weekend retreat for his brother outside their hometown of Santander, in northern Spain. Navarro compared the work to a musical instrument; it was designed to transmit the sensory ambience of the rainy locale, cueing to the sound of rain on the low zinc roof or, like Chillida's *Peine del Viento*, framing the line of the horizon of the distant sea.[13] As in the work of Gallego, his muted Sotian forms cede protagonism to the intensity of awareness he seeks to elicit in the visitor.

In his following public works, Navarro used more traditional techniques of massing to explore these themes. He became particularly obsessed with the formal conceit of a suspended interior dome entirely without visible supports and isolated from surrounding walls. In subverting this traditional form in such a contemporary manner, he sought to provoke a visceral sense of the presence of gravitational force through the illusion of its absence, as he explained in a 1988 interview.[14] The figure appears in three built works: the restoration of a historic watermill on the Segura river in Murcia (1983–8); inside the Asplund-esque drum of the public library in Madrid's Puerta de Toledo (1982–92); and over the main auditorium of the Congress Centre in Salamanca (1985–92). In this last version, the stepped dome hovers over the great square hall like a sheltering canopy. The almost classical masonry weight of the buildings that accommodate these cupolas help to integrate them in their historic settings. In Salamanca, the square volume, dressed in the warm local sandstone, seeks to join its backdrop of Baroque university cloisters and church towers as a contemporary equal.

The most extreme minimalist of De la Sota's students in Madrid is Alberto Campo Baeza (class of 1971), an influential teacher for generations, although he has stood apart from his colleagues at the school for his religious convictions and ties to the Church. His work aspires to an austere, Euclidian abstraction that is closer to the absolute, spiritual values of Neoplatonic idealism than to the relativism of his contextualizing peers. In a 1992 manifesto, he proclaimed: 'I propose an ESSENTIAL Architecture, born of an IDEA, brought into existence by LIGHT and translated into an ESSENTIAL SPACE.'[15]

After experimenting with the crisply cut white volumes of the New York Five and the ordered geometric massing of the Tendenza in a number of public schools in the 1980s, Campo Baeza brought these traits together in the more personal work that followed, where De la Sota's influence became more apparent. The Casa Turégano in Pozuelo de Alarcón, Madrid (1985–8), is organized like the early houses of Richard Meier, with trays of secondary spaces (bedrooms, kitchen, baths and stairs) stacked at the back, overlooking a multi-level living area. This public zone is a three-level cascade of spaces overlooking one another, and large square windows follow this diagonal section around the volume in staggered patterns that recall De la Sota in Tarragona.

Campo's international reputation dates to the more regionally inflected minimalism of the Casa Gaspar in Zahora, Cádiz (1990–92). In response to the strong light and austere but fertile landscape of this coastal province of Andalucía, he further reduced his forms, creating a Miseian courthouse of whitewashed walls set in a field, with a spare living pavilion dividing two walled patios, each arrayed around a pair of lemon trees. The frameless glazed openings are positioned at the corners of the patios, transforming the overlapping criss-cross of walls around them into a brief Neoplasticist ballet.

The most radical defence of a renewed modern practice, crucially conditioned by a postmodern critical perspective, appeared in the work of the Barcelona-based Albert Viaplana and Helio Piñón (both Barcelona, class of 1966; Viaplana was born in 1933, Piñón in 1942). The two startled the profession with a series of unrealized competition designs: austere, elementary volumes, empty of all formal or historic memory and static in structure and fenestration. They were animated, if at all, by movement in section, as in the stepped volume of their competition design for the Valencia College of Architects (1977), where floors overlook one another in staggered set-backs. This rather Organicist strategy, playing against the tight, regular structure, creates a sense of tension that – as with Campo Baeza's Casa Turégano – has its ultimate source in De la Sota's Tarragona project.

The hard-line, underfed drawings for these proposals added to their minimalist allure, as did the lapidary, oracular laments of their project briefs, written by Viaplana. Of the Valencia proposal, he wrote:

Albert Viaplana and Helio Piñón, College of Architects, Valencia, 1977. Competition project.

The zoning, the programme, the competition brief and the site and its surroundings confront us with a restricted role from which there appears, with no possibility of appeal, the building volume. And in this reduction, we find purity, exact, finished, impeccable, sterile. A world of light without a place from which to design. The objective form, the imposing presence of what is called for. The empty force of the desert. With a taste for the Baroque, which these absences indulge. An abstract volume, enclosed in itself, without internal contradictions, without any pretence to redeem the city that spawns it. A magnificent catastrophe.[16]

This talk of architecture without context, of working in the 'desert' of contemporary urban development, pushed to its logical breaking point the concept of contextual design as defined by Moneo's Bankinter, finished in the same year. 'What does contextual design become in the absence of context?' Viaplana implicitly asks. De la Sota reported facing much the same dilemma in his design for a classroom building for the University of Sevilla in 1972.[17] And so did Robert Venturi in 1968, with his competition project for an office building in Washington, DC.[18] The answers of all three were similar: the work becomes introspective and minimal on principle, creating its own context, as it were, out of the prerequisites of structure, zoning, programme and so on, and in the arbitrary play of internal self-reference. Venturi's project prepared the way for *Learning from Las Vegas* (1972), and its surrender to the realities of the contemporary post-urban landscape. But Viaplana and Piñón contemplated this surrender with none of the transgressive glee and cool Pop hauteur of Venturi and Scott-Brown, a distinction that made all the difference for the poetic force of their succeeding work. Valencia and their other early competition projects thus set the stage for a radical renewal of modernism, now contextually inscribed within a fallen post-utopian world.

The Postmodern City

Many of the most profound transformations to come out of the ideas of Aldo Rossi and the Tendenza are found in the urban policies and projects initiated in the 1980s by new left-wing democratic municipalities. The research, theories and design proposals of the Tendenza were primarily focused on the city. Its protagonists advocated the idea that architects should take the lead in urban design, declaring the autonomy of architecture as a discipline against the primacy in post-war planning of the social sciences; legal and technical norms with generalizing, non-specific application; and functionalist concepts of zoning, circulation and massing. In place of these supposedly scientific methods, the Tendenza proposed to study the city in terms of its physical morphology, returning to historic urban fabrics to analyse their constituent parts, their public spaces, blocks and building types. These studies contributed to the re-evaluation of historic city centres, and their urban design proposals helped to establish the traditional urban forms and types of the eighteenth and nineteenth centuries as models for new urban development.[19]

These ideas were promoted in Spain during the 1970s chiefly by the Grupo 2C and their magazine, and the Barcelona Laboratory of Urbanism (LUB), established in 1968 at the school of architecture by the urban planner

Manuel and Ignacio de las Casas, Palomeras housing, Madrid, 1978–83.

Manuel de Solà-Morales. The LUB, in its studies and teaching, delved into the Tendenza's morphological approach, or what Solà-Morales liked to call an 'urbane urbanism'. For its part, the Grupo 2C organized a series of international seminars on urban design in three cities: in Santiago de Compostela, 1976, directed by Aldo Rossi; in Sevilla in 1978; and in Barcelona in 1980. All three cities would become early protagonists in morphological planning initiatives.

Before the new municipal governments were established, the first ventures in morphological urbanism took place in public housing, which was reconsidered as building types for urban form. One example, designed by the brothers Manuel and Ignacio de las Casas (Madrid, class of 1964, 1971), is the Cabeza del Moro complex in Talavera de la Reina (1977–84), which partially took the form of a dense, seven-storey *plaza mayor* realized in red brick. The brothers went on to design a group of several large housing blocks in Palomeras, Madrid (1978–83), where apartments are accessed along open galleries overlooking a long central atrium, modelled on Madrid's popular *corralas* of the eighteenth and nineteenth centuries. Though here colossal in scale, the atriums retain a sense of community and domesticity.

Located in Vallecas, on Madrid's southeastern periphery, the project was part of an emergency housing initiative created by a special act of Congress before Madrid's local government had been formed. The measure responded to the orchestrated protests of residential associations in the nearby shanty town of Palomeras, who were organized by young leftist lawyers, architects and other activists. The right to 'dignified and adequate housing' had just been recognized by the new Constitution of 1978, mandating public authorities 'to regulate land use . . . so as to prevent speculation'.[20]

The neighbourhood associations of Palomeras were part of a national movement organized by Communists and other leftist parties to mobilize potential voters. The groups would have a significant impact on the urban policies of Madrid, Barcelona and other cities. They also introduced many young architects into political action, and to the urban problems created by unfettered speculative growth under Franco. Several of these figures went on to direct urban policy in major cities, notably Eduardo Mangada in Madrid and the architectural historian Víctor Pérez Escolano in Sevilla. Other architects entering socialist politics at this time included Oriol Bohigas, the first delegate of urbanism on the Barcelona City Council, and Xerardo Estévez, elected mayor of Santiago de Compostela. All introduced sweeping changes in urban policy. Their models for action came from the Tendenza and the historic preservation policies of the pioneering 1965 Plan for Bologna, Italy, orchestrated by its Communist city council.

Their first measures were to protect historic urban cores from redevelopment and begin their restoration. Sevilla under Pérez Escolano immediately suspended all existing building permits and planning legislation before passing new rules and cataloguing the historic building stock for protection. Similarly, Mangada's team in Madrid prepared a Special Plan, passed in 1980, that gave protection to 8,000 buildings classified by grades of preservation, from 'integral' to 'structural' and 'contextual'. Mangada also launched a programme to subsidize rehabilitations, carrying out several pilot projects in the popular neighbourhoods of Lavapiés and the Rastro.

In historic cities that became the capitals of new autonomous regions, the regional governments joined municipalities in recovering palaces, religious buildings and the like for representational and administrative uses. In Sevilla, for example, among other works, the Junta of Andalucía, with the architect Jaime Montaner in charge of public works, restored the historic sixteenth-century Hospital de las Cinco Llagas as the new seat of its parliament (1986–92) and installed the presidential offices in the Baroque Palace of San Telmo, restored by the local architect Guillermo Vázquez Consuegra (first phase 1989–92).

Other municipal urban programmes took on large swathes of historic districts for renewal, as in Madrid's Special Plan for the Area of San Francisco el Grande, where a boulevard had been crudely cut through the neighbourhood during the dictatorship. In 1982, Juan Navarro Baldeweg won the city's competition for the site with a proposal that approached the urban problem essentially as an architectural design, devising specific formal solutions for every condition along the boulevard's path. Among the resulting projects for public housing and services, he reserved for himself the library and social services buildings that flank the historic gateway of the Puerta de Toledo. Here, his melding of architecture and urban design is found at its most sophisticated, brilliantly handling the site's complex differences in scale, grade and figure–ground configuration.

Another major intervention in Madrid was organized in collaboration with the central government: Operation Atocha recovered the degraded environs of the Atocha train station, at the southern end of the Paseo del Prado. The city demolished a lugubrious highway flyover in front of the station, a pioneering move to recover public spaces from the former prioritization of high-speed traffic. The state converted the abandoned eighteenth-century San Carlos Hospital, a massive building situated beside the flyover, into the Reina Sofía Museum (1980–86; second phase 1988–92).

These initiatives were coordinated with the state's expansion of the train station itself, including facilities for the new high-speed trains to Sevilla, part of preparations for the 1992 Universal Exposition. In 1984, Rafael

Juan Navarro
Baldeweg, Puerta de
Toledo Library, Madrid,
1982–92.

Moneo won a closely watched competition for the work. His design mixes traditional building type forms with flowing, modern spaces, using the difference in grade between the railway yards and the surrounding streets to sort pedestrian and vehicular traffic flows onto different levels. He converted Alberto de Palacio's historic train shed into a botanical greenhouse and lobby, situating the commuter and high-speed train stations behind it. A grand shed of Corten steel and glass supported by a field of concrete columns spans the high-speed train platforms. Like its Organicist precedents, the hypostyle structure evokes both Islamic types and Wright's Johnson Wax Building. Other place-marking elements include a clocktower and an entry rotunda for the commuter station, both finished in Moneo's

Rafael Moneo, Atocha train station, Madrid, 1984–92.

characteristic pressed brick. As seen from the Paseo del Prado, the rotunda stands out against the sky, a lone symbol of Neoclassical urbanity amid the traffic swirling around it.

The New Ensanches

The new city planners implemented the ideas of the Tendenza at a large scale in new planned urban developments. With surprising consistency, these projects were based on Spain's nineteenth-century *ensanches* with regular gridded streets and blocks. Their aim was to bring the urbanity of the traditional city to peripheral residential developments, although this goal proved elusive. Their principal point of reference was Cerdà's Eixample, which was a central focus of the urban studies of the Grupo 2c and Solà-Morales's Laboratory of Urbanism. Even Aldo Rossi gave it a prominent place in *The Architecture of the City*, where he judged it superior even to Haussmann's Paris.[21] Simplified versions of Cerdà's plan, often with modestly chamfered corners and other formal eccentricities – diagonal streets, circles, plazas, crescents – became the standard formula for new urban layouts in the 1980s and the decades to follow.

These new ensanches resurrected a classic early modern housing type, the perimeter block, a doughnut-shaped, full-block structure that established a regular street wall on its perimeter and enclosed a semi-public central court, generally accessible only to residents. Apartments were organized as in the functionalist era, with through-block units distributed around vertical circulation cores.

The first new ensanche to be built was Pino Montano, located in one of Sevilla's poorest outlying suburbs. In 1979, the year he took office, Pérez Escolano cancelled an existing plan for the site and turned the design over to the architects Cruz and Ortiz. Their scheme mixes groups of square and

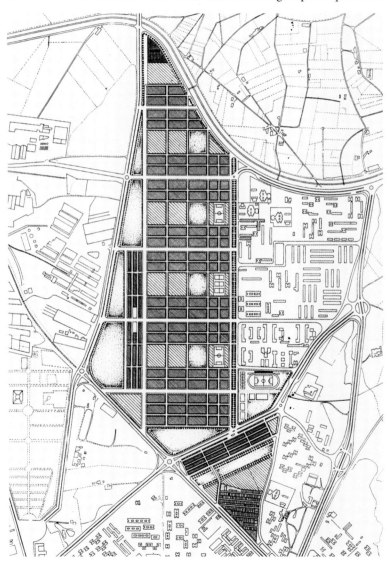

Antonio Cruz and Antonio Ortiz, Pino Montano, Sevilla, 1981–4. Master plan.

elongated residential blocks with wide, open bands where public services are located, creating a hybrid of open planning and the new urbanism. In the residential sections, the perimeter block type made one of its first appearances.

The model of the ensanche was consolidated in Madrid Sur (1985–94), an area situated on the site of the original Palomeras shanty town, near the Pozo del Tío Raimundo. The development comprised 7,000 units of subsidized housing and was built in a single campaign. Forty per cent of the buildings were developed by owners' cooperatives organized by the major trade unions in an attempt to replace speculative development with collective effort. The urban design, with a grid of square blocks overlaid

Antonio Vázquez de Castro, Madrid Sur, 1985–94. Master plan.

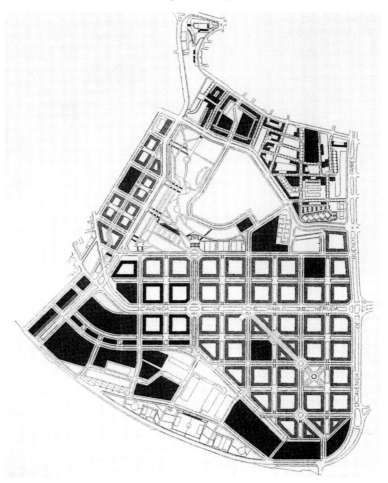

with some variations, is the work of Antonio Vázquez de Castro, one of the authors of Caño Roto three decades earlier. His design specified many formal characteristics of the buildings, including uniform heights and brick finishes, giving the project a coherence despite the varying quality of the buildings themselves.

Reflecting the impish populism of the times, the streets were named after classic films – Cleopatra, Romeo and Juliet, the African Queen. The project appeared during the height of La Movida, Madrid's post-Franco reply to Barcelona's Gauche Divine, a camp movement of libidinous punk transgression, expressed in pop music, comics and other arts. Its best-known figure is the director Pedro Almodóvar, whose breakout film, *Women on the Verge of a Nervous Breakdown*, was released in 1988.

In Pino Montano, Madrid Sur and their successors, the weaknesses of the model soon became apparent. Their streets lacked the urbane liveliness of the nineteenth-century ensanches because they imitated them only in form, while remaining essentially suburban and peripheral in character, as could hardly have been otherwise. The new developments were monolithically zoned for residential use. Commercial spaces were segregated off-site in conventional shopping centres and office parks, with the exception of a few storefronts on principal streets. The perimeter-block type further deadened streets, as it concentrated social life in the central, semi-private court at the expense of the neighbourhood. Secondary streets became residual spaces and were often pedestrianized. Pino Montero and Madrid Sur experienced a high rate of crime soon after they were completed. From a present-day perspective, it is hard to see them as a great improvement over the gardens and terraces of Caño Roto, or the Organicist Ciudad de los Poetas of the 1960s.

Barcelona's Parks and Plazas

Despite the interest of these urban initiatives in Sevilla and Madrid, it was the audacity, sweep and innovative ideas of Barcelona's urban projects that captured the world's attention, as indeed they were designed to do. Directed chiefly by Oriol Bohigas, and linked from the beginning with the ambition to host the 1992 Summer Olympics, the city's programme fell into two initial phases, the Parks and Plazas projects (1980–88) and the preparations for the Olympics themselves (1984–92). The first phase, comprising 145 projects scattered across the city, turned the urban recovery policies of Madrid and Sevilla inside out, focusing not on the preservation of historic buildings and neighbourhoods but on improving public spaces, both within the city centre and in its working-class suburbs. This apparent preoccupation with questions of image rather than substance was intended 'to restore the lost sense of dignity to the urban landscape', as Pasqual Maragall, who succeeded Narcís Serra as mayor in 1982, grandly put it. He explained that the programme was conceived as a response to the 'high expectations' and 'scepticism' created by the victory of a socialist city council in 1979. Working with scant resources and time, the programme offered tangible signs of regeneration before more far-reaching plans could be marshalled into place.[22]

Bohigas presented the Parks and Plazas programme as a radical rejection of conventional planning. 'It is essential to abandon abstract planning based on idealized models that ignore the reality of the urban scene,' he wrote. The 'substitution of the project for the plan' became a reductive – albeit effective – motto for this philosophy, in which 'the project' was a concrete architectural design solution for a particular urban problem.[23]

The projects were designed by architects rather than planning technicians. They brought together previously uncoordinated city services such as lighting, street furniture, landscaping and paving, in unified original works that extended the elegant, well-crafted modernism of Barcelona's design tradition to the street. Many included striking designs for custom lighting masts, benches and the like. In older neighbourhoods, vehicular traffic and surface parking were ejected in favour of pedestrian uses. Asphalt, concrete and bare earthen surfaces were replaced with fine-cut stone. Many also harboured underground parking and, lacking vegetation, became known as 'hard plazas' – a term often used critically. Notable examples include a network of ten small plazas in the barrio of Gràcia, north of the Eixample, by the architects Jaume Bach and Gabriel Mora, or the rehabilitation of the nineteenth century Plaça Reial in the Gothic Quarter by Federico Correa and Alfons Milà.

In a declaration of principle and faith in the programme, Bohigas moved his firm's offices and his own home to the Plaça Reial, establishing an outpost of respectability in the heart of the city's seedy medieval core. The move reflected a basic aim of these cosmetic interventions. Unlike Madrid, it was not considered sufficient to simply improve housing conditions for poor residents. Mayor Maragall explained, 'You have to convince people that they have a stake in their neighbourhood, and I mean middle-class people. You need a minimum critical mass to create that spontaneous expansion of wealth necessary for a certain level of vitality.'[24] This defence of gentrification highlights the socialists' evolution through the 1980s away from their working-class bases and Marxist ideology.

While more modest projects such as these were completed by 1983, Bohigas's team also planned long-term structural improvements for the city centre. The Moll de la Fusta, designed by Manuel de Solà-Morales, was the first element in a chain of operations designed to open the

Óscar Tusquets and Lluís Clotet, 'From the Liceu to the Seminary', El Raval, Barcelona, 1980. Master plan.

Gothic Quarter to the harbour. Future plans included a new commercial port in the Zona Franca, southwest of the city, and the redevelopment of the old port for recreational and urban uses. As a starter, Solà-Morales decked over a highway along the water, part of a new ring road, to create a direct visual and physical connection between the city and the docks.

Elsewhere, Lluís Clotet and Óscar Tusquets were commissioned to develop a preliminary plan for rehabilitating one of the city's most neglected districts, a section of El Raval west of the Ramblas. Their study, titled 'From the Liceu to the Seminary', sought to end the district's isolation, creating points of attraction and organizing vehicular and pedestrian circulation through its narrow streets. They proposed consolidating a new central plaza, and the reuse of several obsolete religious buildings for new cultural facilities. The scheme laid the groundwork for the creation, after the Olympics, of the Centre for Contemporary Culture of Barcelona (CCCB), installed in an eighteenth-century charity hospital by Viaplana and Piñón, and Richard Meier's Barcelona Museum of Contemporary Art (MACBA), prominently sited on the new plaza.

The Parks and Plazas programme also created new public spaces in outlying districts. Works of contemporary art were central elements in these designs, following an international trend in site-specific and public art. Among others, the city commissioned works from Richard Serra, Roy Lichtenstein, Claes Oldenburg and Ellsworth Kelly, as well as local artists including Antoni Tàpies, Joan Brossa and Susana Solano. Bohigas's aim with these collaborations was, he wrote, 'to "monumentalize" these districts . . . to create a central focus, giving them significant popular value. They should be given the urban style they have never had.'[25] The most spectacular of these collaborations is found at the Creueta del Coll Park, completed in 1987, where Bohigas's partners Josep Martorell and David Mackay converted an abandoned quarry into a lush landscape with multiple recreational and festive uses. Suspended over a pool at the base of the quarry's steep and jagged walls is *Elogio del agua* (Homage to Water), a 50-ton, claw-shaped sculpture by Eduardo Chillida held in place by four long, tensed cables anchored into the rock on either side.

Richard Serra's work for the Plaça de la Palmera (1988), built on the site of a demolished factory, was inspired by his site-specific installation *Tilted Arc* (1981) in New York, and was nearly as controversial (the New York work was removed after a divisive court battle in 1989). In Barcelona, working with municipal architects, he cut the park in two with a high, curving wall, more than 100 metres (328 ft) in length, broken into two overlapping sections to create a passage. It was built of thin stuccoed masonry to lower costs and lack the tense energy of *Tilted Arc*'s raw plated steel. Neighbourhood associations had lobbied for a park on the site, as well as a primary school and seniors' centre that were built in later years, but they didn't understand 'The Wall'. Shortly after its completion, a late-night raiding party attempted to demolish it before police intervened. Over time, however, the work has won a grudging acceptance owing to its international recognition.[26]

Other former industrial sites were converted into parks, often incorporating elements of the demolished factories, such as gateways and chimneys. Beside the Sants train station, a recreational waterpark,

Josep Martorell and David Mackay, La Creueta del Coll Park, Barcelona, 1987; Eduardo Chillida, *Elogio del agua* (Homage to Water), 1987. Concrete with iron filaments and red aggregate, steel cables.

Elías Torres and José A. Martínez-Lapeña, Lampeluna street light, 1986. Seen here on the Paseo de las Delicias, Sevilla.

designed by Luis Peña Ganchegui with uncharacteristically postmodern elements, replaced the historic Espanya Industrial textile mills, closed in 1969. The nearby municipal slaughterhouses, occupying four blocks of the Eixample, gave way to a city park presided over by a totem-like statue by Joan Miró. And in Sant Andreu, the young architects Enric Batlle and Joan Roig designed lush gardens along an artificial canal on the grounds of the former Pegaso truck factory.

The city made new public spaces from other raw sources. Along the Via Julia in working-class Nou Barris, municipal architects resolved a sharp, unplanned change in grade with parallel roadways on different levels, and a long central promenade with planted slopes between them. In upper-class Sarrià, Elías Torres and José A. Martínez-Lapeña (both Barcelona, class of 1968) converted a formerly private estate into the public gardens of the Villa Cecilia. Their 'Lampeluna' light standards for the project went into general production and can now be found in many public spaces in Spain.

This period is best remembered for two very different projects, however: the reconstruction of Mies van der Rohe's German Pavilion of 1929, replicated on its original site on Montjuïc (1983–6); and Viaplana and Piñón's seminal plaza at the Sants train station (1981–3). The pavilion had long been a pet project for Bohigas – he had first broached the subject in a letter to Mies in 1957, aged 32, with the backing of the Grup R. The replication was a forensic operation, since original documents were scarce and differed from the built work seen in period photographs. The process of piecing together the design and converting it into a permanent building was carried out by the historian and critic Ignasi de Solà-Morales (Manuel's brother) and the architects Cristian Cirici and Fernando Ramos.

Few public projects in these years made reference to the political values of Catalan nationalism or Republicanism that the dictatorship had suppressed. In lieu of such claims, the impulse to resurrect the tantalizing ghost of Mies's pavilion, which even Sert and his GATEPAC colleagues had managed to miss or ignore in its time, forms part of the city's decades-long effort to claim its place in the international vanguard of modernism, as seen in the opening of Barcelona's Picasso Museum in 1963, created by private collectors and the city over the objections of the central government, and Sert's Miró Foundation of 1974. The sense of redress implicit in this aspiration to modernity pervades Bohigas's urbanism in general, if in more subtle ways, and a public settling of accounts with the regime in these terms was far less divisive than more political issues in the early years of the democracy.

Viaplana and Piñón's plaza at the Sants train station resembled nothing that had come before. The commission pushed the 'Architecture Degree Zero' approach of their provocative competition projects of the 1970s towards its vanishing point. They were asked to design a vast plaza, surrounded by wide streets, in an area on the western edge of the Eixample developed in the 1960s and '70s with little character or cohesion. The plaza was sited on the deck covering the railway tracks in front of the station, a surface that could support little more than a layer of paving, and of course no trees.

Instead of seeking to disguise or overcome these limitations, they characteristically played into them. Using light concrete fill, they subtly moulded and sculpted the continuous stone paving in relief and furnished it with a handful of minimalist elements, suggesting an artificial landscape as desolate as a Beckett stage set. The sparse furnishings and open metal structures promote an awareness of scale, spatial depth and movement. A skeletal pergola, undulating in a single eccentric wave over its 90-metre (295 ft) length, traverses the expanse, with the 'Baldacchino', as they called it in an early text – an open pavilion 15 metres (50 ft) high – situated off to one side.[27] Details such as eccentric bench tables, and the striking project drawings in which the plan, sections and elevations are superimposed, point to the future work of Enric Miralles (Barcelona, class of 1978), the most prodigiously talented architect of his generation. Miralles had apprenticed with Viaplana and Piñón since his student days and was given credit as a collaborator on the plaza. How much the design owes to his influence is a subject of dispute, but it is tempting to see his exuberance pushing against the melancholy rectitude of his professors to produce the project's exquisite formal tension.

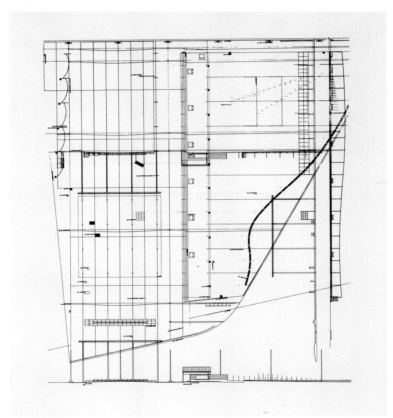

Albert Viaplana and Helio Piñón, plan of Sants Plaza, Barcelona, 1981–3.

Albert Viaplana and Helio Piñón, Sants Plaza, Barcelona, 1981–3.

Though misunderstood and criticized for its harshness, Sants was the most significant work to come out of the Parks and Plazas programme. But it was also antithetical to the premises of Bohigas's humanist urbanism. The design offered a nihilist critique of the limits of those premises under the conditions of contemporary urban development. If Moneo's similarly situated rotunda at the Atocha station in Madrid, opened almost a decade later, proposed a sophisticated reimagining of the Neoclassical amid this landscape, the sun-scorched skeleton of the Baldacchino at Sants dispensed with such illusions.

Olympic Barcelona

Already in 1979, the Barcelona mayor Narcís Serra was manoeuvring to claim the 1992 Olympics, with the help of Juan Antonio Samaranch, the local businessman who was president of the International Olympic Committee. The games would coincide with the five-hundredth anniversary

254

of Columbus' first voyage. Bohigas quickly understood that, like the expositions of 1888 and 1929, 'the Olympic Games could be the instrument for major urban transformations.'[28] The chance to oversee this transformation was the main reason he agreed to direct urban policy in Serra's government.

The city's bid for the games was accepted in 1986, but planning was well advanced in 1984, when Bohigas left the city council with a choice commission in his pocket, the master plan for the Olympic Village, which he developed with his firm MBM (Martorell, Bohigas and Mackay). His role in the city government was taken by his lieutenant and former employee at MBM, the architect Josep A. Acebillo, who became the tsar of Barcelona urban policy for the next dozen years.

For these strategists, many interlocking ambitions came together around the Olympic project. First and foremost, it was an enormous, international public-relations campaign on behalf of the city, with benefits for the Catalan region and the country as a whole. Second, it was to be a launch pad for economic regeneration and the conversion from a declining industrial base to a diversified service economy. Third, the capital investments required for the games would be channelled into long-term benefits, allowing Barcelona to tackle projects, principally the Olympic Village and a new ring road, then otherwise unfeasible, which would fundamentally change the city's structure and development.

The challenge was exhilarating. Public authorities were required to assume extraordinary powers, as well as extraordinary risks in terms of financing and projected returns. But they were also required to take on a daunting programme of work under the pressure of a looming fixed deadline, with no possibility of postponement or appeal; when that time came, they would submit themselves to the judgement of the world.

As a promotional event, the Olympics represented the presentation on the world stage of a new society, democratic, modern and ambitious, as well as youthful and chic, with its Mediterranean culture and spirit proudly on display. High design was everywhere, from the city's architecture and urbanism to the uniforms of Olympic volunteers. Varieties of original local cultural expression ranged from Cobi, the playful Cubist Olympic mascot created by the graphic designer Javier Mariscal, to the spectacular shows for the opening and closing ceremonies, other-worldly fantasies by the local theatrical companies La Fura dels Baus and Els Comedians that evoked mythic themes of Catalan identity rarely seen since the days of Gaudí and the Noucentistes. The event triggered a cataclysm of popular emotion and regionalist fervour, as registered in Freddie Mercury's apotheotic anthem 'Barcelona', commissioned by the city, which he recorded with the local opera star Montserrat Caballé for the event.

As an instrument of structural transformation, the Olympic Village opened the city to its seafront and changed the course of its future growth. Located on the Mediterranean coast northeast of the old city, it was the first step of a concerted municipal effort to redirect development to the industrial and working-class district of Poblenou. Extensive site preparations included clearing a wide swathe of historic industrial buildings, which were razed without contemplation. In their place rose a new residential neighbourhood, with a line of beach and parkland along the waterfront, and an Olympic marina.

The village was one of four principal areas hosting Olympic events, distributed in four quadrants of the city and linked by the new circumferential highway. The Olympic Ring, the main venue, was located on Montjuïc, near the site of the 1929 Exposition, and was organized around an existing Olympic Stadium built in 1936. Two secondary zones gathered other venues: the Diagonal area, to the west, which used existing facilities such as the Camp Nou football stadium; and Vall d'Hebron, to the north and east in the district of Horta, which was a newly developed park-like setting laid out in a master plan by the architect Eduard Bru. The ring road bears mention as another application of the city's project-oriented approach to planning, with city architects working together with engineers. On its inland leg, the Ronda de Dalt, large areas of the trench-cut roadway were covered to reconnect neighbourhoods, and the new spaces were dedicated to public services, plazas and vegetation. On its coastal run, the Ronda Litoral, the highway was planned together with a new coastal park and restored beaches. The road is sunken through the park to mitigate its impact, while landscape architects designed its scenic unfolding from the viewpoint of vehicular-borne users.

The Architecture of the Games

With few exceptions, the architecture of these venues did not rise to expectations. Some of the reasons for this can be seen in the competition for the Olympic Ring on Montjuïc. Perhaps the most interesting submission came from Arata Isozaki, who proposed to raise two parabolic arches over the existing stadium, which would support a curving canopy above the grandstands. His covered arena sported an undulating roof reminiscent of a flying carpet. But the project was cut up and distributed to several of the competitors, which assured, for example, the participation of local firms. The unremarkable general plan, with buildings grouped around an esplanade, was designed by Federico Correa and his team. Bohigas's friend Vittorio Gregotti was awarded the enlargement of the stadium, and Isozaki built the Palau Sant Jordi arena. While still the best work of the complex,

Arata Isozaki, Palau
Sant Jordi sports arena,
Barcelona, 1992. Part
of the Olympic Ring
complex on Montjuïc.

Esteve Bonell and
Francesc Rius,
Velòdrom d'Horta,
Vall d'Hebron,
Barcelona, 1984.

with its lopsided dome seeded with skylights, it is far more conventional than his initial proposal. But of greater impact was a late addition: the telecommunications tower by Santiago Calatrava. The Valencian architect and engineer based in Switzerland was already well into his meteoric rise (Architecture, ETSAV, Valencia, class of 1974; Civil Engineering, ETH Zurich, class of 1979). Original as it was, the work was essentially scaleless and bore no relation to its surroundings, but that hardly mattered for its popular appeal.

These results highlight how the desire to promote local figures came at a time when they were easily overshadowed by the media-savvy designs of emerging international stars, who understood the rising dominance of photogenic image over the actual spatial and sensorial experience of a work. It was also a time of transition: old arguments faltered, and new impulses at the local level were still in their tender-shoots stage of emergence.

Among the outstanding works for the games were the Velòdrom d'Horta in Vall d'Hebron (1984) and the basketball stadium in the working-class suburban municipality of Badalona (1991), both by Esteve Bonell and Francesc Rius (Barcelona, class of 1971, 1967). Both combine strong geometric figures and classical gravitas with a precise modern and minimal vocabulary. Cornice lines become thin horizontal planes that hover over walls of poured concrete or industrially processed stone. The result is a sense of restrained, monumental presence that orders the landscape or cityscape around it.

In the 'tender shoots' category, the most spectacular debut at the Olympics was the archery range at Vall d'Hebron by Enric Miralles and Carme Pinós, his first wife and partner (Barcelona, class of 1978, 1980). The two met at the Barcelona School, where Moneo was an influential teacher to both. Their competition-winning design transformed a modest commission for a pair of pavilions, little more than dressing rooms, into a radical formal manifesto (1989–91, partially demolished). Like the plaza at Sants, the design created an imaginative new world of forms. But its vision represented a repudiation of Viaplana and Piñón's dry minimalism, which Miralles and Pinós swept away in an energizing surfeit of creative inventiveness. The two pavilions were banked into the terrain overlooking the shooting range. In the surviving structure, a series of tilting and bent roof

Enric Miralles and Carme Pinós, Olympic archery range, Vall d'Hebron, Barcelona, 1989–91, partly demolished.

planes jostle together at different angles. Supported by angled columns, they project over a sequence of rhythmically angled and curving walls topped by clerestory windows. The interiors are further convulsed by the sinuously curving back wall and angled partitions. The raw finishes and earthy atmosphere recall the fresh, tactile Mediterraneanism of Sert, while the formal inventiveness and fusion into the landscape bring to mind Gaudí's Park Güell. But the fragmentation of the compositions into repetitive, varied plays of angled and curving elements in both vertical and horizontal planes create a music of their own, complex, dynamic and lyrical. The method could be likened to a hyper-agitation of the modular, cellular designs of Organicism, while anticipating the formal options opened by computer-aided design. These qualities extend to the calligraphic plans, which raise architectural draughtsmanship, on the eve of its disappearance, to the level of a new art form.

The Olympic Village

As a showcase for Barcelona architecture and urbanism, the Olympic Village was a success, despite certain quirks and weaknesses. With a structure based on Cerdà's 113 by 113 metre (370 ft) blocks, the new development reinterpreted the Eixample in contemporary terms, helping to maintain and renew its ineffably Barcelonan character.

Bohigas remained a modernist at heart, and for the village's master plan he and his team sought to fuse the best of the Tendenza and CIAM, combining defined blocks and urban spaces with modern standards of sunlight, ventilation, privacy and open space. Taking his cue from the Plan Macià, developed by Le Corbusier and GATEPAC for Barcelona during the Second Republic, he combined groups of three blocks into superblocks, though without entirely suppressing the intermediate streets. Lines of apartments one unit deep define the superblock's street walls, with interruptions to create what he called 'almost Corridor streets' and 'almost closed blocks'.[29] The landscaped interiors of the superblocks accommodate sections of rowhouses and small point towers, amenities such as playing courts and private gardens, and an underground shopping centre, which was built over a new water-treatment plant. This hybrid plan, more integrated than Cruz and Ortiz's Pino Montero in Sevilla, created strong urban facades facing the coastal park and along the parallel interior boulevard, and a more diffuse cross-grain between these axes.

The Olympic Port, with its large pier and recreational marina, links the district to the seafront. Here Bohigas planted two commercial towers, 154 metres (505 ft) tall, that create a maritime facade for the district and the city as a whole, scaled to its topographic setting between the Tibidabo

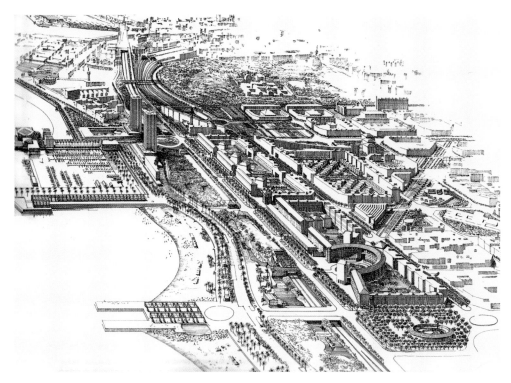

mountain and the sea. The gesture was an homage to the Plan Macià, which proposed a trio of towers overlooking Barcelona's Old Port.

Bohigas develop the master plan in three incremental stages as a way to bring the design-based approach of the Parks and Plazas programme into the planning process. MBM completed the basic outline of the plan in 1986. As site preparations progressed, teams of architects and technical specialists developed each of the four superblocks at a more detailed level under MBM's supervision, followed by the individual designs for buildings and open spaces by two dozen architecture firms. Bohigas defended this system as a way to 'compress in a short period the long process of constructing the city and assure that the new neighbourhood would be a diverse mix of different contributions'.[30] But Acebillo, overseeing the process for the city, fumed at its time-consuming complications.[31]

Built by a public-private holding company, the 2,000 units of housing were destined for the commercial market in order to finance the operation. Past winners of the local FAD architecture prize were invited to design the buildings. The prizes dated to 1958 and brought together three generations of Barcelona architects, including Antoni Bonet, Francesc Mitjans and Ricardo Bofill and his Taller de Arquitectura. Bohigas thought this selection method would contribute to the neighbourhood's variety and instant temporal depth, but even he admitted that many of the contributions were disappointing.[32]

A star line-up of projects stands along the promenade facing the seafront park. Two buildings – one by Óscar Tusquets with Carles Díaz, and another by Lluís Clotet with Ignasi Paricio – use the brick finishes mandated by the master plan to give their late examples of postmodernism a certain tectonic basis. They stand between a work by Correa and Milà and a more modernist block, in a creamy white and grey, by Bonell, Rius and Josep María Gil. A large semicircular crescent is cut out of the next superblock, together with a diagonally cut street. The red-brick buildings along the crescent and a taller, sculptural point tower in its middle were designed by Torres and Martínez-Lapeña. Their sliding exterior wood louvres, a reference to Coderch's early work, give these blocks a refreshing Mediterranean air. The ensemble shows the visual force of a strong figure–ground urbanism over the spatial dispersion of the other superblock interiors.

The restoration of beaches from La Barceloneta to the Olympic Village revived another GATEPAC project, the City of Repose, in its aim to open the seafront to the masses. But Barcelona is not a well-heeled resort town like Nice, and the location of these beaches near the heart of the city – rather than a distant zoned area, as GATEPAC proposed – produced civic conflicts. With the mass tourism of recent decades, beachgoers have had to be discouraged from wandering up the Ramblas in bathing suits, and late-night revellers from the crowded bars of the Olympic Port from invading the

Elías Torres and José A. Martínez-Lapeña, housing in the Olympic Village, Barcelona, 1991.

village's sleeping middle-class residential streets. Meanwhile, isolated from the coast by the waterfront park, the main promenade of the village has failed to attract the lively urban scene for which Bohigas had hoped. With this exception, the Olympic Village has thus been almost too successful, and a bit too innocent in its promotion of mass seaside recreation and amusement.

Dignifying the Urban Fabric

One of the most remarkable, if controversial, achievements of Barcelona's urban policy was to intervene in the architectural quality of private development. Evidently, the character of the city depended greatly on the individual decisions of private speculators. With its control of building licences and development plans, the city could exert considerable influence on these decisions, breaking with another taboo of a laissez-faire approach to the real-estate marketplace.

Throughout their tenure, Bohigas and Acebillo commanded wide leeway in the selection of architects for projects, and they sought to extend this control into the private sector. Following an initial open competition for the site of the former municipal slaughterhouses, Bohigas preferred to commission architects according to his own criteria. This control, Acebillo told the journalist Llàtzer Moix, was intended to maintain the efficacy and momentum of the urban makeover, which he argued could otherwise have become entangled in lengthy debates, controversies and procedures, as had proved to be the case with the competition. But Moix compared this method to 'certain forms of enlightened despotism', and it certainly opened the door to favouritism, bias and worse.[33]

When commercial development resumed with the preparations for the Olympic Games, the Department of Urbanism sought the same control in selecting architects for projects. As Moix delicately put it, 'with certain important speculative ventures, it became a common practice of the municipality to suggest to the builder in question the advisability of hiring this or that darling of the architectural coterie.'[34] While Moix does not identify specific examples, they can perhaps be inferred from some of the results. The partnership of Jordi Garcés and Enric Sòria, whom the city tapped to design a Special Urban Plan for the Carrer de Tarragona boulevard, also designed the plan's key development, the Hotel Plaça d'Espanya (1989–92). Viaplana and Piñón designed the Hilton Hotel on the upper Diagonal, an unlikely client for their brand of radical minimalism (1987–90). They massed the building in two simple parallel slabs dressed in white and black granite, like a Harlequin costume – a cipher that made no concessions to its sponsor. Bonell and Gil's Aparthotel Citadines introduced a refined, contextualizing modernism to the Ramblas (1988–94). Nearby, Torres and Martínez-Lapeña enlarged and refurbished the Corte Inglés department store on the Plaça de Catalunya, with a further addition by MBM (1990–94). One apparent exception to these direct commissions was the design for the L'illa Diagonal, a full-block, multi-use complex, won in a competition by Rafael Moneo and Manuel de Solà-Morales (1986–94). These are all decidedly modern buildings, handsomely finished in stone. They are models of civic dignity that set a new standard for future development, contributing to the renewal of Barcelona's ineffable urban character. Commercial building would remain under the influence of the city in coming years, as municipally sponsored urban plans continued to drive and direct its patterns of growth.

Expo '92 in Sevilla: Developing the South

Just as in 1929, when both Barcelona and Sevilla hosted international expositions, the two cities coincided again with major international events in 1992. An official committee organized to commemorate the five-hundredth anniversary of Columbus' voyage won approval in 1982 for a Universal Exposition in Sevilla, which had a strong historic connection with Columbus and his expedition. The socialist government in Madrid, elected in that same year, put the full force of the Spanish state behind the project. President Felipe González was a Sevilla native and had won control of the Socialist Party from this political base. Despite the challenge of organizing and financing two international events simultaneously, he saw the endeavour as a 'now or never' moment to attack the isolation and endemic poverty of the city and in Andalucía as a whole, and to integrate the region in the government's efforts to transform Spain into a modern European country.

While the exposition (popularly known as Expo '92) and its related projects produced several significant works of architecture and design, such aesthetic ambitions were not as integral to its global concept as they were to Bohigas's Barcelona. The same can be said of its intended impact on the city's urban morphology and the thoroughness of planning for a post-expo future. The difference is tied to the management of the event: unlike Barcelona, architects and urbanists were not involved at the highest levels of planning, which was directed by professional managers and civil engineers. Likewise, the municipal government of Sevilla was marginalized from the development process, which was run from Madrid, with a consequent loss of local focus. The Junta of Andalucía played a supporting role to Madrid, and its director of public works, the architect Jaime Montaner, commissioned a few of the more notable projects.

The most important long-term impact of the expo was on the city's infrastructures and its connections to the rest of the country. The expo was sited across the Guadalquivir river from the historic city, on the island of La Cartuja, an undeveloped tract that had been recovered from chronic flooding. The flood-control programme, begun during the dictatorship and completed in 1982, consolidated a new main channel for the river west of La Cartuja, and converted its historic course beside the city into a secondary channel. Another state-sponsored project diverted the main railway lines and station from the riverside to an underground inland route. For the first time since the nineteenth century, the river recovered its historic and morphological centrality in the city.

The inland rail route was part of the most transformative initiative launched for the expo: the construction of a high-speed train line between Sevilla and Madrid. It was the first leg of a nationwide system, the construction of which continues into the 2020s. The AVE (Alta Velocidad Española, or Spanish High Speed) trains cut travel time between the two cities from seven to three hours. Parallel with the AVE, Madrid replaced the two-lane road to Sevilla with a modern highway. The AVE put Spain on the same technological level as France or Germany and revolutionized travel. The new trains reinforced the growing status of historic city centres and prepared the way for cultural tourism. The project was one of the first in Spain to be partially financed by direct grants from the European Union's Regional Development Fund, a source of financing that would become an important spur for the outpouring of public investments in the following two decades.

Cruz and Ortiz's Santa Justa train station is the visible monument of this endeavour, together with its partner in Madrid, Moneo's Atocha. It stands in isolation in a newly developed area east of the historic city. In the vivid brick massing, the wide streamline curves of the main facade and its cantilevered entry canopy contrast with the tilted shed volume, the jutting roof of which follows the diagonal descent to the sunken train platforms. The composition resonates with memories of Art Deco and Expressionism, Dutch and Scandinavian modernism and the grand stations of the 1930s in Florence, Venice and Rome.

Santiago Calatrava's Alamillo Bridge (1987–92), which spans the old channel of the Guadalquivir at the northern end of La Cartuja, was part of another major infrastructural project: a new ring highway. One of his first bridges, it was commissioned by Jaime Montaner, and it is arguably the most well-known legacy of the expo. Cables supporting the road deck stretch diagonally from one side of a 140-metre (460 ft) pylon, like the strings of a harp, and the pylon tilts back in the opposite direction to counterbalance their eccentric load. Another bridge, La Barqueta, connects

Santiago Calatrava, detail of Alamillo Bridge, Sevilla, 1987–92.

the city more directly to the Expo '92 grounds. Designed by the engineer Juan José Arenas with Marcos J. Pantaleón, its graceful steel arch over the roadway already shows Calatrava's influence.

However, the Alamillo Bridge provoked as much opposition as it did admiration. Calatrava proposed for civil engineering something akin to that which the Tendenza proposed for urban planning: to take structural design beyond the calculus of technical efficiency and conceive it in expressive, formal terms. But these intentions defied the engineer's basic principle of structural economy and scandalized his professional colleagues. They found the bridge over-dimensioned, and the structural solution inefficient and visually misleading: the leaning pylon required massive foundations to do the real work of counterbalancing the eccentric loads. They pointed to the visual weakness of the excessively long upper cables, which reach to a tower that recedes away from them, and joked that it was the road deck that supported the pylon, which they considered entirely superfluous. 'The result is neither engineering nor sculpture. Personally, I find it repugnant,' sentenced the engineer Javier Manterola: 'When the balance between the engineer and the artist is out of kilter, the results can be kitsch, bad or pretentious.'[35]

The Expo Grounds

Like the Olympic Ring on Montjuïc, the design of the exposition site was marred by caution and compromise. The 1986 competition of ideas awarded a double first prize to two antithetical proposals. The first, by Emilio Ambasz, an Argentine architect based in New York and Bologna, was visionary and daring. It also presented certain practical problems, though Ambasz anticipated the scepticism it might provoke with a series of independent feasibility studies. In a pioneering example of bioclimatic design, he envisioned an artificial landscape of lagoons, hills, dense vegetation and rainbow-strewn banks of artificial fog, all designed to mitigate Sevilla's harsh summer heat. Floating pavilions would be erected in the lakes, and visitors would move among them on ferries and water taxis. With few roads and other infrastructures, development costs would be reduced, according to his calculations, and the site would revert to an Edenic garden after the fair. The second winning project offered little save its practicality, laying out avenues and building plots for pavilions in accordance with the competition bases. Surprisingly, the Madrid-based team behind this proposal was headed by a civil engineer, José Antonio Fernández Ordóñez, who was a cultivated and well-connected figure but old-school in his professional practice.

With this strategy of double winners, the exposition organizers took control of the planning process. Julio Cano Lasso, who won the competition for Spain's national pavilion, was asked to oversee a melding of the two proposals that left very little of Ambasz's vision intact. There was a single large lake ringed by pavilions on its shores, and avenues lined with others. The hard streets and full utilities assured an easy conversion of the site into the high-tech research park that was planned to follow the expo. Much of the rest of La Cartuja's 500 hectares (1,235 ac) was dedicated to park land. Responding to Ambasz's climate-control ideas, the organizers hired a local team of university professors to design an array of outdoor climate-control features, including water misting in fabric cooling chimneys, which reportedly lowered average temperatures on site by 3°C.

Among the individual pavilions of participating countries vying for attention, the list of memorable works was topped by Tadao Ando's monumental timber structure for Japan, inspired by traditional Japanese building craft. Of the official works, the Pavilion of Navigation and its observation tower established the national reputation of the local architect Guillermo Vázquez Consuegra (Sevilla, class of 1972). Located beside the river, it is composed of long repeated bays with ribbed vaults that recall Sevilla's medieval shipbuilding halls, the Atarazanas Reales, in a formal language that is unapologetically modern.

La Cartuja languished in the years following Expo '92. The technological research park got off to a slow start, although the addition of university

Emilio Ambasz,
Universal Exposition
of Sevilla, competition
project model, 1986.

facilities helped in later years. Several of the original exposition pavilions were selected for preservation, and some have been repurposed for these new uses, although others remain abandoned. The economic difficulties of La Cartuja, and of the city in general, provoked several other forays into what we might call the 'grand gesture' approach to economic regeneration initiated with the expo. In 1997, Isla Mágica opened around the lake, a publicly supported theme park that likewise proved to be a disappointment. In 1999, the city opened Cruz and Ortiz's Olympic Stadium on the northern end of the island and made unsuccessful bids for the Summer Olympics of 2004 and 2008, and in the years following the fair, the Junta and city promoted a proposal to build an iconic commercial skyscraper on the island. The project came to fruition with Pelli Clarke Pelli's Torre Sevilla. At 180 metres (590 ft) and 37 storeys, it almost cost the city its status as a World Heritage Site because of its impact on the historic skyline. When the real-estate market collapsed in 2008, construction on the tower was halted, and the public savings bank that had backed it went bankrupt amid corruption scandals. This list of failures demonstrates the limits of recurring too often to the 'grand gesture', especially when it is not backed up by the strong planning, economic potential and genuine world interest that Barcelona was able to muster in 1992.

Threshold to a New Paradigm

From Bankinter to Barcelona, postmodernism in Spain proposed two powerful, entwined ideas: to use the city to remake architecture, and to use architecture to remake the city. For a brief time, the architects who helped to build Spain's young democracy succeeded in implementing this dual vision of urbanity. But as the 1980s progressed, the country's political class evolved away from ideological goals and towards a more centrist pragmatism, as seen in Mayor Maragall's apology for middle-class gentrification. Thus, the more lasting accomplishment of the architects involved in institutions of power would be to introduce Spain's new political class to the value – and seductions – of quality architecture and to the importance of the historic patrimony.

In Sevilla, with its managerial planning, the rupture with the urban ideas of the Tendenza was complete. With it was lost a certain high ethical idealism, Marxist or socialist in spirit, that underlay both the Tendenza and the Modern Movement before it and gave design a constraining, ethical framework that would eventually be missed. In this reduced form, architecture became little more than its individual works, as exemplified by the Alamillo Bridge, which functioned like a trophy, the icing on the cake for conventional development strategies.

The international architectural vanguard of the 1980s was accommodating itself to this situation, as can be seen in Calatrava's work. Viaplana and Piñón had diagnosed the problem in their 'desert' of decontextualized capitalist development. But in this arid landscape, Calatrava's iconic landmarks offered a more appealing option than the nihilistic, critical minimalism of the plaza at Sants, or the hollow postmodern nostalgia of Madrid Sur.

The emergence of the icon or 'signature' work, and its author, the 'star architect', which had begun with postmodernism, marked a basic shift in paradigm. Avant-garde movements, with their leaders, followers and factions, were breaking up into their individual protagonists, each with a body of work that functioned like a brand identity, integrating architecture into late capitalism's mechanisms of seduction and self-reproduction. Global connectivity and the rapid interchange between multiple points of cultural reference contributed to the breakup of single, centrist cultural visions. At the same time, the formal discipline of the architectural profession was broken open to new possibilities of formal invention offered by computer-aided design and fabrication, as well as the loosening of modernism's ingrained strictures on formal efficacy and formal contention.

This new paradigm was impossible to ignore by 1992. In the next and final chapter, we will see its impact on the booming public architecture of the next fifteen years. This would be a time of unparalleled creativity, in which Spanish architecture, whether designed by Spaniards or international figures, would take a leading role on the global stage, carried forward by the enthusiasm unleashed with the events of 1992 and the energies that fed the remaking of the country.

However, as the post-1992 history of La Cartuja suggests, such enthusiasm was not always accompanied by sound planning or management. Instead, we find political opportunism, wishful thinking, whims, fancies and high-stakes bets. The pressure to inaugurate within short election cycles often seemed to outweigh the practical usefulness of a project. Flashy architecture encouraged these shortcomings. The economic collapse of 2008 exposed such failings, leaving behind a desolate landscape of magnificent palaces haunted by multiple political sins, from grandiosity and outrageous expenditures to malfeasance and corruption. Irremediably implicated in this reckoning, architecture would have to start over after the crisis, in search of a new animating impulse capable of persuading society, once again, of its powers to reimagine a better future.

chapter nine

Over the Top, 1992–2015

Bring on the Museums, bring on the Academies, bring on the Expositions.
Let there be Education, let there be Urbanity, let there be Frivolity . . .

Eugeni d'Ors, 1907[1]

The events of 1992 might have served as a triumphant climax to Spain's process of democratization and modernization, but in fact they proved to be more of a beginning, setting a precedent for increasingly daring strategies of development coupled with architectural creativity. The most extraordinary product of these new strategies was Frank Gehry's 1997 Guggenheim Museum in Bilbao, which was, like the events of 1992, the capstone of a thorough makeover of the city. It was the bright star in a constellation of initiatives in the 1990s that confirmed architecture's new status, and its worldwide success inspired countless new ventures in the following decade. The results could be disappointing or overreaching, but just as often they were of great interest and quality. They included showcase works such as museums, concert halls and skyscrapers, as well as many smaller works for local communities designed by new generations of architects and serving everyday functions, from medical clinics, schools and libraries to parks, recreational buildings and subsidized housing. The true culmination of these years of exuberance may well have been in 2006, when contemporary Spanish architecture was celebrated in a major show at New York's Museum of Modern Art.[2]

International architecture was changing rapidly in the years leading up to Bilbao. The project that most clearly prefigured the new moment was Richard Rogers and Renzo Piano's Centre Pompidou in Paris (1977), which brought together a new interest in the traditional city with the contrasting attractions of novel, transgressive architecture. As a cultural phenomenon, it was the culmination of the spirit of May 1968, of Archigram, Cedric Price and Prada Poole. City and building came to life together in the form of a permanent happening, with the attributes of a tourist mecca, a cultural magnet and a theatre of urban life. Erupting apparently off-schedule amid the postmodern era, the Centre Pompidou was in fact a harbinger of the future. François Mitterrand's 'Grands Projets' immediately followed, enlarging on

The ensanche de Vallecas, Madrid, in 2010, with construction halted during the economic crisis.

its example and establishing a new model for coupling architectural and political ambitions.

Spain's leading role in this emerging panorama unfolded in two inter-woven stories, one focusing on political initiatives and the other on the development of architecture itself. In the political sphere, the examples of Paris and Barcelona inspired programmes of local boosterism in politicians of every stripe. Regionalist fervour helped inflame such ambitions in many cases. Both Barcelona and Bilbao were the metropolitan centres of auton-omous regions whose governing parties openly dreamed of independence, although they were otherwise moderate and pragmatic, representing the conservative local establishment. Elsewhere, as in the Canary Islands or Galicia, a more subdued regionalism of similar establishment origins also found an outlet in architecture.

Spain's Popular Party (PP) gained ground in these years, extending its reach from the traditional conservative strongholds of Castilla-León and Galicia to win lasting control of both the municipal and regional govern-ments of Madrid and Valencia in the 1990s. In 1996, its leader, José María Aznar, unseated Felipe González as president of Spain, and the two parties would alternate in power in succeeding years. The conservatives assumed as their own many of the socialists' goals of social welfare and protections, and they proved no less inclined to lavish spending on public works. Ambitious designs by renowned architects, and the media attention they attracted, became an integral part of these programmes.

In the other strand of this history, the new expectations raised for public architecture made extraordinary demands on architects, while also giving them unprecedented creative freedom. In the hands of a Frank Gehry or a Zaha Hadid, the practice of architecture became a virtuosic performance, demanding the contradictory talents of establishing a recognizable cre-ative identity and breaking all previous expectations with each new work. Spain's architects responded with their usual scepticism and reserve – with important exceptions – but the new creative climate brought out the best in many. It will suffice, for the moment, to roughly sketch the range of responses: we can contrast the overheated inventiveness of Enric Miralles with the intuitive lyricism of Carme Pinós; the neo-Organicism of Madrid's Luis M. Mansilla and Emilio Tuñón with the neo-Brutalism of Tenerife's Fernando Menis, or the differing immersive sensualities of Madrid's José Selgas and Lucía Cano, and the Catalans RCR (Rafael Aranda, Carme Pigem and Ramón Vilalta): neo-futuristic Pop on the one hand, material and essentialist on the other.

The Road to Bilbao

In Spain's architecture of the 1990s, premonitions of Bilbao's potential are found brewing in Barcelona's museum projects after the Olympics and in Calatrava's work for his native Valencia. Nevertheless, the success of Bilbao depended on a unique combination of circumstances, including luck, timing, talent, desperation and the mysterious alchemies of making a hit in any popular art.

In Barcelona, the regionalist fervour and high cultural aspirations expressed in Eugeni d'Ors 1907 exhortation, which had smouldered under the repression of the dictatorships of Primo de Rivera and Franco, burst into the open again with democracy. In the heat of the preparations for the Olympics, the city and the Generalitat (the revived regional government) launched a host of plans for new and expanded cultural institutions, revindicating Catalan culture and creativity, although most would have to wait until after the games. Some fifteen new cultural projects, public and private, were inaugurated in the decade following the Olympics, while existing institutions were reorganized, modernized and enlarged. The city relied on its A-list of local architects for these assignments, with the exception of more ambitious ventures entrusted to figures with a greater international profile. Thus, we find Tusquets and Clotet restoring Domènech i Montaner's Palau de la Música, including a small addition (1982–9, 2000–2004). Ignasi de Solà-Morales headed a modernization plan for the Liceu opera, which became a reconstruction after a devastating fire in 1994 (1986–99), and the Picasso Museum, which occupied a pair of medieval palaces in the Gothic Quarter, was enlarged with a third palace by Jordi Garcés and Enric Sòria in 1985, and enlarged again by Soria in 1999.

Two of Viaplana and Piñón's best works of this period were for city cultural centres. Both are set in highly determined historic contexts, and in both, the architects use their minimalist formal language to create a sense of poetic estrangement. The Santa Mónica Arts Centre on the lower Ramblas (1985–7) rises from the footprint of a former convent and incorporates the surviving arches of its cloister. The lost building bleeds through the centre's abstract volumes like a ghostly recollection, as in the round opening of the unadorned rectangular facade, situated in the position of a rose window. Access to the entry is via an eccentric blur of raised ramps and decks, further undermining the sense of grounded solidity. As Viaplana writes in the brief, 'Under a cornice, the smile of the Cheshire Cat slowly disappears.'[3]

The architects' conversion of a former charity hospital into the Barcelona Centre for Contemporary Culture (cccb, 1990–94) was one of the major projects envisioned in the plans for El Raval. Here, they replaced the north side of the existing courtyard with a new wing, finished entirely in glass, which contains the vertical circulation. It rises over the cornice line of the existing wings, an extra floor whose facade tilts dramatically over the courtyard, reflecting the neighbouring roofscape into the court. Access to the building is via long ramps that descend to the lobby under the courtyard. Tunnelling under and towering over the older structure, the design dramatizes its late arrival, acting as both a subordinated and subversive intrusion.

Some of Barcelona's more ambitious cultural commissions were not so successful, however. As part of the city's effort to redirect development to the industrial zones of Poblenou, it allocated two adjacent blocks near the Plaça de les Glòries Catalanes for a new concert hall and the National Theatre of Catalunya. But architecture alone could do little to alleviate the isolation and lack of definition of the site, located beside a rail yard. Rafael Moneo's auditorium (1987–99) is a long rectangular volume with an exposed concrete frame and infill panels of Corten steel, emulating Louis Kahn's Yale Center for British Art of 1977. But given the context, the result here seems anonymous and industrial rather than subtly elegant. Ricardo Bofill's theatre reflects the gaudy tastes of its client, the Generalitat of President Jordi Pujol. His design anchors the site with an overscaled Greek temple of precast concrete. Behind its columns, sheer glass walls enclose a full-height lobby that wraps around a second volume containing the theatres and other services.

The Italian architect Gae Aulenti, then amid her triumphant makeover of the Gare d'Orsay in Paris, was hired in 1985 to perform a similar operation on Puig i Cadafalch's Palau Nacional, the bombastic centrepiece of the 1929 Exposition on Montjuïc, which since 1934 had housed important collections, now rechristened as the National Art Museum of Catalunya. Aulenti's most audacious idea was to flood the building's immense elliptical Gran Salón and scatter across this interior lake a handful of pavilions of different ecclesiastical type forms (a Greek cross, an apse, half a basilica and so on), sketching a semblance of the original settings for the artworks they displayed. But this concept was rejected, and the restoration dragged on without much further notice until 2004.

With Richard Meier's Barcelona Museum of Contemporary Art (MACBA, 1985–95), however, the formula of the Guggenheim in Bilbao was almost in place. The brilliantly white, neo-modernist composition was suitably exotic, drawing visitors and new life to El Raval. Unfortunately, the design was equally alien to its Mediterranean environs, as seen in the excessive glazing of the main southern facade, which has caused problems of sunlight control in the galleries. But a spark had been ignited. The anecdotal stories of Meier's first encounters with the Barcelona mayor Pasqual Maragall reveal

Albert Viaplana and Helio Piñón, Barcelona Centre for Contemporary Culture (CCCB), 1990–94. View of central courtyard.

Richard Meier posing in front of his Barcelona Museum of Contemporary Art (MACBA), completed in 1995.

the force of a mutual attraction that extended beyond the particular figures involved. According to one version, Maragall arranged to run into Meier, recently anointed with the Pritzker Prize, at a dinner party in New York. There he 'popped the question', as Alan Riding wrote in the *New York Times*: 'I'd like one of your buildings in my city. What would you like to do?' Riding continues, 'It is a situation that architects usually only dream about, to be sought out by the mayor of a rich European metropolis.'[4] To find Barcelona portrayed by the *Times* as rich, European and metropolitan would have thrilled the Catalan. But with New York recently staggering out of near-bankruptcy and other American cities in crisis, a mayor with a pocketful of projects was remarkable enough.

The scale and ambition of Barcelona and Sevilla's rush towards 1992 had a contagious effect on other cities. Valencia, Spain's third largest metropolis, launched the City of the Arts and Sciences in these years, a monumental complex by native son Santiago Calatrava. Valencia had undergone a major urban transformation in the 1980s at the hands of its first socialist municipal government. After a deadly flood in 1957, Franco's technocrats began a decades-long project to divert the course of the Turia river from the centre of the city to a new channel, the 'southern collector', a mutilation unthinkable today, with plans that included a highway along the former riverbed.

In the face of strong, organized popular opposition, the new democratic government converted the course of the river into a park, designed by Ricardo Bofill and opened in 1988.

Calatrava's project was an initiative of the new regional government, at first in socialist hands. It was located at the eastern end of the new river park, between the city and the port – a grey zone that the project launched into redevelopment. The programme for the initial proposal of 1991 comprised three basic elements: an IMAX theatre and planetarium; a Museum of Science and Technology; and a 382-metre (1,255 ft) telecommunications tower. Despite some initial hesitation, the conservatives of the PP continued and expanded the project after they won regional elections in 1995. They replaced the tower with an opera and added an aquarium with a restaurant designed by Félix Candela, chosen at Calatrava's urging. In 2004, the complex was further expanded with the Ágora, a large events space, and three commercial towers that never found financing. Construction was not completed until 2009 at an estimated cost of €1.3 billion (never officially acknowledged), a staggering sum for the time.[5]

Calatrava's move from works of engineering to buildings brought out a zoomorphic surrealism in his curving designs. Thus, we have the eyeball-shaped dome of the planetarium, with an eyelid in the guise of a moving sunshade. The neo-Gothic dinosaur ribcage of the Science Museum, 150 metres (490 ft) long, is an asymmetrical nave sliced with natural light, thoroughly unsuited to its function. The opera hall is encased in a lobster-like exoskeleton, with a slightly raised, cantilevered lid curving over the structure and ending in a sharp point like a stinger. These three main elements, brilliantly white in their pristine setting, might be compared to the cathedral complex at Pisa, with culture, education and amusement replacing religious faith as a cover for local boosterism, and a will-to-form that triumphs over all practical considerations.

Of the oft-told tale of Bilbao and the Guggenheim, it is sometimes forgotten how improbable the success of the venture actually was. Scarcely known outside Spain, Bilbao was near bankruptcy in the 1980s: its polluted industrial riverfront of steel mills and shipyards was in ruins, one-quarter of its workforce was unemployed and local society was riven by the escalating violence of ETA terrorism. Neither were Frank Gehry or the Guggenheim sure bets. Thomas Krens, the museum's flamboyant director, found obstacles at every turn in his controversial bids to expand the museum as a branded international franchise. He came to Spain fresh from the collapse of proposals for Venice and Salzburg, the latter featuring a spectacular design by Hans Hollein. With Carmen Giménez, the first director of exhibitions at the fledgling Reina Sofía Museum, as his local influencer, he peddled his project to Madrid, Barcelona and Sevilla in the untimely year of 1991.[6] Frank Gehry's untamed designs also provoked scepticism in sober minds. As the Guggenheim went up, the cost of his building for the American Center in Paris drove its client into bankruptcy (1991–4).[7] In Los Angeles, his 1989 proposal for the Disney Concert Hall, a precedent for the Guggenheim, was paralysed by a soaring budget and the doubts of potential backers, led by Eli Broad, who had clashed with Gehry over the delays and uncontrolled costs of his own Gehry-designed home.[8]

In short, Bilbao needed the Guggenheim and the Guggenheim needed Bilbao. Their alliance of *desperados* proved far more powerful than the similar ambitions of Barcelona or Valencia, thanks to Gehry's unprecedented, irresistible design, together with the international clout that a dynamic New York arts institution could bring to a Spanish backwater. Bilbao found Gehry at the culmination of his creative breakthrough. His uninhibited formal explorations, developed in rudimentary models, became possible to draw and fabricate thanks to CATIA, an aerospace engineering design programme, thus launching a new era of computer-assisted formal freedom. Gehry's free-flowing ribbons of reflective titanium, extending along the riverfront and rising to a lopsided crescendo around the soaring central atrium, are both monumental and playful, almost cartoonish, but the design has remained remarkably fresh over time.

Bilbao was already well versed in the attractions of brand-name architecture. As the clean-up of the riverfront progressed, and a new commercial port was built at the mouth of the river, Norman Foster won an international competition to design the stations for a new Metro system (1988–95). James Stirling was hired to design an unrealized intermodal station. Calatrava built a new airport terminal (1990–2000) and the Zubizuri footbridge over the Nervión river (1990–97), a gracefully curving cable structure, although flawed by a transparent glass deck that became treacherous when wet. The demolished factories of the riverfront gave way to a new urban district, the Abandoibarra, first planned by César Pelli in 1993. The area was framed by the rising Guggenheim on one side and the Euskalduna Palace (1992–9) on the other, a congress centre and concert hall designed by a young Madrid couple, Federico Soriano and Dolores Palacios (class of 1986, 1987). Their sophisticated, competition-winning design is a visual and tactile metaphor for the shipyards it replaced, with the main hall encased in a Corten-steel hull, and the multi-level lobbies rising freely around it like shipyard scaffolding.

The Guggenheim was the capstone of this regeneration. It became a motor of economic recovery in its own right, drawing world tourism as well as new business. In its first year, the museum attracted 1.3 million visitors, more than double the most optimistic estimates, and those figures

Frank Gehry,
Guggenheim
Museum, Bilbao,
1991–7.

remained high through the succeeding years.[9] The ironies of this runaway success were many. First, while the project inaugurated a new era of competitive icon-making, it is hard to think of any other subsequent project that has attracted a similar following, with the exception of the ongoing work to complete Gaudí's Sagrada Família in Barcelona. Second, while Basque nationalist leaders underscored their regional identity and independence from the Spanish state with the museum, they did so by embracing what many saw as American cultural imperialism.[10] And although Americans found a renewed national pride in Gehry's achievement, as reflected in Herbert Muschamp's ecstatic review in the 7 September 1997 issue of the *New York Times*, 'The Miracle in Bilbao', they had to admit that this miracle had come about in Spain, and not, for example, in Los Angeles. In fact, this displacement was key to the project's power of attraction.

One final irony came with a dark edge of the absurd. At the press opening in October 1997, attendees were confronted by a stark juxtaposition. A few steps away from Jeff Koons's Sphinx-like floral sculpture *Puppy* near the entrance to the museum, wreaths and police tape marked the spot where ETA gunmen had slain a police officer a few hours before, in a frustrated attempt to sabotage the opening ceremonies. But it was *Puppy*, in all its silliness, that would prevail over the terrorists in the long run. After a prolonged decline, ETA officially renounced terrorism in 2011.

Álvaro Siza,
Galician Centre
for Contemporary
Art, Santiago de
Compostela, 1988–93.

The promise of architecture's new protagonism remained fresh in other works of the 1990s. The Portuguese architect Álvaro Siza's Galician Centre for Contemporary Art in the historic centre of Santiago de Compostela (1988–93) was the most significant work realized by the new regional government in its new capital. In his design, conditioned by an adjacent Baroque monastery, the diverging lines of a perspectival sketch become diverging building volumes that expand from the narrow entry facade, provoking lively interior repercussions. The effect is as if the rules of perspectival space have become entangled in a Mannerist subjectivity.

The 1990s were particularly sweet for Rafael Moneo, then in his fifties. Among many prestigious projects at home and abroad, the decade was framed by two state commissions for Madrid that implicitly recognized his position as Spain's pre-eminent architect: the Thyssen Museum (1989–92), where he rebuilt the gutted interiors of a seventeenth-century palace for a private collection acquired by the state, and the enlargement of the nearby Prado Museum (1996–2007). In 1996, he was also awarded the Pritzker Prize, another first for Spain.

His international projects in this decade are notable for their discreet sophistication. He began close to Harvard with the Davis Museum at Wellesley College (1990–93), followed by Stockholm's Museum of Modern Art and Architecture and a new cathedral for Los Angeles, among others. More spectacular was his competition-winning Kursaal Concert Hall and Congress Centre in San Sebastián, the most clearly iconic work of his career (1990–99). Located on the city's curving bay, the building takes its measure from the surrounding landscape rather than the city behind it. Utzon's Sydney Opera, on which Moneo had worked thirty years before, was a model, as was, surprisingly, Bofill's National Theatre of Catalunya. As with both, Moneo encased the two main halls in larger, independent structures, with soaring lobbies between them. In this case, the outer structures are two slightly tilted prisms of translucent glass, seductively luminous by day and night, that gesture towards the sea at different angles like 'two stranded rocks on the shore', in Moneo's own poetic description.[11]

Moneo's addition to the City Hall of Murcia (1991–8), a regional capital near Spain's southeastern coast, marked the distance covered in the country's evolving democracy in the years following his 1981 Logroño City Hall. Working with a site across a small square from the Baroque transept of the city's cathedral, he responded to its superposition of classical orders with a four-storey portico of irregularly spaced stone piers stacked between the thin floor slabs. The syncopated disorder of the piers made room for a double-height, off-centre ceremonial opening. Again, as in Logroño and Alejandro de la Sota's Civil Government Building, the design sidestepped the authoritarian weight of a centralized balcony, but the tone here was playful rather than sober or tragic, treating civic ceremony as harmless operatic pomp.

Rafael Moneo, Kursaal Concert Hall and Congress Centre, San Sebastián, 1990–99.

After the failure of a flawed open competition to enlarge the Prado Museum organized by the outgoing socialist government in 1995, Moneo won a second round in 1998, this time with the Popular Party in power. His addition comprised a discreet new entry behind Juan de Villanueva's Neo-classical structure, and a connection under the street to a tidy new building that wrapped around a semi-ruined cloister, a surviving fragment of the royal palace of El Buen Retiro that formerly occupied the hillside behind the museum. Moneo's design was exquisitely modest and contextual, with the architect's characteristic elegance of detail, including bronze entry doors to the new building by artist Cristina Iglesias and a stately row of square, fluted brick columns, rather retro-Deco in style. Throughout he used the red brick of the Prado and the palace before it, the same red brick that had become a hallmark of his own work. It was as if the groundbreaking con-textualism of Bankinter had simply been a dress rehearsal for this, the understated culmination of his career.

Apart from Bofill and Calatrava, no Spanish architect has matched Moneo's international reach. The only figure to come close was the young Enric Miralles, but his career was cut short with his premature death from a brain tumour in 2000, at the age of 45. His trajectory blazed brightly through the 1990s as he completed works begun with his first wife and design partner, Carme Pinós (1984–9), and began competing for interna-tional work with his second, the Italian architect Benedetta Tagliabue (1993–2000). His most memorable work with Pinós is the Igualada Cemetery,

Rafael Moneo, addition to Murcia City Hall, 1991–8.

near Barcelona (1985–94). Like the Olympic Archery Range, the design fuses architecture and landscape, with broken lines of repetitive elements, in this case the inclined berms of the mortuary niches that shape and meld into the terraced terrain, creating a descending, winding route to a small plaza. Visitors are immersed in a semi-urban, semi-natural setting, at once earthy and otherworldly.

The partnership with Pinós disciplined and focused Miralles's torrential creativity. His subsequent designs, on his own and then with Tagliabue, were more ambitious and daring, challenging every formal and structural preconception. In one case, the outlandish structure for a basketball stadium in Huesca (1994), in which eccentric roof trusses were supported by cables spanning crosswise below them, collapsed during construction.[12] In another, the 22-storey tower for Gas Natural in Barcelona (1999–2006) incongruously sported a massive horizontal volume cantilevered from its midsection – the 'aircraft carrier', as Tagliabue called it.[13] More successful were the flowing interiors of the National Centre of Rhythmic Gymnastics in Alicante (1993, begun with Pinós), where visitors move on curving ramps and raised platforms around the performance and training spaces, or the student union at the University of Vigo in Galicia (1999–2003), a semi-circular raised structure poised on the edge of a mountainside terrace.

In the mid-1990s, Miralles and Tagliabue won a series of international competitions that culminated with their 1998 commission to build the

Scottish National Parliament in Edinburgh, finished by Tagliabue in 2005. The project was their crowning achievement, although it was plagued by changes in programme, cost overruns and hostile, politically charged press coverage, receiving a degree of public scrutiny unheard of in Spain. Their design is full of brilliant moments, but it fails to cohere as a whole, perhaps precisely because they sought to upend traditional representations of political authority. 'This is not a building in a park,' they wrote, 'but rather the form of people gathering, physically shaping the act of sitting together.'[14] The project thus eschews the iconic for more Organicist ideas of psychosocial and phenomenological space, which can be traced in part, within Miralles's wide-ranging formation, to his early friendship with Alison and Peter Smithson.

Composed intuitively from the inside out, the building is a collage of heterogeneous functional elements: the main debating chamber, visitors' spaces, a tower that houses committee-hearing rooms and a multi-storey slab for MPs' offices. The embracing, curving spaces are naturally lit, often from multiple directions and with the indirect, dappled light of the Organicists' 'essential forest'.[15] This effect is augmented by what Tagliabue describes as the 'visual vibration' of surfaces and details, which is created by the repetitions and variations of visual elements.[16] This can be seen in the sweep of notched, irregular wood desktops for MPs in the debating chamber, or its roof assembly of heavy timber trusses interlaced with thin stainless-steel tension rods. The latter illustrate a characteristic design strategy in which the architects separate assemblies into contrasting components so that each can express a specific tectonic task.

The architects' best-known work in Barcelona, the renovation of the Santa Caterina market in the Gothic Quarter (1997–2005), features a similar layering of structural elements, filtered natural light and visual vibration, transforming the dour, original 1845 structure into a vibrant field of incident, as exemplified in their new roof, an undulating carpet of ceramic tiles splashed with colours taken from fruit and produce. The intervention extended to the market's depressed surroundings. The architects demolished the back of the structure to create a small plaza bordered by two modest new towers of senior housing, and sutured the urban wounds left by an incomplete nineteenth-century boulevard with small, focused interventions. For example, they narrowed the avenue's aborted path to create a pedestrian-scaled gateway framed by new public housing that was literally extended from existing buildings.

EMBT Architects (Enric Miralles and Benedetta Tagliabue), Scottish National Parliament, 1998–2005. View of the debating chamber.

This urban micro-surgery was an advance on the wholesale demolitions of the Bohigas era in El Raval, and postmodern concepts of morphological urban space in general. It permitted renewal and the reduction of unhealthy densities in the Gothic Quarter without erasing its historic identity and

idiosyncrasies. As in the Scottish Parliament project and other works, Miralles and his partners pioneered a singular path forward out of the formal obsessions of the era, with a creative flair that few could match. Pinós and Tagliabue continued to develop their individual lines of work from these premises. One can only wonder how Miralles himself might have evolved. As fate would have it, he was buried in the Igualada Cemetery, in a tomb overlooking its small plaza from an upper terrace, beside a solitary cypress.

Returning to Madrid, Moneo's two museums were followed by other state initiatives, in which the governing Popular Party used limited competitions to open its horizons to international figures. Richard Rogers joined Madrid's Estudio Lamela, a commercial firm in its second generation, to win the commission for the new T4 terminal at Barajas Airport (1998–2006), an extravaganza of custom-made structural and mechanical elements under undulating skylit roofs. Jean Nouvel enlarged the Reina Sofía Museum (1999–2005), with a behemoth of richly coloured metal finishes overlooking a busy boulevard. In a notable private venture, the collection of museums around the Prado was joined by Jacques Herzog and Pierre de Meuron's CaixaForum (2001–8), a cultural centre sponsored by the Caixa savings bank. The Swiss architects raised a protected brick industrial building off the ground and extended it upwards with several floors finished in rusted steel plate, a provocative approach to contextualism and the conventions of historic preservation that was a precedent for their Elbphilharmonie in Hamburg (2017).

As the economy heated up in the late 1980s, private clients began exploring the new cache of brand-name architecture, beginning modestly with

EMBT Architects (Enric Miralles and Benedetta Tagliabue), Santa Caterina market, Barcelona, 1997–2005.

Minoru Yamasaki's Torre Picasso (1988), and an interior makeover of a historic building by Hans Hollein for the Santander Bank (1988–93). When the boom faltered in the late 1990s, a welter of bankruptcies and fraud cases exposed the cut-throat business culture behind it. At the centre of these scandals was Philip Johnson and John Burgee's Puerta de Europa, a pair of leaning towers framing the northern end of the Paseo de la Castellana (1989–96), which stood unfinished for years.[17]

Madrid was the incubator and epicentre of the last of the great urban operations of the socialist era, designed to 'socialize' Spain's housing sector, combating rising prices and speculation, though its ultimate consequence was precisely the opposite. The central government had provided abundant housing subsidies throughout the 1980s, but a new four-year plan, launched in 1992 for nearly 500,000 units, was coordinated with aggressive public methods of urban development and the nationwide deployment of non-profit building cooperatives organized by the principal trade unions. These new strategies had been pioneered at Madrid Sur, which also provided the ensanche model of urban plans based on the perimeter-block housing type, with the addition of lower-density variations such as rowhouses.

The housing cooperatives proposed to operate on the same large scale as the country's major promoters. The expansion of the PSV, organized by the socialist Unión General de Trabajadores (UGT), was particularly aggressive, enrolling some 20,000 families for 76 projects throughout Spain. But it was disastrously managed and declared bankruptcy in 1993, discrediting the cooperative concept.[18] More successful were the consortiums: public corporations organized by regional and municipal authorities to execute large urban projects. The consortiums provided sites for both subsidized and open-market housing and used the power of expropriation to control land prices and force land held in speculation onto the market. In 1990, the regional government of Madrid met with the union cooperatives and the leftist municipalities of thirteen working-class bedroom communities of the capital's so-called 'Red Belt'. They joined forces to plan the construction of new districts that would eventually contain 120,000 housing units, more than half of which would be subsidized.[19] The new districts were integrated in a regional plan that included mass transit and 'areas of centrality' for offices, shopping, industry and education, as well as parks and nature reserves, all connected and separated by new highways. As seen from these motorways, the new ensanches stand out at the edges of existing towns, their uniform – contained massing and crisply defined edges – in vivid contrast to the usual formless sprawl of suburban development elsewhere.

The city of Madrid, governed since 1991 by the Popular Party, launched a similar development programme in 1994 that proposed to build a ring of some sixteen new ensanches, ultimately urbanizing all the remaining open land within the city limits, with a capacity of more than 300,000 new homes.[20] In these interventions, the ensanche model of Madrid Sur was reduced to little more than a bureaucratic instrument for subdividing land.

Municipalities throughout Spain made similarly ambitious plans, and these stimulus measures combined with other expansive economic factors to trigger the housing bubble of the 2000s. Annual figures for new housing projects began to reach record levels in 2001, topping out at over 760,000 units in 2006 alone, more than in all of the four other major European countries combined. From 1997 to 2007, the average cost of a home tripled.[21] Commercial building experienced a similar boom. The skylines of Spanish cities in the first years of the new century were studded with construction cranes, but when the supply of credit collapsed in 2008, it brought the entire Spanish economy down with it.

The New Century

Like the runaway housing market, the euphoria of public architecture in the 1990s only increased in the following decade, as did the booming inversions in transportation and other infrastructures. One study estimates the excess public expenditures on projects deemed unnecessary, underused, excessively costly or economically inviable at roughly €81 billion for the period between 1995 and 2016 (although the bases of such calculations are open to debate).[22] Among the projects listed as wasteful are many significant works of architecture.

Madrid's conservative local governments offer prominent examples. Among other major ventures, there were three failed bids to host the Olympics, a pharaonic dig that buried an existing highway under the Manzanares river and reverted the site to parkland, and an unrealized fourteen-building City of Justice studded with star turns by Foster, Rogers, Hadid and the like, as well as programmes to convert public housing into a showcase for international architects and the experiments of younger talents. The Olympic bids left behind a stadium by Cruz and Ortiz, who enlarged their 1994 athletic stadium as the centrepiece of an aborted Olympic Ring, and Dominique Perrault's 'Magic Box', a tennis stadium with three covered courts and roofs that tilt open on hydraulic pistons (2002–8; estimated cost €300 million).[23]

In Madrid's most transformative project, the recovery of the riverfront created a new green axis through the city that set the stage for future growth. Known as Madrid Río, the 6-kilometre (4 mi.) park was made possible by burrowing 25 kilometres (15 mi.) of curving highways and connections under the river, a grandiose urban spectacle in its own right (2004–11; cost more than €4 billion).[24] The park was designed by the Madrid studio of Francisco Burgos and Ginés Garrido (Madrid, class of 1985, 1989), with the Dutch landscape architects West 8 and others. Its southern end is anchored by the Matadero, a sprawling, lively cultural centre installed by the city in former municipal slaughterhouses (neo-Mudéjar industrial sheds from the early twentieth century), which were renovated by a roster of young local architects (2006, ongoing).

In the same years, the Municipal Housing Company commissioned a host of international architects to design subsidized housing in the new ensanches and elsewhere. The results were not always stellar, with many projects by second-tier firms or old glories such as Archigram's Peter Cook or Pei Cobb Freed. Among the best was a muscular block by David Chipperfield. Several challenged the reigning perimeter-block typology. Thom Mayne returned to the carpet housing of Caño Roto in the 1950s for a block in the new ensanche of Carabanchel (2006), although his clusters of individual houses, each with its own small patio, are built over the obligatory parking decks rather than on firm ground. The Mirador, or Lookout, by Dutch architects MVRDV was more irreverent (2001–5). In concept, the design flipped the perimeter block on its end to create a 22-storey tower slab with a large rectangular hole cut through its midsection, a vertical patio 40 metres (130 ft) above the street. The slab is a collage of differentiated blocks, characterized by different apartment layouts, openings and finishes, piled up over one another with the random precision of a Mondrian, while red-painted exterior stairs and galleries crawl up around them. Dominating Madrid's northern skyline in the ensanche

de Sanchinarro, the project is the undisputed star of the city's housing campaigns, a monument, thrilling and depressing by turn, to the hubris and excess of the moment.

Other Spanish cities continued to take enormous risks, bidding to outdo one another in architectural boldness, although often a competition jury of architects and other 'experts' pushed them into these adventurous positions. A 2001 competition-winning design for a congress centre in Córdoba by Rem Koolhaas's Office for Metropolitan Architecture (OMA) proposed confronting the historic city centre from across the Guadalquivir river with a steel and glass behemoth 360 metres (1,180 ft) long, but the project never got off the ground. In 1999, another jury selected Peter Eisenman's proposal for the City of Culture of Galicia in Santiago de Compostela, a complex scaled to rival Calatrava's City of the Arts and Sciences. His design superimposed and manipulated a series of reference patterns, including a plan of medieval Santiago, the ribs and outline of a scallop shell, the symbol of the city, and the topography of the hillside site. The result, wrote the critic Suzanne Stephens, was 'an artificial landscape of thrashing, gnashing stone creatures restlessly rising up from the earth'.[25] Eisenman's forms had little relation to the programme, which in turn had little relation to actual needs, according to its critics: the local architect Pedro de Llano asked why a city of 90,000 needed an opera house to rival those of Valencia and Milan, for example.[26] Construction was halted in 2012 with the complex two-thirds complete, at an expenditure of more than €400 million.

Like Sevilla, with its post-expo Olympic bids and other attempts to spur development, Barcelona too sought to repeat the high of 1992, in its case with the 2004 'Universal Forum of Cultures', a patently self-invented 'world event' designed solely to mobilize a new urban development, the extension of Cerdà's boulevard of the Diagonal to the sea, on the city's desolate north-eastern limits. The forum campus at the end of the boulevard had to span the coastal highway and a modernized wastewater treatment plant, a feat accomplished by converting it into an 11-hectare (27 ac) pedestrian plat-form composed of spreading fingers of multicoloured asphalt, rising, falling and bifurcating across the site. Guiding its forms was a vision of the Diagonal as a natural force, like a stream of lava, pushing towards the water, as described by the architect Josep Lluís Mateo, who participated in the cigar-stoked weekend charettes where the concept was conceived, together with Enric Miralles and Josep A. Acebillo, Barcelona's chief planner.[27] The idea was clearly Miralles's, although it was developed after his death by Elías Torres, José A. Martínez Lapeña and others.

The work is a mutant version of hard plazas like Sants, where Miralles had begun his career, and the two projects frame Barcelona's vertiginous

MVRDV, the Mirador, a subsidized housing block in the ensanche de Sanchinarro, Madrid, 2001–5.

formal evolution in these years. A careful 'good taste' had often limited the aesthetic ambition of local designers, including Viaplana and Piñón's exquisite 'distaste' at Sants. Miralles opened the city towards more earthy, expansive and expressive forms, closer to the spirit of Gaudí and the local artists Joan Miró and Antoni Tàpies. This new spirit is also seen in the chief commercial work associated with the forum, Jean Nouvel's 142-metre (465 ft) Torre Agbar on the Diagonal (today known as the Torre Glòries), originally built for Barcelona's public water authority (1999–2005). The design is a shimmering, multi-hued, torpedo-shaped glass 'geyser', in Nouvel's description – another force of nature.[28] Other projects around the forum site include Herzog & de Meuron's triangular Edificio Fórum and the Diagonal Mar Park, designed for a Gerald Hines housing development by Miralles and Tagliabue and inspired by traditional Chinese parks and gardens (2002).

As the building bubble climbed towards its climax, the list of initiatives of similar ambition grew longer. One of the last to make it to fruition was the Universal Exposition of Zaragoza in 2008, which focused on the theme of water. Notable legacies include a new train station by Carlos Ferrater and Zaha Hadid's Bridge Pavilion, a bundled tubular structure that splays across the Ebro river to the exposition site. Easily overlooked was the fluvial park that wraps around the expo grounds along a large meander of the river, designed by Iñaki Alday and Margarita Jover, who opened their Barcelona studio in 1996. With its innovative concepts of flood management and waste-water treatment based on natural processes, it anticipated

Elías Torres and José A. Martínez-Lapeña, Esplanade, Barcelona Forum, 2004. Photovoltaic array.

Jean Nouvel,
Torre Agbar
(today Torre
Glòries),
Barcelona,
1999–2005.

the environmental, territorially scaled thinking that would offer architects one post-crisis strategy for the future, as shall be discussed later.

Among the endeavours left by the wayside, Valencia announced various development plans to connect its old port and coastline to the city centre, culminating with a tower-strewn master plan cobbled together from proposals by Jean Nouvel and Meinhard von Gerkan, who tied as winners of a 2007 competition. The remains of these ambitions are found in the old commercial port, converted into a recreational marina, with David Chipperfield's VIP clubhouse for the 2007 America's Cup races and a Formula One racetrack. Outside Valencia stand the ruins of Sociopolis, a residential district planned beside the redirected channel of the Turia river, amid the irrigated gardens of the Valencian plain. Designed by the local architect Vicente Guallart, it mixed residential towers, most by well-known architects, with 'urban gardens'. Begun in 2006, work halted in 2012, leaving behind a handful of half-occupied towers and construction skeletons. Zaha Hadid's 2003 urban design for the Zorrotzaurre peninsula in Bilbao met a similar fate, as did a so-called Environmental City outside Soria, planned by Francisco Mangado with Félix Arranz and promoted by the regional government of Castilla-León, which drew criticism precisely for occupying a protected natural environment.

The new century brought other singular buildings that were difficult to ignore. In Barcelona, a raw hub of development at its southwestern border with Hospitalet de Llobregat, centred around the new Fira convention centre campus by Toyo Ito (2003–8), included hotels by Richard Rogers, Nouvel and Ito himself. Nearby is David Chipperfield's City of Justice (2001–10). In Madrid, there were sprawling new corporate campuses for Santander Bank (Kevin Roche, 2004), the privatized state company Telefónica (Rafael de La-Hoz Castanys, son of the post-war architect Rafael de La-Hoz, 2007) and the Banco Bilbao Vizcaya (or BBVA, Herzog & de Meuron, 2003–19). In a lucrative deal, Real Madrid football club sold its former practice grounds on the upper reaches of the Paseo de la Castellana for a development of four skyscrapers, each 250 metres (820 ft) high, which changed the city's skyline. The architects were Foster & Partners, Henry Cobb of Pei Cobb Freed, César Pelli and the local studio of Enrique Álvarez-Sala and Carlos Rubio Carvajal (all completed 2007–9).

Outside the capitals, Oscar Niemeyer's cultural centre in Avilés, in the northern region of Asturias (2011), must be mentioned, as well as the Metropol Parasol in Sevilla by the German architect Jürgen Mayer (2005–11), whose 'parasols', comprising layers of laminated wood cut-outs, shade a raised terrace over a market in the Plaza de la Encarnación. Among the many other projects left by the wayside with the financial collapse of 2008, Zaha Hadid's library for the University of Sevilla stands out, because it was halted by citizen opposition rather than financial problems. Challenged in court by local residents for occupying part of a neighbourhood park, the incomplete structure was demolished by court order in 2012.[29] With its demise, the era of the architectural icon in Spain could be said to have been definitively laid to rest.

Spanish Architects of the New Century

Young architects flourished in the boom years of the 1990s and early 2000s. Work was abundant, and many open competitions encouraged beginner practitioners, who also found teaching positions in the thriving schools that offered a modest economic base for launching a practice. Architecture became one of the most sought-after university careers. Among the students, more than half were women by the turn of the century, and women entered the profession for the first time in significant numbers, although most often in partnership with their husbands, as seen in the early careers of Pinós and Tagliabue. However, with the collapse of 2008, new contracts for public and private buildings disappeared for more than a decade.[30] Many found refuge in teaching abroad, particularly in the United States, and in foreign commissions, leading a second exodus of talent comparable to that of 1939.

Spanish architecture enjoyed international prominence in these years, but the profession remained insular, following its own internal course of development and responding to international trends – including those on display in Spain itself – on its own terms. As in the 1980s, its guild-like nature, with its hereditary chains of masters and disciples, proved to have an inertia of its own. Spain's best young architects were by no means provincial, but the story of their different evolutions takes us back, in its origins, to the questions raised in the 1980s by the developing interest in the work of Alejandro de la Sota and the insistence on an essential functionalism, whether technical, poetic, minimalist or otherwise. These various positions were assumed in resistance to the seductions of the postmodern or the iconic, which could seem, from this collegial perspective, as rhetorically empty and unnecessary as the inflated 'national' styles that horrified De la Sota in his own time.

A prime example of this evolution is found in the joint careers of Luis Moreno Mansilla and Emilio Tuñón (both Madrid, class of 1982). They established their practice while working for Rafael Moneo (1983–93), with whom their work is in constant dialogue. In the Museum of Archeology and Fine Arts in the Castillian city of Zamora (1989–96), Roman artefacts are hung on raw poured-concrete walls raked with natural light from above, a variation on the hard brick walls of Moneo's museum in Mérida. But the composition is a tightly packed set of opaque nestling boxes that contain the galleries and the Corbusian circulation ramps between them. This packed container becomes legible in the gridiron of skylights on the roof, visible from the heights of the city above them, with their repeated rhythmic runs, short and long, facing this way and that.

In succeeding projects, the two unpacked the germinal compositional elements latent in this design, exploring the potentials of pattern and cellular assembly that would take them towards a new Organicism. Their first step in this direction was the patterned facade of a concert hall for a historic plaza in León (1995–2002). Again, like Moneo at the Murcia City Hall, their facade is composed of varied openings, distributed seemingly at random across several levels in a play of theme and variations. This facade fronts a shallow stack of exhibition galleries, independent of the simple rectangular concert hall behind them, forming a perversely tectonic version of a Venturian billboard. Pattern took on spatial form in the Museum of Fine Arts in Castellón (1997–2001), where a series of double-height galleries at the centre of the building drop through several floors in a diagonal cascade, each overlooking the one below.

In their best-known work, the MUSAC, a museum of contemporary art in León (1997–2003), Mansilla and Tuñón further developed this concept of repetitive and interlocking cellular spaces. The floor plan is composed entirely of the reiteration of a single, irregular element: two squares that meet at an angle to form a bent rectangular space. The concrete-walled cells nestle together in rows to form a continuous carpet, with an irregular, undulating exterior profile. The architects explain that adding or subtracting units does not change the essential character of the design, which is found, like a game, in the rules generating its forms rather than in the forms themselves.[31] The principal facades are clad in opaque glass set in random vertical bands of colours taken from the stained glass of León's Gothic cathedral – another arbitrary Venturian strategy – creating a photogenic image with little relation to the work's internal character.

The partnership came to an end with Mansilla's premature death in 2012, at the age of 52, leaving Tuñón to complete their most prestigious commission, the Gallery of the Royal Collections in Madrid, opened in 2023, a series of elongated granite volumes terraced into the ramparts below the Royal Palace and Cathedral.

Mansilla and Tuñón's use of pattern and variation, or Pop methods of representation, establish a degree of distance between the architects and the results of their designs, like scientists performing an experiment, a position that has a long tradition in modern art and architecture. In their case, the sense of disengagement that these methods produce should perhaps be understood in contrast to the 'exacerbated', wilful form-making of figures such as Calatrava or Miralles. Tuñón discusses this renunciation in an essay where he adapts the motto of Herman Melville's Bartleby, 'I would prefer not to,' as his own.[32]

Such renunciations were a common starting point for this generation and later, but they left few ready options for young architects anxious to make a splash. One solution was to arm a technically based, functional approach in an intellectual argument of sufficient theoretical and historic

Luis Moreno
Mansilla and Emilio
Tuñón, Museum
of Contemporary
Art (MUSAC), León,
1997–2003.

depth to have an impact in the international academic community. This was the strategy of Iñaki Ábalos and Juan Herreros (Madrid, class of 1978, 1985), who in books such as *Technique and Architecture* (1998) presented the theoretical arguments for a De la Sotian approach to design. For example, they advocated a distancing of the architect from the design process through the critical selection of catalogue parts, an eminently De la Sotian approach that they compared to the working method of Andy Warhol and opposed to the High-Tech movement's custom industrial designs. They clad a house for the painter Luis Gordillo outside Madrid (1994–6) in off-the-shelf metal 'Robertson' panels, a De la Sota favourite but generally used for cheap office blocks. Their larger works took Oiza's Banco Bilbao as a prototype, utilizing glass and metal towers with a squarish footprint and rounded corners, as in the Woermann residential tower in Las Palmas de Gran Canaria (2004), where the top two floors slant off to one side for a Pop effect. Ábalos, too, wrote a memorable book, *The Good Life: A Guided Visit to the Houses of Modernity* (2001), where he related emblematic domestic designs of the twentieth century to the different strains of philosophy that each could be said to embody.

Such theoretical speculations helped guide the architects towards broader issues of architecture's role in social, environmental and territorial terms.

This opening began with the unpromising commission for a waste sorting plant at Madrid's Valdemingómez landfill near Vallecas, which they converted into a manifesto for sustainable design (1997–8). The building itself was recyclable, with a demountable steel structure, recycled polycarbonate cladding panels and a sod roof, while the large shed interior included catwalks over the sorting belts for the civic enlightenment of visiting schoolchildren.

The two partners separated in 2006, and Ábalos established a new practice with the Polish architect Renata Sentkiewicz (Cracow University of Technology, 1998). He began teaching at Harvard, where he became chair of the architecture department (2013–16). In their work and teaching, Ábalos and Sentkiewicz pushed forward from Valdimingómez, seeking in questions of environmental responsibility a new paradigm for architecture that Ábalos baptized as 'thermodynamic'.[33] Using continuous environmental data flows for design and performance, buildings would become something like living organisms, continually exchanging energy with their surroundings. This rather literal Organicism often resulted in hybrid building types, in which structures took on characteristics of landforms and vegetation. A proposed art museum for Zhuhai, China (2014), combined a large concrete base, acting as a thermal cold bank, and a forest of tree-like canopies that shade the accessible roof. The Logroño high-speed train station, opened in 2018, straddles the tracks with an irregular triangulated space frame, its roof rippling down to the park that covers the underground platforms as a seeded slope with a water feature. Herreros, for his part, has gone on to build works such as a restrained vertical slab of a building for the Munch Museum on the Oslo waterfront (2009–21).

If, for these first two studios, an architecture of renunciation required a degree of cool distance from the design process, other architects sought a greater intensity of engagement that shared affinities with Minimalism and Arte Povera in their insistence on replacing representation with the immediate experience of the artistic object. None took this further than the partnership of María Fraile and Javier Revillo (Madrid, class of 1984; Pamplona, class of 1983), who began their association in 1991 while working in Moneo's studio. Of their Agricultural Trade Fair Pavilion outside Zamora (1993–6), they declared their aim to 'annul singularity, in so far as it is possible, and the figuration of architectural elements, to dilute and neutralize them in favour of the general space'.[34] The pavilion's two large free-span halls are defined by the regular rhythm of the exposed steel structure, perimeter columns and roof trusses. The entry hall is enclosed in panels of luminous, translucent polycarbonate, with sheets of clear glass at ground level that establish a connection with the exterior, while rows of trench skylights illuminate the second hall.

María Fraile and Javier Revillo, Agricultural Trade Fair Pavilion, Zamora, 1993–6.

The Miesian order and simplicity of the design is not quite the sublimated idealism of Ortiz-Echagüe and Echaide's SEAT buildings of the early 1960s, but it certainly has Zen undertones, mixing the hard realism and immediacy of its industrial finishes with a Japanese sense of spatial emptying, or *ma*, in which the architects limit themselves to issues of scale and proportion, texture, light and detail, or the most elementary choreography of the spatial experience. In a 1993 essay, 'The Interpretation of Space', Revillo challenged even the concept of perspectival space, maintaining that it situates the spectator outside what is essentially a representation.[35] Instead, the two compared the geometric order of the Trade Fair Pavilion to the rows of the ploughed fields around it, a space of immersion that engulfs and embraces the viewer. Other works of note by the two include a sports centre in Valdemoro, near Madrid (1992–8), and a multi-use congress centre in Villadecans, opened in 2005. This line of intense minimalism took many forms. One strain combined a sensorial richness of materials with monumental sculptural concision, as seen in the major projects of Francisco Mangado, who studied and now teaches at the architecture school in Pamplona (class of 1981), where his chief mentor was Rafael Echaide. The black granite exterior and simple, precise modelling of his Baluarte Congress Centre in Pamplona (1998–2003) give the two long L-shaped arms of the building a density of mass that is heightened by large void of the plaza they embrace.

Other takes on a contained, powerful minimalism came from students of Alberto Campo Baeza. The couple Sol Madridejos and Juan Carlos Sancho

(Madrid, class of 1983, 1982) have explored his more metaphysical approach to sculpted form and light, and its sources in the sculpture of Eduardo Chillida. In their city hall for the town of San Fernando de Henares, east of Madrid (1995–99), the solid plane of the rear facade, finished in Roman travertine, is interrupted on the upper floor by a deep cubic balcony lined with translucent onyx panels backed by glass, in a bid to make its contained space and reflected light as palpable as the solid stone, according to the architects.[36] The two interviewed Chillida for *El Croquis* in 1996, where he talked about the concept of the fold as a generative formal principle.[37] From this, they began to explore different procedures for generating three-dimensional forms through cuts and folds in a two-dimensional plane, which they put to the test in a group of buildings on a 5,000-hectare (12,355 ac) hunting estate in Almadén, in the province of Ciudad Real (2000). While they used rectilinear manipulations for the main house and a trophy pavilion, they designed a free-standing chapel through diagonal cuts and folds over a six-sided rectangular box. Each intervention in the box produced deformations throughout the whole. The result, realized in concrete, was a complex triangulated structure, at once expressive and mathematically exact.

Some of Campo Baeza's younger students were drawn to a tougher minimalism that is best understood in context, as seen in a public housing project in Madrid's ensanche de Vallecas by Estudio Entresitio, led by María Hurtado de Mendoza (Madrid, class of 1993) with her brother José María (1999) and César Jiménez de Tejada (1992). Their design rebelled against the ensanche's pantomime of traditional urbanism, rejecting both the drab brick blocks of open-market housing and the attempts by their contemporaries to liven up the formula with bright colours and jazzy formal moves.

With the cooperation of Madrid's housing authority, they substituted the site's perimeter-block zoning for a narrow 22-storey tower. Clad in a monolithic skin of black 'anthracite' zinc, the tower is an unsettling presence, alien to its surroundings, a contrast that vibrates with a hard immediacy.

Entresitio's ventures into the neo-Organic were no less powerful. Their medical clinic in the working-class Madrid suburb of San Blas (2006) also turned its back on the neighbourhood. In lieu of windows, thirteen glazed patios, with plants and splashes of cobalt blue tile, are scattered through its porous maze of corridors, double-height waiting areas and examining rooms. The irregular profile of the exterior, with its 'towers' and walls of board-formed concrete, recall classic Organicist 'village' compositions, while the scattered natural light of the interiors revive the Organicists' 'essential forest'.

A pared-down approach also helped to launch the post-crisis international practice of Fabrizio Barozzi and Alberto Veiga, an Italian–Spanish team that has been based in Barcelona since 2004. Their work has evolved from the starkly expressive, multi-gabled Philharmonic Hall of Szczecin in Poland (2007–14) to a more contained intensity that recalls the Romantic classicism of central Europe, where they have won several open

Sol Madridejos and Juan Carlos Sancho, chapel for a hunting estate, Almadén, province of Ciudad Real, 2000.

competitions, as in the Bündner Kunstmuseum in Chur, Switzerland (2011–16). Barozzi came to Spain from Venice on an Erasmus scholarship, and Veiga studied under Francisco Mangado in Pamplona.

We find the minimalist option opening into more unexpected creative territories in the work of RCR Architects and SelgasCano, who apply radical experiments with materials and sensorial experience to the search for immediacy we first encountered in the work of Fraile and Revillo. Rafael Aranda, Carme Pigem and Ramón Vilalta of RCR met at the Vallès architecture school, graduating in 1987, and returned to their native Olot, in the foothills of the Pyrenees, to begin designing houses for their neighbours

Estudio Entresitio, public housing in the ensanche de Vallecas, Madrid, 2004–9.

and small service buildings for local parks. The fundaments of RCR's creative sensibility are found in Minimalist art, traditional Japanese culture and an earthy vision of a lush, inhabited natural world, inspired in the volcanic terrain, forests and farmsteads of Olot. These sources come together in a kiosk and changing rooms for a local swimming hole in Olot's Tussols-Basil Fluvial Park (1995–8). The bathhouse is an exquisite sculptural object lost in the woods near the riverbank, with curbing corners and subtle inflections realized in vandal-resistant Corten steel and sandblasted stainless steel, crafted by a local foundry.

Their work took a new turn in two projects for Les Cols, a two-star Michelin restaurant housed in an eighteenth-century farmhouse in Olot. The architects used a single material, steel plate, for the restaurant interiors (2001–2), seeking to expand the material's conventional vocabulary of sensorial effects and associations. The walls of the front dining room are of oxidized steel, and the floors are unfinished steel planks, mixing the natural colours of different mills: deep blues, purples, reds and browns. Against this soft, earthy background, tables and chairs are finished in a luminous pale gold. RCR designed the tables from two plates of steel, 8 millimetres (⅜ in.) thick, which rise from the floor and fold open like leaves. The 5-millimetre plates of the chairs are ingeniously bent and folded like origami to form seat, back and a single armrest. RCR's Pavilions (2003–5) are a suite of guest rooms in the wooded gardens, each a raised pavilion built entirely of thick, frameless glass – again, walls, floors, ceilings and even baths – and set amid garden courts walled in stalks of steel and translucent glass. The rooms contain no more than a bed and retractable curtains. Following the social ceremony of dining, the Pavilions propose an intimate, meditative state of sensory awareness, an Edenic re-encounter of the body with nature. Other immersive environments created by the architects include a child-care centre in Manlleu (Barcelona, 2001–4), where skylit baths and coat rooms, walled in tinted glass in a rainbow of colours, transform space and light into palpable, almost liquid substance. The studio's major work to date is the Soulages Museum in Rodez, France (2008–14), where major galleries are finished in dark varnished steel. In 2017, the trio received the Pritzker Prize.

In the work of SelgasCano, the concept of sensory immersion and immediacy turns dayglo Pop, plastic, hedonistic and surreal. José Selgas and Lucía Cano met at the Madrid School of Architecture (both class of 1992); Cano is the daughter of Julio Cano Lasso, one of several siblings in the profession. The exterior walls and interior partitions of their El Batel Auditorium and Conference Centre in the ancient port of Cartagena (2004–11) are entirely composed of plastics (polycarbonate, Plexiglas and ETFE), brightly coloured, translucent and artificially illuminated from

within. These surfaces transform interiors into abstract, luminous fields of colour that flatten spatial depth. Human figures stand out in this setting like actors in a cartoon or inside a mobile phone's illuminated screen. The lime-white rubber floors and white walls of the 100-metre (328 ft) interior promenade that ramps down from the entry to the main auditorium are interrupted by the deep red of a long metal ramp, suspended on tension rods, that ascends to the upper level. Brilliant orange gashes in the luminous walls open niches for the information desk and a bar. The main auditorium, in contrast, is steeped in deep underwater blues, including backlit translucent side walls with a shimmering mirror-film backing. Despite the sensory extremes of these spaces, the basic building forms are elemental, a line of rectangular volumes comparable to industrial sheds. The technology behind their innovative use of plastics draws on building systems developed for Spain's agricultural industry, where thousands of hectares are cultivated under plastic greenhouses.

If the sensorial minimalism of Fraile and Revillo or RCR, and their search for a heightened awareness of everyday reality, can be seen as a reaction against the increasing encroachment of visual media and the seductive fascination of the illuminated screen, SelgasCano react by conjuring that altered reality into existence, trading ascetic astringency for something closer to the ludic altered reality of Prada Poole. The couple are also the authors of congress centres in Badajóz (2005) and Plasencia (2005–17), both in the region of Extremadura. In 2015, they built the Serpentine Pavilion in London's Hyde Park, and they have designed co-working spaces for Second Home in London (2014) and Hollywood, California (2019).

Questions of materiality, while a major theme for Spanish minimalists, were also taken up in more adventurous designs, as seen in the work of AMP architects in the Canary Islands and Antón García-Abril in Madrid. Felipe Artengo, Fernando Menis and José María Rodríguez-Pastrana formed AMP in Tenerife in 1981. In the Presidency Building for the head of the regional government in Santa Cruz de Tenerife, they developed an expressive, muscular neo-Brutalism inspired by the abrupt volcanic landscapes of the islands (competition 1986; redesign and construction 1993–2001). Building materials included large slabs of multicoloured volcanic rock, planks of native tea pine, centuries old, and concrete worked up into creases, folds, waves and other manipulations. The architects would climb into the formwork to insert jagged shards of wood, or set it on fire to draw out its knots and veins. Halfway through the design, they incorporated into the central court the glazed galleries and stairs, in chestnut and tea, of the Hamilton Patio, the remains of a seventeenth-century mansion, which they discovered disassembled in a government warehouse.

Salvage was an integral part of AMP's hands-on methods. In Berlin, they converted an old coal barge into a floating swimming pool on the Spree (2003–4), where the blue underwater lighting transformed the floating decks and pool into a miniature island resort. In Santa Cruz, they persuaded the regional government to convert an obsolete gas deposit into 'El Tanque',

SelgasCano, El Batel Auditorium and Conference Centre, Cartagena, 2004–11. View along sloping entry gallery with underside of suspended metal ramp to upper level.

a multi-use arts space (1997). Menis had family ties to members of the regional government, and AMP's influence contributed to other cultural projects, such as Herzog & de Meuron's TEA museum and cultural centre in Santa Cruz (1999–2007). (In the same period, although unrelated, Calatrava built a concert hall in Santa Cruz (2003), and Óscar Tusquets designed the Alfredo Kraus Concert Hall in Las Palmas, 1992–7).

While the Presidency Building had a conventional concrete frame structure, in subsequent work AMP used masses of poured concrete as primary structural and formal elements. In the Magma Arts and Congress Centre in Adeje, Tenerife (largely developed by Menis, 1996–2005), monumental piers of jack-hammered concrete, tinted with local volcanic ash, encircle the multi-use hall, the waves of its white fibre-cement-board roof billowing between them, like a wilder version of Le Corbusier's chapel at Ronchamp. Menis left AMP in 2004 and continued in this direction, as in his Concert Hall in Jordanki, Poland (2008–15), where the jack-hammered concrete exposed the lumps of recycled broken brick used as aggregate, contributing to the auditorium's acoustic performance.

Antón García-Abril of Ensemble Studio (founded in 2000) also jumps into the building process, although his approach is more like that of a showman. One of his first stunts was to erect a neo-Megalithic portico of unfinished granite slabs for the facade of a private cultural centre and offices in Santiago de Compostela (SGAE Headquarters, 2005–7). The oversized boulders, culled from quarry debris, were pitched up into an irregular colonnade without mortar or other connections, leaning this way and that like an untidy bookcase. For the Casa Hemeroscopium, his home outside Madrid (2005–8), he stacked up a vertiginous, spiralling cage of varied surplus beams for highway bridges, including a section of an irrigation aqueduct filled with water, which he precariously balanced against one another like a juggler. Living quarters occupy a simple glazed container at the base of the structure. García-Abril now teaches at the Massachusetts Institute of Technology (MIT), where he and his wife, the Spanish architect Débora Mesa, founded POPlab in 2012, a research institute dedicated to developing new techniques of prefabrication. One of their first experiments was the family home in Brookline, Massachusetts, assembled from Styrofoam beams finished with metal studs and cement board (2015).

To the list of those drawn to a greater formal exuberance or complexity, we can add the heirs of Miralles, those who explore different versions of what I have called neo-Organicism, and others who, like Iñaki Ábalos, develop their positions in more theoretical or academic terms. Of the Miralles circle, Carme Pinós stands out for her beautifully constructed, lyrical works, in which compositional elements come together in dynamic couplings and triads. The two L-shaped volumes of the galleries in the

Fernando Menis,
Concert Hall, Jordanki,
Poland, 2008–15.

CaixaForum of Zaragoza (2008–15) cantilever out from the central structure on different levels, looking out in different directions like a couple dancing the tango. Other examples include the Cube Tower in Guadalajara, Mexico (2002–5), and Barcelona's Massana School of Art and Design (2008–17). Benedetta Tagliabue, for her part, maintains the EMBT imprint in Barcelona, with works including the Spanish Pavilion for the 2010 World's Fair in Shanghai, and waterside public spaces for the HafenCity district of Hamburg (2002–11). Two of Miralles's former employees, Ricardo Flores and Eva Prats, who opened their studio in 1998, create sensitive dialogues between past and present in the reuse of existing buildings, as in the Sala Beckett Theatre in Barcelona's Poblenou district (2011–14).

Neo-Organicist options include a tendency to break programme elements into independent, loosely connected volumes, as in Entresitio's Casa #1.130 outside Madrid (2013), where indoor and outdoor spaces intermingle. In the repetitive programmes of social housing, building masses are often broken up into cellular assemblies with an added element of idiosyncrasy, as in the random colour patterns of units in a project by Atxu Amann, Andrés Cánovas and Nicolás Maruri in Madrid's new ensanche of Carabanchel (2009). On a nearby block, Dosmasuno Architects (Néstor Montenegro, Ignacio Borrego and Lina Toro) added extra bedrooms to their basic one-bedroom units by simply projecting them off the building's exterior wall, in a haphazard pattern of surprising cantilevers (2008). At a larger scale, in the master plan for Madrid's unrealized City of Justice in the ensanche of Valdebebas (2005), the fourteen buildings were all circular, of different diameters, and distributed across the site tangentially, like the cogs and wheels of an old movie projector; its authors were Javier Frechilla and José Manuel López-Peláez (Madrid, class of 1970).

For architects with a more theoretical approach, a common strategy has been to open their thinking to other disciplines and wider social and cultural concerns. Alejandro Zaera and Farshid Moussavi of Foreign Office Architects (FOA) began their practice using concepts from advanced mathematics as tools for design innovation. Zaera (Madrid, class of 1987) met the Iranian-born Moussavi at Harvard, and the two apprenticed with Rem Koolhaas before settling in London in 1993, where they taught at the Architectural Association. In their competition-winning design for the Yokohama Passenger Ship Terminal in Japan (1995–2002), they conceived the multi-level, mixed-use pier as a continuous folded surface, a complex topological figure that splits and opens in mouth-like ramps from level to level to suggest an uninterrupted spatial flow. FOA's work in Spain includes a waterfront park with an outdoor auditorium for the Barcelona Forum (2004), and the Institute for Legal Medicine, the only completed building in Madrid's City of Justice (2009), which is based on the topological figure of the torus or doughnut. In the ensanche of Carabanchel, they built a housing block clad entirely in stalks of bamboo, with the look of a habitable haystack (2008). The bamboo fills the continuous facades of folding shutters, which screen shallow galleries and floor-to-ceiling glass. Zaera was named professor at Princeton in 2008 and briefly served as dean of the School of Architecture (2012–14), though his tenure there was embattled and ended in controversy. The couple separated in 2009 and now maintain separate practices.

Like García-Abril, Andrés Jaque has attracted attention in the United States using the strategies of the showman, though his stance is more critically attuned, as seen in the name of his studio, Office for Political Innovation, which was founded in 2004. His stunts include the Escaravox in the main plaza of Madrid's Matadero (2012), for which he customized a 40-metre (130 ft) mobile irrigation rig, adding plastic seating, shading and a sound system to create a flexible performance space and outdoor hangout. In 2015, he built another machine for the Museum of Modern

Carme Pinós,
CaixaForum,
Zaragoza, 2008–15.

Ecosistema Urbano,
Air Tree, new ensanche
de Vallecas, Madrid,
2004–7.

Art's PS1 in Queens, New York, a transparent, portable waste-water treatment plant with a capacity of 13,640 litres (3,000 gal.). His growing portfolio of recent projects include a Madrid restaurant that unites dining and kitchen in an 'urban technofarm' (Run Run Run, 2019). He was named dean of Columbia University's architecture school in New York in 2022.

Belinda Tato and José Luis Vallejo of Ecosistema Urbano, founded in Madrid in 2000, also began their careers with a hit: the so-called prosthetic trees for the ensanche de Vallecas. They have since developed a worldwide, multidisciplinary practice based on community participation in urban design and focusing on issues of social space and environmental planning. They currently teach in the architecture programmes of Harvard and

Columbia, respectively. The prosthetic trees – open drum-shaped structures erected at three intersections along Vallecas's semi-pedestrian Bulevar de la Naturaleza (Nature Boulevard) – were designed as temporary structures to create the beneficial microclimatic effects of a tree cover lacking in the still-nascent development, as well as offering social gathering spaces (2004–7). One was lined with potted vegetation, another ringed by tubular chimneys with fans and water misting to create cooling downdrafts. The devices are set amid a cluster of public housing, with a few adventurous designs by younger architects. The studio's current work focuses on techniques of what they call 'the self-organization of citizens'.[38] For the redevelopment of the main square in the town of Hamar in Norway (2011–13), their design process included public brainstorming sessions supported by workshops, lectures from international figures, exhibits, mock-ups, digital projections and an online network and database of citizen ideas.

This brief survey, taken from a period of unprecedented creativity and abundance, has left out many. The intention has been to present the range of approaches as seen in representative cases, rather than attempting to include every significant studio and its work. This extraordinary flourishing came to an end with the economic crisis of 2008, but the crisis produced a new, though marginal, architectural culture of its own. Ecosistema's network-based, participatory design process was part of a generational movement represented by a new type of architectural studio: the collective, such as Madrid's Zuloark, Basurama or PKMN, in which the hierarchy of the traditional office was replaced with network-based collective work. As the crisis deepened, these collectives became active in new social and political movements, which were similarly non-hierarchical, democratic organizations sustained by social media and networking. Prominent among the latter was the 'Okupa' movement, in which neighbourhood collectives and activists occupied abandoned buildings and converted them into local cultural centres, and appropriated empty lots to create community gardens. There grew to be as many as eighty such occupied sites in Madrid, as well as squats in empty housing and organized resistance to forced evictions. Two prominent examples, ultimately accepted by authorities, were the Tabacalera, a ruinous eighteenth-century tobacco-packing plant in central Madrid, and the large public space of the Campo de la Cebada (Oat Field), where Zuloark and other architectural collectives had a prominent role in the garden's design and operation.[39]

The wave of collective action culminated with 'M-15', a protest settlement occupying Madrid's central Puerta de Sol, which began on 15 May 2011 and lasted two months. The settlement anticipated Occupy Wall Street and similar actions elsewhere, and gave rise to new leftist political parties such as Podemos, founded in 2014. In 2015, coalitions of these parties won municipal elections in Madrid and Barcelona, led respectively by Manuela Carmena, a retired judge and labour rights lawyer during the Transition, and Ada Colau, a young anti-eviction organizer. Their measures included citizen participation in urban design plans, such as the redevelopment of Madrid's Plaza de España, and citywide environmental programmes. Podemos, for its part, entered the national government, joining a coalition led by the Socialist Party in 2017.

In this chapter we have seen how Spain's architects of the twenty-first century have conceived their work in resistance to the dominant international theme of the icon, which at the same time so fascinated the country's politicians. This resistance prepared the way for a reappraisal of architecture's role in society following the 2008 crisis. The outlines of such a vision are visible in the ideas of collective organization, community participation and broad, multidisciplinary environmental and territorial thinking discussed above. Other hints are found, for example, in RCR's focus on a sensibility of place, in the low-profile renovations of Flores and Prats and others, whose interventions commingle with a palimpsest of pre-existing conditions, or in the thermodynamic, holistic environmental thinking of Ábalos and Sentkiewicz. In these practices and others, the design of a building as a discrete object is not the central focus. Rather, the project becomes the locus of a holistic, multidimensional investigation that seeks to understand all the forces at play around the given locus, and then propose a strategy to positively influence those forces through an intervention. Such an approach is nothing new in architecture. Understanding and addressing the complexities of a given project has always been an essential part of the design process, as we have seen with particular clarity in the case of Oriol Bohigas's urban policies for Barcelona, or even in the conception of the Guggenheim Museum in Bilbao. But in Spain's present situation, the tendencies noted above suggest that a shift of emphasis away from built, formal results and towards a larger field of vision may be the best way to understand what architecture – as a discipline, a culture and a way of thinking – can best offer society in the face of its most pressing current challenges.

Epilogue

One of the most striking characteristics of Spanish architecture observed in these pages has been a recurring oscillation between opposing poles of flamboyant display and austere reticence. In the first chapter, the formal and decorative richness of works produced in search of a 'national' style, whether at the hands of Antonio Palacios or Antoni Gaudí, with their flights of grandiosity, betray the insecurities and ambitions of a diminished Spain in the international context of imperial competition. Calls for austerity came in reaction to these perceived excesses, from the Noucentistes in Barcelona, the Free Institution of Teaching (ILE) in Madrid and the young modernists of the 1920s and '30s.

This cycle recurs through the following decades, revealing a larger pattern to the abrupt shifts of direction appearing with each new generation as Spain's dramatic political and social upheavals sweep old arguments off the table time and again. Thus, the monumentalism of the early dictatorship is succeeded by the practical functionalism of the 1950s, and the Organicist flowering of the prosperous 1960s provokes nascent countercurrents in the following decade, from Prada Poole's pneumatic domes to the incipient High-Tech of Sáenz de Oiza's Bank of Bilbao. Reacting against both functionalism and Organicism, the public architecture of the new democracy proposed a new sort of monumentality, combining the complexity of the historic context with the banality of the Tendenza and its type forms. Since the 1990s, the two poles of minimalism and free iconic invention have developed simultaneously, with the caveat that the most radical forms of minimalism, such as those by the likes of Viaplana and Piñón or Fraile and Revillo, are as demanding in the intensity of their formalism as anything by Enric Miralles, for example.

Spanish architecture is nevertheless further unified on both sides of this divide by another common characteristic, first presented here in the form of the structural rationalism of Viollet-le-Duc, a model for Gaudí and the Modernistes. This concept was still central by the end of the twentieth century, although it had evolved or broadened from a focus on the logic of construction to a more general emphasis on the technical, embracing mechanical services, suppliers' catalogues and other aspects of modern construction.

On one hand, Spanish architects defended traditional styles against the forms of modernism by understanding them as a constructive system rather than a decorative programme, as seen in the work and ideas of Secundino Zuazo, Luis Moya and Rafael Moneo. Part of the resistance of early Madrid modernists such as Luis Lacasa to the work of Le Corbusier can be understood in these terms. From the perspective of their allegiance to the formal logic of masonry construction, for reasons of training and local conditions, Le Corbusier's abstract planes of plastered brick seemed like a shoddy pastiche.

On the other hand, while the logic of construction served to justify traditionalist positions, such technical arguments were also used to contest them, from Bergamín's praise of the standardized steel windows and cork insulation of his Casa del Marqués de Villora to Aizpurúa's dismissal of traditional architects as 'pastry chefs'. After the Civil War, Alejandro de la Sota was one of the most radical exponents of Bergamín's 'not making architecture'. But the centrality of technique, or what Moneo has called a 'disciplinary practice', is an often-unspoken principle underlying all Spanish architecture and has led to some of its most inventive works, as seen in SelgasCano's adoption of the technology of greenhouse agriculture in their projects.

This primacy of technique contrasts to the design process of Frank Gehry's Guggenheim in Bilbao, for example, conceived in working models and engineered afterwards by technical specialists. For Gehry, the titanium skin was one option selected among others in the search for a material capable of adapting itself to his formal concept. Moneo's Roman Museum in Mérida, however, is inconceivable without its brick fabric. Form and technical means were inseparable in its conception. The same could be said for virtually any work of architecture in Spain.

Ultimately, this technical focus has its roots in the idea that architecture is as much a science as an art. In this sense, Spanish architecture continues the defence of Reason and the spirit of the Enlightenment that characterized its beginnings amid the shadows of a decadent and defeated post-imperial Spain (indeed, those shadows have also extended well into the twentieth century). But considered on its own terms, this hard reliance on the facts of the case, the material conditions of design and the constraints of manifest reality, has surely enriched Spanish architecture, giving its best works a distinctive depth and intensity.

References

Quotes are translated from Spanish and edited by the author unless noted.

chapter one A Short History, 1750–1925

1 General John Aitchison, *An Ensign in the Peninsular War: The Letters of John Aitchison* (London, 1981), p. 187.
2 See for example: Leonardo Benevolo, *History of Modern Architecture* (Cambridge, MA, 1977); Kenneth Frampton, *Modern Architecture: A Critical History*, 4th edn (London, 2007).
3 Raymond Carr, *The Civil War in Spain, 1936–1939* (London, 1986), pp. 2–3.
4 Ibid., pp. 13–15.
5 Fernando de Terán, *Historia del urbanismo en España III: siglos XIX y XX* (Madrid, 1999), p. 61.
6 Pío Baroja, 'Cuenca', *Arquitectura*, 2 (June 1918), pp. 28–9.
7 Sigfried Giedion, *Building in France, Building in Iron, Building in Ferro-Concrete* [1928] (Santa Monica, CA, 1995), pp. 146–57.
8 A. and M. J. Arnaiz, 'Andaba suelto un arquitecto loco con delirios de grandeza', in *Madrid no construido*, ed. Colegio Oficial de Arquitectos de Madrid (Madrid, 1986), pp. 120–23.
9 Julio Arrechea, *Arquitectura y romanticismo: el pensamiento arquitectónico en la España del XIX* (Valladolid, 1989), p. 29.
10 For the nationalist hermeneutics of Gaudí's works, see Juan José Lahuerta, *Antoni Gaudí: arquitectura, ideología y política* (Madrid, 1993).
11 Robert Hughes, *Barcelona* (New York, 1992), p. 377. For the relation to Carlism, see Carr, *Civil War*, p. 11.
12 Walter Benjamin, 'Paris, Capital of the Nineteenth Century', in *The Arcades Project* (Cambridge, MA, and London, 1999), pp. 8–9.
13 Ibid.
14 Gerald Brenan, *The Spanish Labyrinth: The Social and Political Background of the Spanish Civil War*, 2nd edn (Cambridge, 1974), pp. 30–34.
15 Eugeni d'Ors, *Glosari* (Barcelona, 1907), quoted in Ángel Urrutia, *Arquitectura española del siglo XX* (Madrid, 1997), p. 186.
16 Oriol Bohigas, *Desde los años inciertos* (Barcelona, 1989), p. 8.
17 Rodolfo Ucha Donate, *Cincuenta años de arquitectura española* (Madrid, 1980), pp. 71–2.
18 Carlos Flores, *Arquitectura española contemporánea* (Madrid, 1988), vol. I, p. 97.
19 Luis Lacasa, *Luis Lacasa: escritos, 1922–1931* (Madrid, 1976), p. 87.

chapter two The First Modernists, 1910–25

1 Jorge Guillén, 'Azorín', in *Aire nuestro III: homenaje* (Barcelona, 1978), pp. 424–5.
2 'Modern' and 'rational' and their derivatives were used interchangeably in the 1920s and '30s as terms of reference to the new architecture in Europe and Spain, as seen in the 1928 issue of the *La Gaceta Literaria* edited by Fernando García Mercadal (15 April 1928). Both terms had migrated from engineering and the applied sciences, but by the 1950s, 'rationalism' was

usually used as a historic term referring to architecture before the Civil War, as in Juan Daniel Fullaondo, ed., 'El Racionalismo español', *Nueva forma*, 33 (October 1968), dedicated to the early work of Sert, Zuazo, Gutiérrez Soto and others. The term 'modern' was then used more exclusively for contemporary architecture, alongside other, more specific stylistic terms such as 'organic' and 'functional'.

3 Juan Daniel Fullaondo and María Muñoz, *Historia de la arquitectura contemporánea española*, vol. I: *Mirando hacia atrás con cierta ira (a veces)* (Madrid, 1994), p. 363.

4 Gabriel Ruiz Cabrero, *El Moderno en España, 1948–2000* (Cambridge, MA, and Sevilla, 2001), p. 11.

5 Oriol Bohigas, *Modernidad en la arquitectura de la España republicana*, revd edn (Barcelona, 1990), pp. 12–14.

6 GATEPAC (attributed to Josep Lluís Sert), 'Raíces mediterráneas de la arquitectura moderna', *AC*, 18 (1935), in *Textos de crítica de arquitectura comentados*, ed. Ginés Garrido and Amdrés Canovas (Madrid, 2003), vol. I, pp. 115–24.

7 Raymond Carr, *Spain, 1808–1939* (Oxford, 1966), p. 469.

8 Ibid., p. 473.

9 Ibid., p. 528.

10 Raymond Carr, *The Civil War in Spain, 1936–1939* (London, 1986), p. 12.

11 Francisco Azorín, 'Las casas', *Arquitectura*, 3 (June 1918), pp. 48–50.

12 Unless otherwise noted, all architects mentioned in this chapter are graduates of the Madrid school of architecture.

13 Bernardo Giner de los Ríos, *Cincuenta años de arquitectura española, 1900–1950* (Madrid, 1980), pp. 70–71.

14 Francisco Giner de los Ríos, 'Conferencia Pedagógica: Local y mobiliario en la escuela', *Boletín de la Institución Libre de Enseñanza*, VI/127 (31 May 1882), p. 134.

15 Manuel Bartolomé Cossío, 'Notas sobre construcción escolar', *Boletín de la Institución Libre de Enseñanza*, XXXV/318 (30 September 1911), pp. 257–64.

16 Giner, *Cincuenta años*, pp. 70–72.

17 Ibid., p. 76.

18 Sofía Diéguez Patao, *La generación del 25: primera arquitectura moderna en Madrid* (Madrid, 1997), p. 52; Álvaro Ribagorda, 'Una ventana hacia Europa: La Residencia de Estudiantes y sus actividades culturales (1910–1936)', *Circunstancia*, 14 (September 2007), www.ortegaygasset.edu, accessed November 2010; Luis Buñuel, *My Last Sigh* (New York, 1983), pp. 41–50.

19 Diéguez Patao, *La generación*, p. 44.

20 Ibid., p. 45.

21 Ibid.

22 Giner, *Cincuenta años*, pp. 87–9.

23 Leopoldo Torres Balbás, 'Mientras labran los sillares', *Arquitectura*, 2 (June 1918), pp. 31–4.

24 Miguel de Unamuno, *En torno al casticismo* (Madrid, 1996), pp. 166–70.

25 José Ortega y Gasset, 'Unamuno y Europa, fábula', *El Imparcial* (27 September 1909), p. 3.

26 Torres Balbás, 'Las Nuevas formas de la Arquitectura', *Arquitectura*, 11 (June 1919), pp. 145–8. Le Corbusier did not start publishing *L'Esprit nouveau*, the magazine where the articles for *Vers une architecture* first appeared, until 1920.

27 Leopoldo Torres Balbás, 'Tras una nueva arquitectura', *Arquitectura*, 62 (August 1923), pp. 263–8.

28 Ibid.

29 Carlos Flores, *Arquitectura española contemporánea*, 2nd edn (Madrid, 1988), vol. I, pp. 158–9.

30 Teodoro de Anasagasti, 'Notas de un viaje. Praga', *La construcción moderna* (1914), cited in Ángel Urrutia, *Arquitectura española del siglo XX* (Madrid, 1997), p. 213.

31 Teodoro de Anasagasti, 'Sobre el cine y el hormigón armado', *La construcción moderna* (February 1919), p. 345.

32 Sigfried Giedion, 'L'Architecture contemporaine en Espagne', *Cahiers d'art*, 3 (1931), pp. 157–64.

33 Lilia Maure, *Secundino Zuazo, arquitecto* (Madrid, 1987), p. xiv.

34 José Moreno Villa, 'El arquitecto Zuazo Ugalde: Autocrítica', *Arquitectura*, 94 (February 1927), p. 67.

35 Flores, *Arquitectura española contemporánea*, vol. I, pp. 145–9.

36 Luis Lacasa, *Luis Lacasa: escritos, 1922–1931* (Madrid, 1976), p. 78.

1 Pedro Vaquero, 'La Argentinita', *García Lorca y las canciones populares antiguas*, liner notes to *Colección de canciones populares* [Collection of Popular Songs], arranged by Federico García Lorca. La Argentinita: voice, castanets; García Lorca: piano (Madrid, 1990; original, Madrid, 1931), www.sonifolk.com, accessed July 2011.

2 Bernardo Giner de los Ríos, *Cincuenta años de arquitectura española, 1900–1950* (Madrid, 1980), pp. 129–45.

3 Justo Oliva Meyer, 'Turismo y arquitectura: la modernidad como respuesta', *Vía arquitectura*, 1 (1997), pp. 24–43.

4 For example, Fernando García Mercadal, 'Algunas consideraciones sobre las plantas de la Exposición de las Artes Decorativas', *Arquitectura*, 78 (October 1925), pp. 240–44; Rafael Bergamín, 'Exposición de Artes Decorativas de París: impresiones de un turista', *Arquitectura*, 78 (October 1925), pp. 236–9.

5 Sofía Diéguez Patao, *La generación del 25: primera arquitectura moderna en Madrid* (Madrid, 1997), pp. 307–21.

6 José Carlos Mainer, 'Geometría lírica: la arquitectura en las letras españolas hacía 1930', in *GATCPAC y su tiempo: política, cultura y arquitectura en los años treinta*, ed. Fundación DoCoMoMo Ibérico (Barcelona, 2005), pp. 21–33.

7 *La Gaceta Literaria*, 32 (15 April 1928), cover.

8 Unless otherwise noted, all architects mentioned in this chapter are graduates of the Madrid school of architecture.

9 Javier de Luque, 'Madrid, 1931', *AC: documentos de actividad contemporánea*, 2 (1931), p. 37.

10 Diéguez Patao, *La generación*, pp. 288–96.

11 Luis Lacasa, *Luis Lacasa: escritos, 1922–1931* (Madrid, 1976), pp. 128–49; Fernando García Mercadal, 'Encuesta sobre la nueva arquitectura', *La Gaceta Literaria*, 32 (15 April 1928), in Ángel Urrutia, *Arquitectura española contemporánea: documentos, escritos, testimonios inéditos* (Madrid, 2002), pp. 169–73.

12 Mercadal, 'Encuesta sobre la nueva arquitectura', pp. 169–73.

13 Lacasa, *Escritos*, p. 146.

14 R. B. [attrib. Rafael Bergamín], 'Eso no es arquitectura', *Arquitectura*, 63 (July 1924), pp. 208–11.

15 R. B. [Bergamín], 'Casa del Marqués de Villora en Madrid', *Arquitectura*, 113 (September 1928), pp. 282–8.

16 Bergamín, 'Un poco de historia', in 'Sesion de critica de arquitectura: El Viso', *Arquitectura*, 101 (May 1967), pp. 22–34.

17 Martín Domínguez, 'Le Corbusier, en recuerdos y presupuestos personales', *Nueva forma*, 64 (May 1971), pp. 35, 52, 58, 60, 62–5.

18 For the auditorium's programming, see Chus Cantero, 'El concepto de la extensión universitaria a lo largo de la historia', *Colección Observatorio Atalaya* (Sevilla, 2006), pp. 77–8.

19 Eduardo Torroja, *The Structures of Eduardo Torroja: An Autobiography of Engineering Accomplishment* (New York, 1958), p. 14.

20 Carlos Fernández Casado, 'Félix Huarte – estructuras', *Arquitectura*, 154 (October 1991), pp. 17–19.

21 Eduardo Torroja, 'Estructura de la cubierta del Hipódromo de la Zarzuela', *Informes de la construcción*, 137 (January–February 1962), pp. 154–6.

22 Javier Frechilla and José Manuel López-Peláez, *Luis Gutiérrez Soto, arquitecto* (Madrid, 1997), p. 10.

23 Ian Gibson, *En busca de José Antonio* (Barcelona, 1980), pp. 218–20.

24 Francisco Javier Muñoz Fernández, 'Un nuevo moblaje para una nueva arquitectura: espacio y modernidad en el País Vasco anterior a la guerra', Congreso Internacional de Imagen y Apariencia (Murcia, 2008), http://congresos.um.es.

25 Casto Fernández-Shaw, 'Estación para el servicio de automóviles', *Arquitectura*, 100 (August 1927), pp. 301–3.

26 Mainer, 'Geometría lírica', p. 32.

27 Luz Feduchi, 'Breve historia de Rolaco y su incidencia en el diseño de Madrid', in *Diseño industrial en España*, ed. Daniel Giralt-Miracle, Juli Capella and Quim Larrea (Madrid, 1998), pp. 83–4.

28 Lilia Maure, *Secundino Zuazo, arquitecto* (Madrid, 1987), p. 24.

29 Carlos Sambricio, 'Hermann Jansen y el concurso de Madrid de 1929', *Arquitectura*, 303 (1995), pp. 8–15.

30 Joaquín Medina Warmburg, 'Irredentos y conversos: Presencias e influencias alemanas: de la neutralidad a la postguerra española (1914–1943)', in *Modelos alemanes e italianos para España en los años de la postguerra*, ed. José Manuel Pozo (Pamplona, 2004), pp. 32–3.

31 Maure, *Zuazo*, pp. 308–9.

32 Ibid., p. 315.

33 Ibid., pp. 308–9.

chapter four **The Provinces and Barcelona: Stylists versus Revolutionaries, 1929–39**

1 Rafael Alberti, *La arboleda perdida: memorias* (Barcelona, 1975), pp. 277–8. Edited for brevity by David Cohn.

2 Sofía Diéguez Patao, *La generación del 25: primera arquitectura moderna en Madrid* (Madrid, 1997), pp. 157–8.

3 Ibid., pp. 158–9.

4 Ángel Urrutia, *Arquitectura española del siglo xx* (Madrid, 1997), p. 281.

5 José Antonio Sosa Díaz-Saavedra, ed., *Arquitectura moderna en Canarias, 1925–1965* (Santa Cruz de Tenerife, 2002), p. 46, n. 4; Joaquín Medina Warmburg, 'Imágenes de la ciudad hanseática: Richard Ernst Oppel, arquitecto entre Hamburgo y Canarias', *Basa*, 23 (2000), pp. 120–37.

6 Warmburg, 'Imágenes de la ciudad hanseática, pp. 120–37.

7 María Isabel Navarro Segura, '*Gaceta de Arte* y el proyecto de una arquitectura y un urbanismo modernos', in *Gaceta de Arte, 1932–1935*, ed. Federico García Barba (Santa Cruz de Tenerife, 1989), p. 32.

8 María Isabel Navarro Segura and Álvaro Ruíz Rodríguez, *La arquitectura como escenografía: José Enrique Marrero Regalado, 1897–1956*, exh. cat., Colegio Oficial de Arquitectos de Canarias (Santa Cruz de Tenerife, 1992), p. 58.

9 Ibid., p. 135.

10 Pedro García Cabrera, 'Casas para obreros', *Gaceta de Arte*, 4 (May 1932), p. 3.

11 Enrique Granell, 'ac contra todos', in *GATCPAC y su tiempo: política, cultura y arquitectura en los años treinta*, ed. Fundación DoCoMoMo Ibérico (Barcelona, 2005), p. 189.

12 The Eastern Group is often called 'GATCPAC', substituting the 'E' of España for the 'C' of Catalunya, but this name only appeared on the group's storefront on the Passeig de Gràcia before the nomenclature of the different regional divisions had been agreed upon. Thereafter, the Catalans signed their collective projects as 'GATEPAC GE' (Grupo Este). See Antonio Pizza, 'La experiencia del GATCPAC en el contexto de la arquitectura española', in *GATCPAC y su tiempo*, pp. 13–19. For this reason, unlike many Catalan historians, I have not used the initials GATCPAC to refer to the Barcelona Group.

13 Pizza, 'La experiencia del GATCPAC', p. 15.

14 *AC: documentos de actividad contemporánea*, 1 (1931), p. 13.

15 Luis Moya, 'Idea sobre un genio en la edad juvenil', *Nueva forma*, 40 (May 1969), p. 105.

16 José Manuel Aizpurúa, '¿Cuándo habrá arquitectura?', *La Gaceta Literaria* (1 March 1930), reprinted in José Ángel Sanz Esquide, *Real Club Náutico de San Sebastián, 1928–1929* (Almería, 1995), pp. 65–7.

17 Francisco Javier Muñoz Fernández, 'Un nuevo moblaje para una nueva arquitectura: Espacio y modernidad en el País Vasco anterior a la guerra', Congreso Internacional de Imagen y Apariencia (Murcia, 2008), http://congresos.um.es.

18   Siegfried Giedion, 'L'Architecture contemporaine en Espagne', *Cahiers d'art*, 3 (1931), pp. 157–64.
19   José Ángel Sanz Esquide, *La tradición de lo nuevo en el País Vasco: la arquitectura de los años treinta* (Barcelona, 1988), p. 329.
20   Felipe Ximénez de Sandoval, 'El telón de los caídos' [The Curtain of the Fallen], *Rastoria 1*, Asociación Cultural 'Rastro de la Historia' ['Traces of History' Cultural Association], n.d., www.rumbos.net, accessed July 2008.
21   Gabriel Celaya, *Poesía y verdad: papeles para un proceso* (Barcelona, 1979), pp. 149–50.
22   José-Carlos Mainer, 'Geometría lirica: la arquitectura en las letras españolas hacía 1930', in *GATCPAC y su tiempo*, pp. 32–3.
23   Ibid.
24   Ibid.
25   Ernesto Giménez Caballero, *Arte y estado* [1935] (Madrid, 2009), pp. 139, 149.
26   Carlos Flores, *Arquitectura española contemporánea* (Madrid, 1988), vol. 1, pp. 185–6.
27   *AC*, 9–10 (1933).
28   *AC*, 8 (1932), p. 39.
29   Josep M. Rovira, *José Luis Sert, 1901–1983* (London, 2003), pp. 49–52.
30   Josep Lluís Sert, 'Arquitectura sin "estilo" y sin "arquitecto"', *D'aci i d'allà*, XXII/179 (1934), in *Textos de crítica de arquitectura comentados*, ed. Ginés Garrido and Amdrés Canovas (Madrid, 2003), vol. 1, pp. 125–7.
31   GATEPAC, 'Raíces mediterráneas de la arquitectura moderna', *AC*, 18 (1935), in *Textos de crítica de arquitectura comentados*, pp. 115–24.
32   Ernesto Giménez Caballero, *Arte y estado* (Madrid, 2009), pp. 147–51.
33   See also Le Corbusier, 'España', *Residencia de estudiantes*, 8 (June 1999), www.residencia.csic.es, accessed November 2010.
34   Rovira, *Sert*, p. 204; Kenneth Frampton, *Modern Architecture: A Critical History*, 4th edn (London, 2007), p. 160.
35   Rovira, *Sert*, p. 234.
36   Ibid., p. 79.
37   GATEPAC, 'El GATCPAC ante la transformación social actual', *AC*, 23–4 (1936), p. 8.
38   GATEPAC, 'Problemes de la revolució', *AC*, 2 (June 1937).

chapter five Modernism Expunged: The Civil War and Its Aftermath, 1936–50

1   Carlos Barral, *Los años sin excusa: memorias II* (Barcelona, 1978), pp. 33–4. Edited for brevity by David Cohn.
2   Raymond Carr, *The Civil War in Spain, 1936–1939* (London, 1986), pp. 122–5.
3   Henry Vicente Garrido, ed., *Arquitecturas desplazadas: arquitecturas del exilio español*, exh. cat., Ministerio de Vivienda (Madrid, 2007), pp. 212, 266–7.
4   Dirección General de Arquitectura, 'Orden por la que se imponen sanciones a los arquitectos que se mencionan', *Boletín de la Dirección General de Arquitectura* (9 July 1942).
5   Jaume Claret Miranda, *El atroz desmoche: la destrucción de la Universidad española por el franquismo, 1936–1945* (Barcelona, 2006).
6   Francisco Giral, *Ciencia española en el exilio, 1939–1989: el exilio de los científicos españoles* (Barcelona, 1994), p. 370.
7   José Manuel Pozo, J. Alberto Mínguez and Cristina Sanz, eds, *Javier Lahuerta Vargas: docencia y Oficio de la Arquitectura* (Pamplona, 1996), pp. 41–5.
8   Miguel Ángel Baldellou, 'Desarraigo y encuentro: las arquitecturas del exilio', *Arquitectura*, 303 (1995), p. 16.
9   Garrido, *Arquitecturas desplazadas*, pp. 196–7.
10   Ibid., p. 178.
11   Bernardo Giner de los Ríos, *Cincuenta años de arquitectura española, 1900–1950* [1952] (Madrid, 1980), pp. 193–5.

12 Ángel Urrutia, *Arquitectura española del siglo xx* (Madrid, 1997), p. 327; Tereixa Constenla, 'Retratos tras el consejo de guerra', *El País* (4 April 2010), www.elpais.com.

13 Jesús García Calero, 'La muestra "Zuazo, arquitecto del Madrid de la ii República" provoca un vivo debate sobre la memoria histórica', *ABC* (10 October 2006), www.abc.es.

14 'Luis Gutiérrez Soto: biografía y obra', *Arte España: portal de la historia del arte*, www. arteespana.com, accessed November 2010.

15 José Ramón Menéndez de Luarca Navia Osorio, 'Recuerdo de Martín Domínguez en Cornell', in *Martín Domínguez Esteban*, ed. Pablo Rabasco and Martín Domínguez Ruz (Ithaca, NY, 2015), pp. 204–6.

16 Centro Vasco de Arquitectura, 'Teodoro de Anasagasti y Algan, 1880–1938', Fondos del Archivo Histórico, http://ehai-cva.com, accessed November 2010.

17 Francisco J. Sáenz de Oiza, Javier Sáenz Guerra and Rosario Alberdi, *Francisco Javier Sáenz de Oiza*, exh. cat., Ministerio de Fomento (Madrid, 1996), p. 3; Francisco González de Canales and Nicholas Ray, *Rafael Moneo: Building, Teaching, Writing* (New Haven, CT, 2015), p. 21.

18 Inés Sánchez de Madariaga, *Matilde Ucelay Maórtua: una vida en construcción* (Madrid, 2012).

19 Carlos Sambricio, 'Eduardo Torroja y la vivienda antes y después de la Guerra Civil Española', *Informes de la construcción*, LV/488 (November–December 2003), pp. 66–9.

20 Sánchez de Madariaga, *Matilde Ucelay Maórtua*, p. 52.

21 Andrés Fernández Rubio, 'Murió Blanco Soler, director de la Academia de Bellas Artes', *El País* (30 January 1988).

22 Oriol Bohigas, *Desde los años inciertos* (Barcelona, 1989), p. 201.

23 Dirección General de Arquitectura, 'Presentación', *Revista nacional de arquitectura*, 1 (1941), in Ángel Urrutia, *Arquitectura española contemporánea: documentos, escritos, testimonios inéditos* (Madrid, 2002), pp. 235–6.

24 Enrique Granell, 'La inesperada visita del falangista Muguruza', in *Textos de crítica de arquitectura comentados*, ed. Ginés Garrido and Andrés Cánovas (Madrid, 2003), vol. I, p. 150.

25 Antón Capitel, 'Madrid, los años 40: ante una moderna arquitectura', *Cuadernos de arquitectura*, 121 (1977), p. 9.

26 Pedro Muguruza, 'Ideas generales sobre ordenación y reconstrucción nacional', Inaugural Address at the First Assembly of Architects (Madrid, 1939), quoted in Granell, 'Muguruza', p. 155.

27 Granell, 'Muguruza', pp. 149–52.

28 Ibid., p. 152.

29 Junta de Reconstrucción de Madrid, 'Ordenación General de Madrid' (Madrid, 1942), in Luis Azurmendi, 'Orden y desorden en el plan de Madrid del 41', *Cuadernos de arquitectura*, 121 (1977), p. 17.

30 Natalia Junquera, 'El reto maldito de arrebatar a Franco el Valle de los Caídos: los forenses del Gobierno creen casi imposible exhumar a los republicanos', *El País* (23 September 2010).

31 Luis Moya and Vizconde de Uzqueta, 'Sueño arquitectónico para una exaltación nacional', *Vértice*, 36 (September 1940), pp. 7–12.

32 Capitel, 'Madrid, los años 40', p. 10.

33 Luis Moya, 'Orientaciones de arquitectura en Madrid', *Reconstrucción* (December 1940), pp. 10–15.

34 Moya and Álvarez-Uzqueta, 'Sueño', pp. 7–12.

35 Capitel, 'Madrid, los años 40', p. 10.

36 Ángel Urrutia, 'Entrevista con Luis Moya', in Urrutia, *Documentos*, p. 247.

chapter six **The Return to Modernism, 1949–60**

1 Vittorio Gregotti, 'España arquitectónica 1968', in *Arquitectura contemporánea española*, ed. Luis Domènech i Girbau (Barcelona, 1968), p. 27.

2 Rosa Montero, 'Miguel Fisac, el gran superviviente', *El País Semanal*, 1,426 (25 January 2004), pp. 14–19.

3   For Madrid, César Ortiz-Echagüe, *Cincuenta años después* (Pamplona, 2001), p. 6; for
     Barcelona, Oriol Bohigas, *Desde los años inciertos* (Barcelona, 1989), p. 334.

4   Federico Correa, *Federico Correa: arquitecto, crítico y profesor* (Pamplona, 2002), p. 52.

5   Francisco Prieto Moreno, 'Discurso de apertura', *Revista nacional de arquitectura*, 90 (June
     1949), p. 236.

6   Juan de Zavala, 'Tendencias actuales de la arquitectura', *Revista nacional de arquitectura*, 90
     (June 1949), pp. 264–8.

7   Gio Ponti, 'El arquitecto Gio Ponti en la Asamblea', *Revista nacional de arquitectura*, 90
     (June 1949), p. 269.

8   Antonio Pizza, 'Entrevista Póstuma', UPC – *Butlletí de la Universitat Politècnica de Barcelona*,
     7 (1984).

9   Ponti, 'Arquitecto Gio Ponti en la Asamblea', p. 269.

10   Alejandro de la Sota, '1a Bienal Hispanoamericana', *Boletín de información de la Dirección
     General de Arquitectura*, IV (1952), p. 18.

11   Antonio Pizza and Josep M. Rovira, *Coderch, 1940–1964: en busca del hogar* (Barcelona, 2000),
     p. 92.

12   Opus Dei Awareness Network, 'An Interview with Miguel Fisac: An Insight into the Early Years
     of Opus Dei' (2000), www.opuslibros.org, accessed July 2004. See also Montero, 'Miguel Fisac'.

13   Francisco Arques Soler, *Miguel Fisac* (Madrid, 1996), p. 35.

14   Alberto Moncada, 'La evolución del Opus Dei en España' [The Evolution of the Opus Dei in
     Spain], VI Congreso Español de Sociología (1999), www.opuslibros.org, accessed July 2004.

15   Ángel Urrutia, 'Entrevista con Miguel Fisac' (1979), in Urrutia, *Arquitectura española
     contemporánea: documentos, escritos, testimonios inéditos* (Madrid, 2002), pp. 411–12.

16   Arques Soler, *Fisac*, pp. 35–6.

17   Antonio Moragas, 'Deu anys del Grupo R', *Serra d'Or* (November–December 1961), in Urrutia,
     Documentos, p. 291.

18   Carme Rodríguez and Jorge Torres, *Grup R* (Barcelona, 1994), p. 80.

19   Bohigas, *Años inciertos*, pp. 95–6, 131.

20   Oriol Bohigas, *Entusiasmos compartidos y batallas sin cuartel* (Barcelona, 1996), p. 61.

21   Bohigas, *Años inciertos*, p. 343.

22   Carlos Flores, *Arquitectura española contemporánea* (Madrid, 1988), vol. I, p. 8.

23   José Luis Fernández del Amo, *Fernández del Amo, arquitectura, 1942–1982*, exh. cat., Museo
     Espanol de Arte Contemporaneo (Madrid, 1983), pp. 40–41.

24   Pablo Serrano, 'Testimonio', ibid., p. 21.

25   Gabriel Ureña, *Las vanguardias artísticas en la postguerra Española: 1940–1959* (Madrid, 1982),
     p. 130.

26   Alejandro de la Sota, *Alejandro de la Sota, arquitecto* (Madrid, 1989), p. 34; italics are De la Sota's.

27   Luis Fernández-Galiano, Justo F. Isasi and Antonio Lopera, *La quimera moderna: los Poblados
     Dirigidos de Madrid en la arquitectura de los 50* (Madrid, 1989), p. 99.

28   Ortiz-Echagüe, *Cincuenta años*, p. 6.

29   José Manuel López-Peláez, 'Oiza y el reflejo del Zeitgeist', *El Croquis*, 32–3 (1988), p. 186.

30   Juan Daniel Fullaondo, 'La Escuela de Madrid', *Arquitectura*, 118 (October 1968), pp. 11–23.

31   Colegio Oficial de Arquitectos de Madrid, eds, *J. M. García de Paredes: arquitecto (1924–1990)*
     (Madrid, 1992), p. 29.

32   Bruno Zevi, *Historia de la arquitectura moderna* (Buenos Aires, 1954), pp. 10–11.

33   Raúl Rispa, ed., *Arquitectura del siglo XX: España* (Sevilla, 2000), p. 168.

34   Fernández-Galiano et al., *La quimera moderna*, pp. 16–17, 200–202, 207.

35   Ibid., pp. 11–14.

36   Francisco J. Sáenz de Oiza, Javier Sáenz Guerra and Rosario Alberdi, *Francisco Javier Sáenz de
     Oiza*, exh. cat., Ministerio de Fomento (Madrid, 1996).

37   Carlos Sambricio, ed., *La vivienda en Madrid en la década de los 50: el Plan de Urgencia Social*
     (Madrid, 1999), p. 67.

38   Oriol Bohigas, 'Cap a una arquitectura realista', *Serra d'Or* (April–May 1962), pp. 17–20,
     in Urrutia, *Documentos*, pp. 335–43.

39 José Manuel del Pozo, ed., *Ortiz-Echagüe in Barcelona* (Barcelona, 2000). Additional details are from notes taken at Rafael Ortiz-Echagüe's lecture at Roca Gallery, Madrid, 23 January 2019.
40 Bohigas, 'Cap a una arquitectura', in Urrutia, *Documentos*, p. 341.

chapter seven The Organicist Eden, 1960–75

1 Claude Parent, 'Fullaondo est mort', *L'Architecture d'aujourd'hui* (October 1994), p. 16.
2 Stanley Payne, *The Franco Regime, 1936–1975* (Madison, WI, 1987), p. 463.
3 Vittorio Gregotti, 'España arquitectónica', in *Arquitectura contemporánea española*, ed. Luis Domènech i Girbau (Barcelona, 1968), p. 26.
4 Fernando Higueras, 'Diez residencias de artistas', www.fernandohigueras.org, accessed July 2022.
5 Iñaki Ábalos, 'Fernando Higueras, infinito', *El País* (5 July 2008), www.elpais.com.
6 Luis Fernández-Galiano, 'La corona de pámpanos', *Arquitectura Viva*, 115 (2007), p. 112.
7 [Francisco J. Sáenz de Oiza and Juan Huarte], 'Conversaciones sobre *Nueva Forma*', in *Nueva forma: arquitectura, arte y cultura, 1966–1975*, ed. Gonzalo Armero, exh. cat., Centro Cultural de la Villa (Madrid, 1996), p. 58.
8 Domènech i Girbau, ed., *Arquitectura contemporánea*, p. 172.
9 Antón Capitel, ed., *Arquitectura española años 50–años 80*, exh. cat., Ministerio de Obras Públicas y Urbanismo (Madrid, 1986), p. 26.
10 José Antonio Corrales, *Obra construida*, Lecciones/documentos de arquitectura 5 (Pamplona, 2000).
11 Ábalos, 'Fernando Higueras'.
12 A. González Amézqueta, 'La Iglesia Parroquial de Almendrales', in *J. M. García de Paredes: arquitecto (1924–1990)*, ed. Colegio Oficial de Arquitectos de Madrid (Madrid, 1992), p. 22.
13 Kenneth Frampton, 'Towards a Critical Regionalism: Six Points for an Architecture of Resistance', in *The Anti-Aesthetic*, ed. Hal Foster (Port Townsend, WA, 1983), p. 17.
14 Alejandro de la Sota, *Alejandro de la Sota, arquitecto* (Madrid, 1989), p. 74.
15 Francisco Arques Soler, *Miguel Fisac* (Madrid, 1996), p. 252.
16 For the 1940s, see Oriol Bohigas, *Desde los años inciertos* (Barcelona, 1989), pp. 326–37; for 1957, Cristina Sanz, 'Entrevista biográfica', in *Javier Lahuerta Vargas*, ed. José Manuel Pozo, J. Alberto Mínguez and Cristina Sanz (Pamplona, 1996), p. 124; and for 1964, Antón Capitel, 'Mis memorias de la Escuela de Arquitectura', *Notas de Antón Capitel* (7 May 2009), http://acapitel.blogspot.com.es, accessed October 2023.
17 Capitel, 'Mis memorias'.
18 Bohigas, *Años inciertos*, pp. 310–11.
19 Llàtzer Moix, 'Muere Oriol Regàs, aventurero, alma de Bocaccio y promotor cultural', *La Vanguardia* (8 March 2011).
20 On Bofill's arrest, see Antoni Banyuls i Pérez, 'Arquitectura per al turisme: la utopía urbana de Bofill i el taller d'arquitectura a La Manzanera (1962–1985)', *Aguaits*, 19–20 (2003), pp. 129–61, http://rua.ua.es.
21 José Agustín Goytisolo, *Taller d'arquitectura* (Barcelona, 1977), pp. 5–6.
22 Ricardo Bofill and Taller de Arquitectura, 'Edificio de apartamentos Castillo de Kafka', www.ricardobofill.es, accessed July 2022.
23 Ricardo Bofill, 'La Ciudad en el Espacio', www.ricardobofill.es, accessed July 2022.
24 Ricardo Bofill et al., *Hacia una formalización de la ciudad en el espacio* (Barcelona, 1968).
25 Ramón del Solo, 'Taj Mahal: la primera visita a España', http://bluesvibe.com, accessed July 2022.
26 Ricardo Bofill, 'Walden-7', www.ricardobofill.es, accessed July 2022.
27 Ibid.
28 José Miguel de Prada Poole and Fabián López Ulloa, 'José Miguel de Prada y las estructuras neumáticas en España, 1960–1980', in *Geometría y proporción en las estructuras: ensayas en*

honor de Ricardo Aroca, ed. Pepa Cassinello, Santiago Huerta, José Miguel de Prada Poole and Ricardo Lampreave (Madrid, 2010), p. 378.

29 For an eyewitness account, see Toal Muiré, 'Instant City, Ibiza', *Architectural Design* (December 1971), pp. 762–7. For the organizers' account, see Fernando Benito and Carlos Ferrater, 'Ciudad Instantánea', *Hogares modernos*, 63 (November 1971), p. 51.

30 Pepa Bueno, 'Esto se hincha', in *Encuentros de Pamplona 1972: fin de fiesta del arte experimental*, ed. José Díaz Cuyás, exh. cat., Museo Nacional Centro de Arte Reina Sofía (Madrid, 2009), p. 244.

31 Bueno, 'Esto se hincha', p. 244. Notes from the author's conversation with José Luis Alexanco, 16 February 2017.

32 Museo Reina Sofía, *Encuentros de Pamplona 1972*, www.museoreinasofia.es, accessed June 2010, copy in author's archive.

33 Santos Juliá, 'PCE: el orgullo de un nombre', *El País* (April 2017), http://elpais.com.

chapter eight **Building Democracy, 1975–92**

1 Ángeles González-Sinde, 'Jesús del Pozo, el hombre que me vestía', *El País* (August 2011), https://elpais.com.

2 Manfredo Tafuri, *Architecture and Utopia: Design and Capitalist Development* (London and Cambridge, MA, 1976).

3 Antón Capitel, 'Un paseo por la Castellana', *Arquitecturas bis*, 23–4 (July–September 1978), pp. 2–9.

4 Rafael Moneo, 'Aldo Rossi: The Idea of Architecture and the Modena Cemetery', *Oppositions*, 5 (Summer 1976), pp. 1–30.

5 Rafael Moneo, 'On Typology', *Oppositions*, 13 (Summer 1978), pp. 22–44.

6 Rafael Moneo, *Rafael Moneo: apuntes sobre 21 obras* (Barcelona, 2010), p. 79.

7 Juan Soriano, 'El Museo Romano de Mérida es para mí una pieza especial y de singular valor' (September 2011), www.hoy.es.

8 Colin Rowe and Robert Slutzky, 'Transparency: Literal and Phenomenal', in *The Mathematics of the Ideal Villa and Other Essays*, ed. Colin Rowe (Cambridge, MA, 1976), pp. 159–83.

9 Rafael Moneo, 'Entrados ya en el último cuarto de siglo . . .', *Arquitecturas bis*, 22: *After Modern Architecture* (May 1977), pp. 2–5.

10 Charles Jencks, *The Language of Post-Modern Architecture*, 3rd edn (New York, 1981), p. 90.

11 Óscar Tusquets and Lluís Clotet, 'Memoria', in *Arquitectura española contemporánea*, ed. Eduardo Bru and José Luís Mateo (Barcelona, 1984), p. 118.

12 Aldo Rossi, 'Mi exposición con arquitectos españoles', *2C: construcción de la ciudad*, 8 (March 1977), p. 25.

13 Peter Buchanan, 'A través del cristal: una casa de Juan Navarro Baldeweg', *AV Monografías*, 14 (1988), pp. 76–7.

14 Sara de la Mata, Fuensanta Nieto and Enrique Sobejano, 'Entrevista a Juan Navarro Baldeweg', *Arquitectura*, 274 (September–October 1988), pp. 114–31.

15 Alberto Campo Baeza, 'Essentiality: More with Less', *Architecture and Urbanism (A+U)*, 264 (September 1992), p. 12, edited by David Cohn.

16 Albert Viaplana and Helio Piñón, 'Colegio de Arquitectos de Valencia: concurso de Anteproyectos, 1977', *El Croquis*, 28 (1987), p. 31.

17 Alejandro de la Sota, *Alejandro de la Sota, arquitecto* (Madrid, 1989), p. 152.

18 Robert Venturi, Denise Scott-Brown and Steven Izenour, *Learning from Las Vegas* (Cambridge, MA, 1972).

19 Victoriano Sainz Gutiérrez, *El proyecto urbano en España: génesis y desarrollo de un urbanismo de arquitectos* (Sevilla, 2006), p. 89.

20 Constitución Española, Artículo 47, Boletín Oficial del Estado [Spanish Constitution, Article 47, Official Bulletin of the State] (Madrid, 1978), www.boe.es, accessed August 2022.

21 Aldo Rossi, *The Architecture of the City* (Cambridge, MA, 1982), pp. 150–51, 193–4.

22 David Cohn, 'Profile: Pasqual Maragall, Mayor of Barcelona', *Architectural Record* (August 1992), pp. 112–13.

23 Oriol Bohigas, 'Per una altra urbanitat', in *Plans i projectes per a Barcelona 1981/1982*, ed. Bohigas, Albert Puigdomènech, Josep Acebillo and Jaume Galofré (Barcelona, 1983). Quote from English supplement, pp. 1–5, edited by David Cohn.

24 Cohn, 'Profile'.

25 Bohigas et al., *Plans i projectes*, p. 4.

26 José Ángel Montañés, '"El muro" de la Verneda, en pie', *El País* (8 August 2010).

27 Albert Viaplana and Helio Piñón, 'Plaça de Sants', in *Plans i projectes*, ed. Bohigas et al.

28 Oriol Bohigas, *Desde los años inciertos* (Barcelona, 1989), pp. 142–3.

29 Josep Martorell, Oriol Bohigas, David Mackay and Albert Puigdomènech (MBM Architects), *The Olympic Village: Architecture, Parks, Leisure Port* (Barcelona, 1991), p. 15.

30 Ibid.

31 Bohigas, *Años inciertos*, pp. 152–3.

32 MBM, *The Olympic Village*, p. 15.

33 Llàtzer Moix, *La ciudad de los arquitectos* (Barcelona, 1994). pp. 47–50, 93.

34 Ibid., p. 101.

35 Llàtzer Moix, *'Queríamos un Calatrava': viajes arquitectónicos por la seducción y el repudio* (Barcelona, 2016), pp. 96–8. Other comments are from my conversations with architects in Sevilla during this period.

chapter nine **Over the Top, 1992–2015**

1 Eugeni d'Ors, *Glosari* [1907], quoted in Ángel Urrutia, *Arquitectura española del siglo XX* (Madrid, 1997), p. 186.

2 Terence Riley, *On-Site: New Architecture in Spain*, exh. cat., Museum of Modern Art (New York, 2006).

3 Albert Viaplana and Helio Piñón, *Obra Viaplana / Piñón* (Barcelona, 1996), p. 36.

4 Alan Riding, 'A Modern "Pearl" Inside Old Barcelona', *New York Times* (10 May 1995), www.nytimes.com.

5 Joaquín Ferrandis, 'La Ciudad de las Artes ha costado cuatro veces lo que se presupuestó', *El País* (16 March 2011), www.elpais.com.

6 Kim Bradley, 'The Deal of the Century', *Art in America* (1 July 1997).

7 John Morris Dixon, 'Gehry's American Center in Paris', *Architect* (March 2010), www.architectmagazine.com.

8 Bernard Weinraub, 'Hollywood Ending for Music Palace', *New York Times* (2 August 2003).

9 Mikel Ormazabal, 'El Guggenheim supera su récord de visitas con 1,3 millones', *El País* (4 January 2018).

10 Bradley, 'Deal of the Century'.

11 Rafael Moneo, 'Kursaal Auditorio y Centro de Congresos', http://rafaelmoneo.com, accessed March 2021.

12 Andrés Fernández Rubio, 'La constructora del polideportivo que se hundió en Huesca culpa a los arquitectos', *El País* (17 April 1993).

13 Blanca Cia, 'Gas Natural vuelve a la Barceloneta, a una torre de cristal de 80 metros', *El País* (9 January 2003).

14 David Cohn, 'Scottish Parliament, Edinburgh', *Architectural Record* (February 2005), pp. 98–111.

15 Luis Fernández-Galiano, 'La corona de pámpanos', *Arquitectura Viva*, 115 (2007), p. 112.

16 Cohn, 'Scottish Parliament'.

17 Roger Cohen, 'Missing Millions – Kuwait's Bad Bet – A Special Report: Big Wallets and Little Supervision', *New York Times* (28 September 1993).

18 David Cohn, 'Valdebernardo und die Krise der PSV', *Bauwelt*, 28 (25 July 1997), pp. 1588–91.

19 David Cohn, 'Der große sozialistische Entwurf', *Bauwelt*, 28 (1997), pp. 1592–99; David Cohn, 'El desafío de la periferia', *Expansión* (24 October 1998), *Fin de Semana*, pp. 12–13.

20 Cohn, 'El desafío de la periferia', pp. 12–13.

21 Sandra López Letón, 'La burbuja que embriagó a España', *El País* (25 October 2015).

22 Juan Romero et al., 'Aproximación a la geografía del despilfarro en España: balance de las
    últimas dos décadas', *Boletín de la Asociación de Geógrafos Españoles*, 77 (July 2018), pp. 1–51,
    www.age-geografia.es.

23 Ana del Barrio, 'Nadie quiere gestionar la Caja Mágica: las pistas llevan vacías desde hace
    meses', *El Mundo* (27 February 2020), www.elmundo.es.

24 Luca Costantini, 'El delegado de la M-30 eleva a 9.400 millones el coste final de los túneles de la
    vía', *El País* (5 October 2017).

25 Suzanne Stephens, 'City of Culture of Galicia Archive and Library', *Architectural Record* (July
    2011), pp. 62–78, www.architecturalrecord.com.

26 Francisco Peregil, 'Monumento a la incoherencia', *El País* (12 November 2011).

27 David Cohn, 'Magma Diagonal', *Arquitectura Viva*, 94–5 (2004), p. 195. The 'cigar-stoked
    charettes' were described to me by Benedetta Tagliabue and Josep Lluís Mateo in interviews.

28 Jean Nouvel, 'Torre Agbar', *Ateliers Jean Nouvel*, www.jeannouvel.com, accessed August 2021.

29 Alfonso Álvarez-Dardet, 'Sevilla dice adiós a un 'zaha hadid', *El País* (24 August 2012).

30 Ministerio de Transportes, Movilidad y Agenda Urbana, 'Publicaciones de construcción de
    edificios (licencias municipales de obra)', www.mitma.gob.es, accessed January 2022.

31 David Cohn, 'Razón y forma', 2G, 27: *Mansilla + Tuñón: obra reciente* (2003), pp. 6–19.

32 Emilio Tuñón, 'I Would Prefer Not To', *Circo*, 194 (2004), www.emiliotunon.com.

33 David Cohn, 'Controlled Energy Exchange: Interview with Iñaki Ábalos', *Speech*, 5 (2010),
    pp. 210–27.

34 David Cohn, *Young Spanish Architects* (Basel, 2000), p. 38.

35 Javier Revillo, 'Interpretación del espacio', *Revista arquitectura*, 296 (March 1993), pp. 146–50.

36 David Cohn, 'Madridejos und Sancho', *Bauwelt*, 43–4 (24 November 2000), pp. 40–47.

37 Sol Madridejos and Juan Carlos Sancho, 'A Brief Conversation with Eduardo Chillida',
    El Croquis, 81–2 (1996), pp. 14–23.

38 Ecosistema Urbano, 'Who We Are', www.ecosistemaurbano.com, accessed April 2022.

39 O. F. Noticia, '20 centros "okupas" permanecen abiertos en Madrid pese a la oleada de cierres
    del último año', *20 Minutos* (10 January 2014), www.20minutos.es.

Select Bibliography

This is a reduced, general bibliography for those interested in further reading. Titles not previously mentioned in the reference notes are either general sources for this book, or recommended reading.

Ábalos, Iñaki, *The Good Life: A Guided Visit to the Houses of Modernity*, revd edn (New York, 2017)
—, and Juan Herreros, *Tower and Office: From Modernist Theory to Contemporary Practice*
    (Cambridge, MA, 2003)
Alonso, Paco, and Javier Saénz Guerra, 'Ciclo Maestros Modernos: Saénz de Oiza', Conferencia
    Madrid (13 June 2017), https://vimeo.com, accessed June 2022
Arean, Antonio, José Ángel Vaquero and Juan Casariego, *Madrid: arquitecturas perdidas, 1927–1986*
    (Madrid, 1995)
Armero, Gonzalo, ed., *Nueva Forma: arquitectura, arte y cultura, 1966–1975*, exh. cat., Centro Cultural
    de la Villa (Madrid, 1996)
Arrechea, Julio, *Arquitectura y romanticismo: el pensamiento arquitectónico en la España del XIX*
    (Salamanca, Valladolid, 1989)
Bevan, Bernard, *History of Spanish Architecture* (London, 1938)
Bohigas, Oriol, *Desde los años inciertos* (Barcelona, 1999)
—, *Entusiasmos compartidos y batallas sin cuartel* (Barcelona, 1996)
—, *Modernidad en la arquitectura de la España republicana*, revd edn (Barcelona, 1990)
—, Peter Buchanan and Vittorio Magnago Lampugnani, *Barcelona: City and Architecture, 1980–1992*
    (New York, 1991)
—, Albert Puigdomènech, Josep Acebillo and Jaume Galofre, eds, *Plans i projectes per a Barcelona*
    1981/1982 (Barcelona, 1983)
Bru, Eduardo, and José Luís Mateo, *Arquitectura española contemporánea/Spanish Contemporary*
    Architecture (Barcelona, 1984)
Busquets, Joan, *Barcelona: The Urban Evolution of a Compact City* (Barcelona, 2006)
Capitel, Antón, ed., *Arquitectura española años 50–años 80*, exh. cat., Ministerio de Obras Públicas y
    Urbanismo (Madrid, 1986)
Centellas Soler, Miguel, *Los pueblos de colonización de Fernández del Amo: arte, arquitectura y*
    urbanismo (Barcelona, 2010)
Cohn, David, *Young Spanish Architects/Junge spanische Architekten* (Basel, 2000)
Colegio Oficial de Arquitectos de Madrid, et al., eds, *Revista Arquitectura/Revista Nacional de*
    Arquitectura, 100 años, 1–382 (1919–2019), www.coam.org.es, accessed October 2023
Col·legi d'Arquitectes de Catalunya, *Arquitectura para después de una guerra: 1939–1949*, exh. cat.,
    Col·legi d'Arquitectes de Catalunya (Barcelona, 1977)
Díaz Cuyás, José, et al., eds, *Encuentros de Pamplona 1972: fin de fiesta del arte experimental*, exh. cat.,
    Museo Nacional Centro de Arte Reina Sofía (Madrid, 2009)
Diez-Pastor, Concha, *La generación del 25: primera arquitectura moderna en Madrid* (Madrid, 1997)
Domènech Girbau, Luis, ed., *Arquitectura contemporánea española* (Barcelona, 1968)
Fernández-Galiano, Luis, ed., *Spain Builds* (Madrid, 2006)
Fernández-Galiano, Luis, Justo F. Isasi and Antonio Lopera, *La quimera moderna: los Poblados*
    Dirigidos de Madrid en la arquitectura de los 50 (Madrid, 1989)
Flores, Carlos, *Arquitectura española contemporánea*, revd edn (Madrid, 1988)
Frampton, Kenneth, ed., *Contemporary Spanish Architecture: An Eclectic Panorama* (New York, 1986)

Fundación Arquitectura COAM (Colegio Oficial de Arquitectos de Madrid), ed., *Arquitectura de Madrid* (Madrid, 2003), https://guia-arquitectura-madrid.coam.org, accessed June 2022

Fundación DoCoMoMo Ibérico, ed., *Arquitectura moderna y turismo: 1925–1965, Actas, IV Congreso, Fundación DoCoMoMo Ibérico* (Valencia, 2003)

—, ed., *GATCPAC y su tiempo: política, cultura y arquitectura en los años treinta* (Barcelona, 2005)

García Barba, Federico, ed., *Gaceta de Arte, 1932–1935* (Santa Cruz de Tenerife, 1989)

GATEPAC (Josep Lluís Sert et al.), eds, *AC: documentos de actividad contemporánea, nos 1–25 [1931–7]* (Barcelona, 2006)

Gausa, Manuel, Marta Cervelló and Maurici Pla, *Barcelona: A Guide to Its Modern Architecture, 1860–2002* (Barcelona, 2002)

Giménez Caballero, Ernesto, *Arte y estado* (Madrid, 2009)

Giner de los Ríos, Bernardo, *Cincuenta años de arquitectura española, 1900–1950* [1952] (Madrid, 1980)

González de Canales, Francisco, and Nicholas Ray, *Rafael Moneo: Building, Teaching, Writing* (New Haven, CT, 2015)

Grupo 2C (Salvador Tarrago et al.), eds, *2c: construcción de la ciudad, 1–22* (1972–85), https://issuu.com, accessed June 2022

Güell, Xavier, *Contemporary Spanish Architecture: The Eighties* (New York, 1994)

Hernando, Javier, *Arquitectura en España: 1770–1900* (Madrid, 1989)

Hughes, Robert, *Barcelona* (New York, 1992)

Lacasa, Luis, *Luis Lacasa: escritos 1922–1931* (Madrid, 1976)

Lahuerta, Juan José, *Antoni Gaudí: arquitectura, ideología y política* (Madrid, 1993)

Mackay, David, *Modern Architecture in Barcelona, 1854–1939* (New York, 1989)

Márquez, Fernando, Richard Levene and Antonio Ruíz Barbarin, eds, *Arquitectura española contemporánea, 1975–1990* (Madrid, 1989)

Martín Frechilla, Juan José, and Carlos Sambricio, eds, *Arquitectura española del exilio* (Madrid, 2014)

Martorell, Josep, Oriol Bohigas, David Mackay and Albert Puigdomènech, *The Olympic Village: Architecture, Parks, Leisure Port* (Barcelona, 1991)

Maure, Lilia, *Zuazo, arquitecto del Madrid de la Segunda república*, exh. cat., Biblioteca Nacional de España (Madrid, 2006)

Moix, Llàtzer, *Arquitectura milagrosa* (Barcelona, 2010)

—, *La ciudad de los arquitectos* (Barcelona, 1994)

—, '*Queríamos un calatrava*': viajes arquitectónicos por la seducción y el repudio (Barcelona, 2016)

Navascués, Pedro, *Arquitectura española, 1808–1914* (Madrid, 1993)

Piñón, Helio, *Reflexión histórica de la arquitectura moderna* (Barcelona, 1981)

Pizza, Antonio, and Josep M. Rovira, *Coderch, 1940–1964: In Search of Home* (Barcelona, 2000)

—, *GATCPAC, 1928–1939: una nova arquitectura per una nova ciutat/A New Architecture for a New City*, exh. cat., Museu Historia de Barcelona and Col·legi d'Arquitectes de Catalunya (Barcelona, 2006)

Pozo, José Manuel, ed., *Los brillantes 50: 35 proyectos* (Pamplona, 2004)

—, ed., *Ortiz-Echagüe in Barcelona* (Barcelona, 2000)

Rabasco, Pablo, and Martín Domínguez Ruz, eds, *Arniches y Domínguez/Arniches and Domínguez*, exh. cat., Museo ICO (Madrid, 2017)

Regás, Rosa, et al., eds, *Arquitecturas bis, 1–52* (1974–85), https://issuu.com, accessed June 2022

Riley, Terence, *On-Site: New Architecture in Spain*, exh. cat., Museum of Modern Art (New York, 2006)

Rispa, Raúl, ed., *Twentieth Century Architecture: Spain*, exh. cat., Spanish Pavilion, Expo 2000, Hanover (Sevilla, 2000)

Rodríguez, Carme, and Jorge Torres, *Grup R* (Barcelona, 1994)

Rovira, Josep M., *José Luis Sert, 1901–1983* (London, 2003)

Sainz Gutiérrez, Victoriano, *El proyecto urbano en España: génesis y desarrollo de un urbanismo de arquitectos* (Sevilla, 2006)

Saliga, Pauline, and Marta Thorne, eds, *Building in a New Spain: Contemporary Spanish Architecture*, exh. cat., Art Institute of Chicago (Chicago, IL, 1992)

Sambricio, Carlos, ed., *La vivienda en Madrid en la década de los 50: el Plan de Urgencia Social* (Madrid, 1999)

San Antonio Gómez, Carlos de, ed., *Revista Arquitectura, 1918–1936*, exh. cat., Ministerio de Fomento
(Madrid, 2001)
Sánchez de Madariaga, Inés, *Matilde Ucelay Maórtua: una vida en construcción* (Madrid 2012)
Sanz Esquide, José Ángel, *Real Club Náutico de San Sebastián, 1928–1929: José Manuel Aizpurúa y
Joaquin Labayen* (Almería, 1995)
Solà-Morales, Ignasi de, *Architecture in Barcelona* (Barcelona, 1992)
—, *Architettura minimale a Barcelona/Minimal Architecture in Barcelona* (Milan, 1986)
—, *Eclecticismo y vanguardia: el caso de la arquitectura moderna en Catalunya* (Barcelona, 1980)
Solà-Morales, Ignasi de, et al., *Birkhäuser Architecture Guide Spain, 1920–1999* (Basel, 1998)
Sosa Díaz-Saavedra, José Antonio, ed., *Arquitectura moderna en Canarias: 1925–1965* (Santa Cruz de
Tenerife, Las Palmas de Gran Canaria, 2002)
De la Sota, Alejandro, *Alejandro de la Sota, arquitecto* (Madrid, 1989)
Terán, Fernando de, *Historia del urbanismo en España III: siglos XIX y XX* (Madrid, 1999)
Torroja, Eduardo, *The Structures of Eduardo Torroja: An Autobiography of Engineering
Accomplishment* (New York, 1958)
Urrutia, Ángel, *Arquitectura española contemporánea: documentos, escritos, testimonios inéditos*
(Madrid, 2002)
—, *Arquitectura española del siglo XX* (Madrid, 1997)
Viaplana, Albert, and Helio Piñón, *Obra: Viaplana-Piñón* (Barcelona, 1996)
Vicente Garrido, Henry, ed., *Arquitecturas desplazadas: arquitecturas del exilio español*, exh. cat.,
Ministerio de Vivienda (Madrid, 2007)
Zarza Ballugera, Rafael, et al., eds, *Kindel: fotografía de arquitectura*, exh. cat., Fundación COAM
(Madrid, 2007)

Acknowledgements

My first and greatest debt in this endeavour is to my editor, Vivian Constantinopoulos, who has seen to completion a project that has been much too long in the writing by any reasonable standard. To her I offer my deepest gratitude.

I am also deeply grateful for the extraordinary support, both practical and vital, of the writer and editor Karin Taylhardat, who dedicated countless hours and her multiple talents and intelligence to help me overcome the limits of my failing eyesight in the final preparations of the book. My friend the artist Pedro Nuñez and my research assistant, the architect Laura Miguel Pastor, were essential in this period, too.

Adela García-Herrera and Luis Fernández-Galiano, my former editors at *Arquitectura Viva*, first recommended me to Reaktion Books for this project. Their long-time colleague, the historian Jorge Sainz, has provided valuable support and advice over the years. I also thank the architectural historian Antonio Pizza, the critic Llátzer Moix and the architect Jorge Díaz of the College of Architects in Tenerife, as well as the historians Pablo Rabasco, Antonio Cobo and Luis Alfonso Basterra, who all responded generously to my doubts and questions.

This book owes much to the architects I consulted, including the late Manuel de las Casas, his daughter, Iciar de las Casas, Martín Domínguez Ruiz, Ignacio Feduchi, Manuel Gallego, Rafael de La-Hoz, Rafael Moneo, Manuel Paredes, Helio Piñón, Carme Pinós, Javier Sáenz Guerra, Benedetta Tagliabue and Elías Torres, among others. Invaluable too have been those who, over the years, gave generously of their time for magazine articles that preceded this book. It has been a great pleasure to renew contact with many of them in gathering images for the present publication.

Photo archivists have been extraordinarily helpful and generous. I would like to thank in particular Alberto Sanz, director of Historic Services at Madrid's College of Architects, and Charles Doran of the Princeton University Libraries. I offer special thanks to the photographers Enrique Carrazoni, Melchor Sarasketa, Horacio Moreno and Jorge Nerea, to the architect Emilio Ambasz and to the many other private foundations and families who have generously loaned material.

I also thank the many other colleagues and friends – not forgotten, though not mentioned here – who have offered encouragement and advice along the way.

Photo Acknowledgements

The author and publishers wish to thank the organizations and individuals listed below for authorizing reproduction of their work.

© Adalberto Benitez, VEGAP, Madrid: p. 97; Agence Photographique, Réunion des musées nationaux. © Succession Picasso – Gestion droits d'auteur. © RMN – Gestion droit d'auteur François Kollar: Agence photo RMN-Grand Palais: p. 119; Courtesy of Alberto Campo Baeza: p. 238 (Photo: © Hisao Suzuki); Archive JMGP: pp. 170 (Lent by Ángela García de Paredes. Photo: Lluís Casals), 200 bottom (Lent by Ángela García de Paredes. Photo: Schommer); Archive Manuel de las Casas: p. 240; Archivo BAU: pp. 91 bottom, 92 centre (Photo: Marín Chivite); Archivo Francisco Javier Sáenz de Oiza: pp. 167 bottom, 188; Archivo Fundación Pablo Neruda: p. 132; Archivo General de la Universidad Complutense de Madrid (AGUCM 10/22-01): p. 120; Archivo General de la Universidad de Navarra/Fondo Javier Carvajal Ferrer: p. 194; Archivo José Miguel de Prada Poole: pp. 215, 216; Archivo Martín Domínguez Esteban: pp. 73 (Period photograph by Otto Wunderlinch), 74 (Period photograph by Otto Wunderlinch), 127 (Cooperativa Fotográfica, La Habana *c.* 1957); Arxiu Josep Lluís Sert/Fundació Joan Miró, Barcelona: pp. 112, 116, 134; Biblioteca de la Escuela Técnica Superior de Arquitectura, Universidad Politécnica de Madrid: p. 144 (Photo: Foto Ángel); Biblioteca Nacional de España: pp. 40, 59 (Colección Zuazo), 75 (Colección Zuazo), 87 (Colección Zuazo); © Centro Carlos Pérez Siquer: p. 206; César Portela: p. 232; Comunidad de Madrid: p. 246; Creative Commons: pp. 26 (Tudoi61/CC BY-SA 4.0), 141 (Sigils/ CC BY-SA 3.0 ES), 250 (Xaxat/ CC BY-SA 3.0 ES), 257 top (Victoriano Javier Tornel García/ CC BY-SA 2.0), 265 (Jebulon/ CC0 1.0); Courtesy of Cruz y Ortiz Arquitectos: p. 218 (Photo: © Duccio Malagamba), 245; David Cohn: pp. 20 top, 48, 54, 151, 157, 196, 201, 211, 212, 223, 244, 258, 270, 279, 287, 290, 291, 292, 299, 300, 304, 305, 309 top and centre; Collection of David Cohn: pp. 60, 142; Courtesy of EMBT: p. 286 (Photo: Alex Gaultier); © Emilio Ambas: p. 267; Courtesy of Emilio Tuñón: p. 297 (Photo: © Luis Asin); © Enrique Carrazoni: p. 92 bottom; Courtesy of Fernando Menis: p. 307 (Photo: Jakub Certowicz); © Ferran Freixa, VEGAP, Madrid, 2022: p. 254; Fisac Foundation: pp. 158 left and right, 204; Flickr: p. 25 (Hans Nerstu); © Photographic Archive Francesc Catala-Roca: Arxiu Històric del Col·legi d'Arquitectes de Catalunya, with the collaboration of COAC: pp. 160, 176; Francisco Javier Sáenz Guerra: pp. 167 top, 190; Fundación Alejandro de la Sota: pp. 164 (Foto FE2), 166, 202, 203; © Fundación César Manrique: p. 199; Courtesy of Fundación Fernando Higueras: pp. 180, 187, 198; © Giuliano Mezzacasa: p. 200 top; With permission of Helio Piñón: pp. 237, 253; © Historical Archive of Col·legi d'Arquitectes de Catalunya (AHCOAC): pp. 111 (GATCPAC Archive), 133 (Bonet Castellana Archive); Horacio Moreno Rosillo: p. 84; Instituto del Patrimonio Cultural de España (IPCE): pp. 72 (Period photograph by Otto Wunderlich), 76 top (Juan Miguel Pando, 1961), 174 (Juan Miguel Pando), 175 (Juan Miguel Pando); Instituto Eduardo Torroja: p. 76 bottom (Torroja, Eduardo, *The Structures of Eduardo Torroja – An Autobiography of Engineering Accomplishment*, F. W. Dodge Corporation, New York, 1958, p.6); iStock: p. 293 (Axel Bueckert); © Javier Azurmendi: pp. 243, 280; Jorge Nerea: p. 198 top; Courtesy of José Manuel Gallego: p. 235; Courtesy of Juan Carlos Sancho: p. 301; Juan Miguel Pando, IPCE, Ministerio de Cultura y Deporte, Spain: pp. 174, 175; Kindel (Joaquín del Palacio), courtesy of his family: pp. 143, (Reference: CTQ-47-A), 177; Le Corbusier Foundation: p. 62 (Ref. No. FLC Photo L1 (2) 10-6); © Lluís Casals, VEGAP, Madrid, 2022: pp. 96, 257 centre, 275 (Archivos COAC/ Photo: © Lluis Casals), 276; © Lluís Casals, José Antonio Coderch de Sentmenat, VEGAP, Madrid, 2022: p. 156; © Manel Armengol: p. 284; © Mark Lamster: p. 131; MBM Architects: p. 260; © Melchor Saraskota: pp. 71, 86; © Microsoft Bing Maps Platform: p. 261 (With permission from Microsoft Corporation); Ministerio de agricultura y Pesca, Alimentación, y Medioambiente, Mediateca: p. 129 (Fondo Colonización,

Index

Page numbers in *italics* refer to illustrations.

NB: Where two last names are used, these are listed alphabetically by the first name, such as 'Campo Baeza, Alberto' or 'Puig i Cadafalch, Josep'.